Photoshop® CS
TOP 100
Simplified®
Tips & Tricks

by Denis Graham

From
maranGraphics®

&

Wiley Publishing, Inc.

Visual

Photoshop® CS: Top 100 Simplified®
Tips & Tricks

Published by
Wiley Publishing, Inc.
111 River Street
Hoboken, NJ 07030-5774

Published simultaneously in Canada

Copyright © 2004 by Wiley Publishing, Inc.,
Indianapolis, Indiana

Certain designs, text, and illustrations Copyright
© 1992-2004 maranGraphics, Inc., used with
maranGraphics' permission.

maranGraphics, Inc.
5755 Coopers Avenue
Mississauga, Ontario, Canada
L4Z 1R9

Library of Congress Control Number: 2003116108
ISBN: 0-7645-4182-X
Manufactured in the United States of America
10 9 8 7 6 5 4 3 2 1

1K/SQ/QR/QU/IN

Trademark Acknowledgments

Important Numbers

For U.S. corporate orders, please call maranGraphics at
800-469-6616 or fax 905-890-9434.

For general information on our other products and
services or to obtain technical support please contact
our Customer Care Department within the U.S. at
800-762-2974, outside the U.S. at 317-572-3993 or
fax 317-572-4002.

Permissions

maranGraphics
Certain text and Illustrations by maranGraphics, Inc.,
used with maranGraphics' permission.

Wiley Publishing, Inc.

U.S. Corporate Sales	U.S. Trade Sales
Contact maranGraphics at (800) 469-6616 or fax (905) 890-9434.	Contact Wiley at (800) 762-2974 or fax (317) 572-4002.

CREDITS

Project Editor:
Sarah Hellert

Acquisitions Editor:
Jody Lefevere

Product Development Manager:
Lindsay Sandman

Copy Editor:
Marylouise Wiack

Technical Editor:
Dennis R. Cohen

Editorial Manager:
Robyn Siesky

Editorial Assistant:
Adrienne D. Porter

Manufacturing:
Allan Conley
Linda Cook
Paul Gilchrist
Jennifer Guynn

Special Help:
Dave Huss

Screen Artists:
Lynsey Osborn
Jill A. Proll

Book Design:
maranGraphics, Inc.

Production Coordinators:
Nancee Reeves
Erin Smith

Layout:
Beth Brooks
LeAndra Hosier

Illustrators:
Ronda David-Burroughs
David E. Gregory

Proofreader:
Christine Pingleton

Quality Control:
Susan Moritz

Indexer:
Sherry Massey

Vice President and Executive Group Publisher:
Richard Swadley

Vice President and Publisher:
Barry Pruett

Composition Services Director:
Debbie Stailey

ABOUT THE AUTHOR

Denis Graham, a confessed Photoshop junkie, lives in Norman, Oklahoma, with his wife, Monica, and three kids, Christina, Jessica, and David. Denis has authored *Photoshop Elements 2: Top 100 Simplified Tips & Tricks* and the book you're holding, and has worked as Technical Editor on ten Photoshop, Elements, and Illustrator books for Friends of Ed publishing.

AUTHOR'S ACKNOWLEDGMENTS

Thanks to God, my wife, and Wiley Publishing. For some reason, all three seem to think I'm a little something special.

maranGraphics is a family-run business
located near Toronto, Canada.

At **maranGraphics**, we believe
in producing great computer
books—one book at a time.

Each maranGraphics book uses
the award-winning communication
process that we have been
developing over the last 28 years.
Using this process, we organize
screen shots and text in a way
that makes it easy for you to
learn new concepts and tasks.

We spend hours deciding the
best way to perform each task,
so you don't have to! Our clear,
easy-to-follow screen shots and
instructions walk you through
each task from beginning to end.

We want to thank you for
purchasing what we feel are
the best computer books money
can buy. We hope you enjoy using
this book as much as we enjoyed
creating it!

Sincerely,

The Maran Family

Please visit us on the Web at:
www.maran.com

HOW TO USE THIS BOOK

Photoshop® CS: Top 100 Simplified® Tips & Tricks includes the 100 most interesting and useful tasks you can perform in Photoshop. This book reveals cool secrets and timesaving tricks guaranteed to make you more productive in Photoshop.

Who is this book for?

Are you a visual learner who already knows the basics of Photoshop, but would like to take your Photoshop experience to the next level? Then this is the book for you.

Conventions in This Book

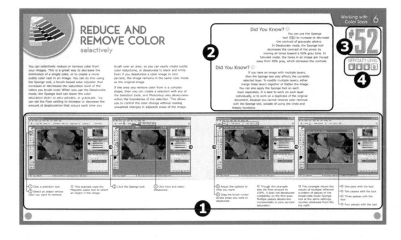

❶ Steps

This book walks you through each task using a step-by-step approach. Lines and "lassos" connect the screen shots to the step-by-step instructions to show you exactly how to perform each task.

❷ Tips

Fun and practical tips answer questions you have always wondered about. Plus, learn to do things in Photoshop that you never thought were possible!

❸ Task Numbers

The task numbers, ranging from 1 to 100, indicate which self-contained lesson you are currently working on.

❹ Difficulty Levels

For quick reference, symbols mark the difficulty level of each task.

Demonstrates a new spin on a common task

Introduces a new skill or a new task

Combines multiple skills requiring in-depth knowledge

Requires extensive skill and may involve other technologies

TABLE OF CONTENTS

1   Working with Layers

2   Working with Drawing Tools

TABLE OF CONTENTS

 Adjusting Photos

Working with Color Tools

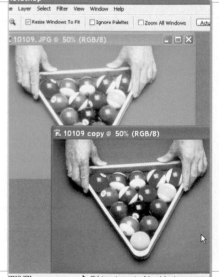

Creating Effects with Filters

Preparing Images for Print and the Web

9 Speeding Up Your Work

10 Designing with ImageReady Tools

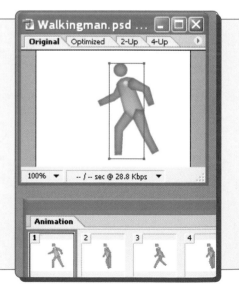

CHAPTER 1

Working with Layers

You can create, design, and manipulate your graphic art in numerous ways by using layers in Photoshop CS (Creative Suite). You can separate an image so that each element is on an individual layer. For example, you can make the bottom layer your background image, and then place an image of a person on a separate layer from the background. The image you see onscreen looks like one solid image, but each image you place on a layer is separate from the other images, and is editable. Without layers, images are flat, solid images, and anything you paint, draw, or paste in the image becomes a permanent part of the image.

In Photoshop CS, you can use layers to create elaborate designs. You can change any layer without affecting the other images on the other layers. You can also move the image around and change the layer order, add special effects, draw, erase, color, or distort whatever the layer contains, without affecting the other layers. You can link, merge, and hide layers, for even more versatility. Layers add an enormous amount of flexibility to Photoshop CS, and with tools including Layer Styles, Layer Sets, and Blending Modes, you can achieve amazing results very quickly.

You can expect many advantages to using layers and the related tools, and Photoshop CS will meet your needs.

TOP 100

ZOOM IN
on multiple documents at once

You can add a new variation to an old tool when you work with multiple images. When you work with photos, you often use the Zoom tool to get a closer view of an image. For example, when you work with multiple images at the same time, you must often zoom in on the images separately to maintain a similar magnification. This can be repetitious when you do a lot of detail work.

You can now use a new Photoshop CS Zoom feature. When you select the Zoom tool, the Zoom All Windows check box appears on the Options bar. If you select this option, Photoshop CS magnifies each open file by the same amount simultaneously when you use the Zoom tool. You can move in on each open file at the same time by selecting the Zoom tool, and clicking one of the open images. You can right-click an image to use the Zoom tool from the pop-up menu; Photoshop only magnifies that image, and ignores the Zoom All Windows.

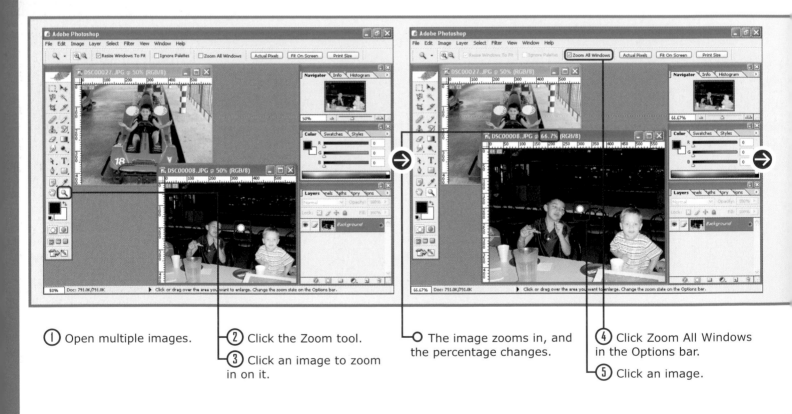

① Open multiple images.

② Click the Zoom tool.

③ Click an image to zoom in on it.

○ The image zooms in, and the percentage changes.

④ Click Zoom All Windows in the Options bar.

⑤ Click an image.

Did You Know? ※

To increase or decrease the magnification, you can click the status bar in the lower-left corner of the screen, and type a percent.

Did You Know? ※

You can zoom in or zoom out even if you have another tool selected. Just press Ctrl+Spacebar to zoom in or Ctrl+Alt+Spacebar to zoom out. When you do this, the current tool turns into ⊕ or ⊖ to reflect your choice.

Shortcuts! ※

You can view the actual pixels of your image by double-clicking the Zoom tool button (🔍). You can use the Fit on Screen zoom option by double-clicking the Hand tool button (✋). You can also quickly access the Zoom tool by pressing the Z key on the keyboard.

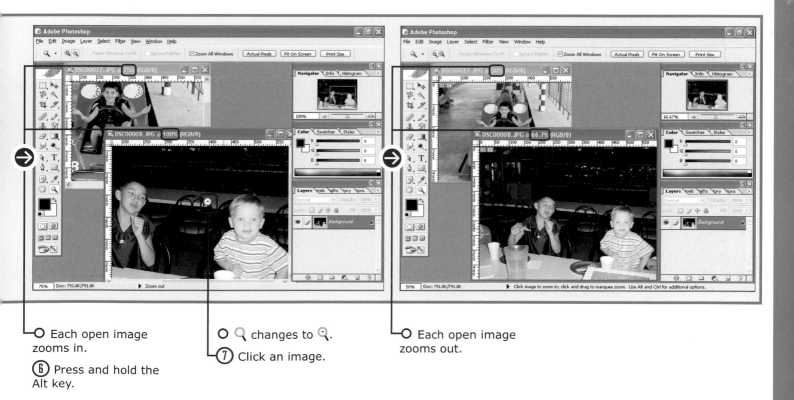

O Each open image zooms in.

⑥ Press and hold the Alt key.

O 🔍 changes to ⊕.

⑦ Click an image.

O Each open image zooms out.

Use GRIDS AND RULERS
to align objects

You can accurately adjust placement of text and objects in your multi-layer images using the Photoshop CS grids and rulers.

When you activate the rulers under the View menu, ruler guides appear on the side and top of your image canvas. This guide can help you to size and place objects within your image.

When you activate the grids, a grid-line overlay appears on the image. With this overlay, you can align and place objects at specific locations in your image. You can set the grid and ruler sizes by

clicking Edit, and then Preferences. In the Preferences dialog box, you can select options to change the ruler measurements, grid sizes and colors, and other options.

You can change the zero center point of your rulers by clicking and dragging from the upper-left corner of the ruler and positioning the center point in your image. Double-clicking the corner again resets the zero point to the upper-left corner of the image. This is useful for measuring distance from a specific point in an image.

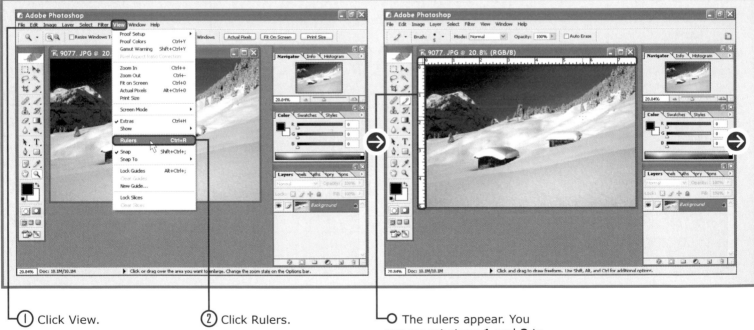

① Click View.

② Click Rulers.

○ The rulers appear. You can repeat steps **1** and **2** to hide the rulers.

Apply It ☀

You can change the ruler settings without going to the Preferences dialog box. Double-click the ruler. In the dialog box that appears, click the Ruler ⚊ in the Units section and choose your measurement unit.

Apply It ☀

You can access an option called Snap to Grid. This option causes the edge or center of a relocated object to snap to the nearest gridline it approaches. Click View, and then click Snap to enable the Snap function. Then click View, Snap To, and then Grid to activate Snap to Grid. This is a great way to create specific layout points for image objects, or designing a table-like grid for placement.

Did You Know? ☀

You can use the grid to straighten photos. Open a crooked scanned photo. Turn on your grid overlay. Click Image, Transform, and then Rotate. Use the Rotate command to align the edges of your image to your grid. This can allow for more precise alignment, because the gridlines are absolutely vertical and horizontal.

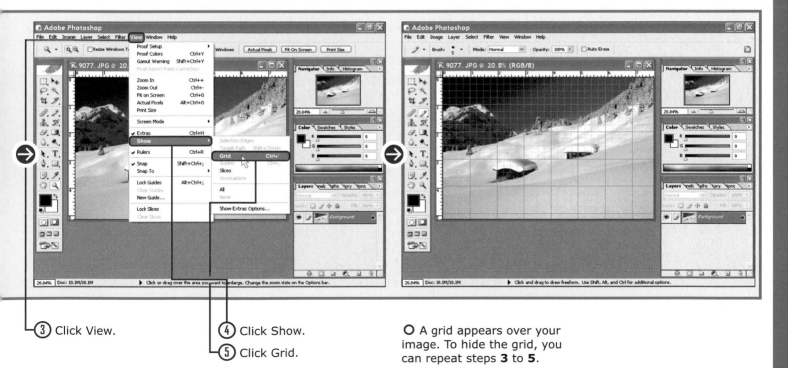

③ Click View.

④ Click Show.

⑤ Click Grid.

O A grid appears over your image. To hide the grid, you can repeat steps **3** to **5**.

Improve workflow by
ORGANIZING AND
RENAMING LAYERS

A Photoshop project can quickly build up a large number of layers in the image, causing confusion or clarity problems. You can organize and name these layers to improve your workflow. Photoshop files can often contain a few to several dozen different layers, and when you organize them, you can speed up the process of locating and using specific layers.

You can place your layers in a particular order, to keep similar objects adjacent to each other for easier reference. For example, you may have

multiple layers of text in an advertisement layout. You can place the text layers next to each other for easy onscreen editing. You can also rename the layers to reflect the content to quickly locate them in the Layers palette.

You cannot rename or move the Background layer: it is a special layer that is locked in place. If you try to move it, then a dialog box informs you that it is locked. Renaming or moving the Background layer causes it to convert into a normal layer.

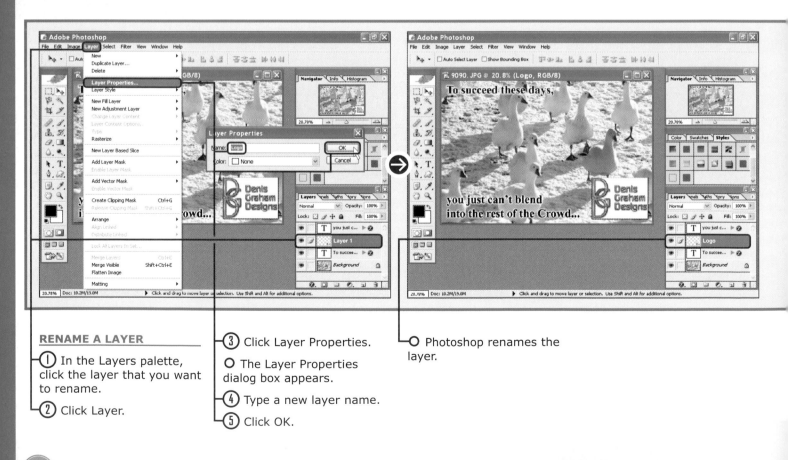

RENAME A LAYER

① In the Layers palette, click the layer that you want to rename.

② Click Layer.

③ Click Layer Properties.

○ The Layer Properties dialog box appears.

④ Type a new layer name.

⑤ Click OK.

○ Photoshop renames the layer.

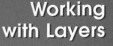

More Options! ※

In the Layer Properties dialog box, you can click the Color ▾ to color-code your layers. With this feature, you can locate images on layers by their color, and you can group layers that have a similar theme with the same color for better organization.

Caution! ※

Rearranging layers that have blending modes can dramatically change your image. Layers with blending modes applied to them modify all layers below them, so changing their position also changes the layers affected by the blending modes. Doing this can alter the final look of your image from what you intended.

Did You Know? ※

You can easily rename your layer by double-clicking the layer in the Layers palette. The Layer Properties dialog box appears. Type a new name, and click OK.

DIFFICULTY LEVEL

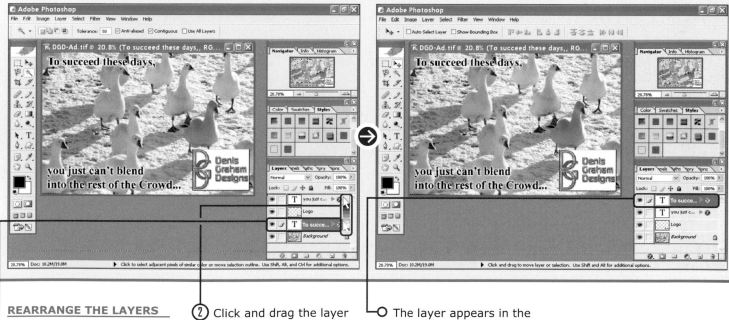

REARRANGE THE LAYERS

① In the Layers palette, click the layer that you want to move to a different stacking order.

② Click and drag the layer to the new position.

○ The layer appears in the new position.

Jazz up images with
LAYER STYLES

You can improve the appearance of your images by using layer styles. Styles can add dimension and special effects to your objects. You can apply styles to any layer except your Background layer. You can only apply styles to a background if you first convert it to a regular image layer.

You have ten layer styles categories from which to choose. Each style comes with multiple options and adjustments, which create an almost unlimited number of combinations for you to use. There is no set formula for using styles, and experimentation is the best way to see how they work.

The more common styles, like the bevels, shadows, and glows, have specific uses. In addition, patterns, color overlays, and other extras can be combined with them to create incredibly complex and detailed effects.

You can still edit text and shapes after you apply styles. Unlike most filters, styles can work on vector graphics, such as text and shapes, without first requiring rasterization of the vector graphic. This offers a great advantage if you need to edit later on.

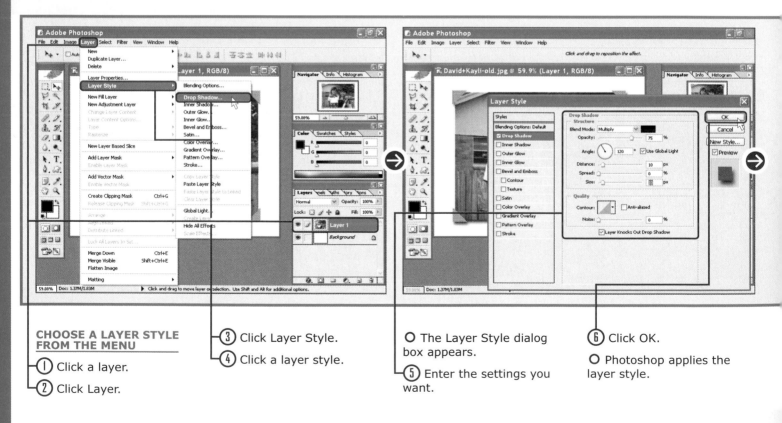

CHOOSE A LAYER STYLE FROM THE MENU

① Click a layer.

② Click Layer.

③ Click Layer Style.

④ Click a layer style.

○ The Layer Style dialog box appears.

⑤ Enter the settings you want.

⑥ Click OK.

○ Photoshop applies the layer style.

Did You Know? ※

You can use a style from the Styles palette; however, it resets any styles already applied, and applies the style you select. This ensures that the style you selected is applied as shown in the palette. If you want to add to a current style, see task #5.

Did You Know? ※

You can copy and paste layer styles. In the Layers palette, right-click a layer with a style applied. The menu that appears includes the Copy Layer Style and Paste Layer Styles options. With these two options, you can copy any style from one layer and apply the exact same style and settings to another layer. This is very convenient for styles you use often.

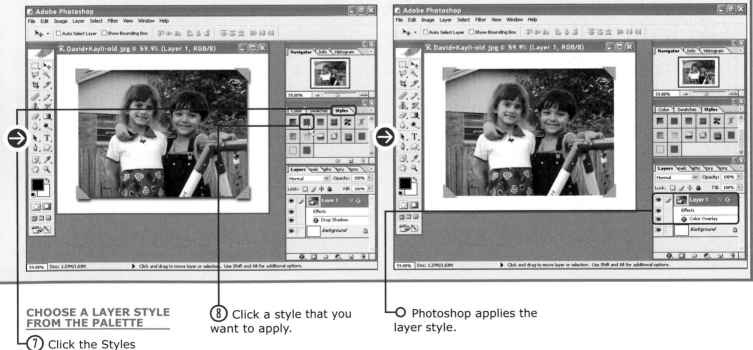

CHOOSE A LAYER STYLE FROM THE PALETTE

⑦ Click the Styles palette tab.

⑧ Click a style that you want to apply.

–O Photoshop applies the layer style.

Make quick adjustments to
LAYER STYLES

You can make changes or additions to your layer styles after you apply them to your image. One of the best features of layer styles is that they do not permanently affect your images, shapes, or text. You can edit their design, copy and paste them, and even delete some of the effects or the entire layer style. If you do not like what you have done, you can easily change it, without having to re-create the style entirely.

To adjust a layer style, you can open the Layer Style dialog box. It contains all ten of the available effects, and you can access the settings specific to each one, all in the same dialog box. Simply select your style effect, and make the adjustments. You can also toggle the effect on or off with a single mouse click. With a Preview option, you can even preview the changes before you apply them.

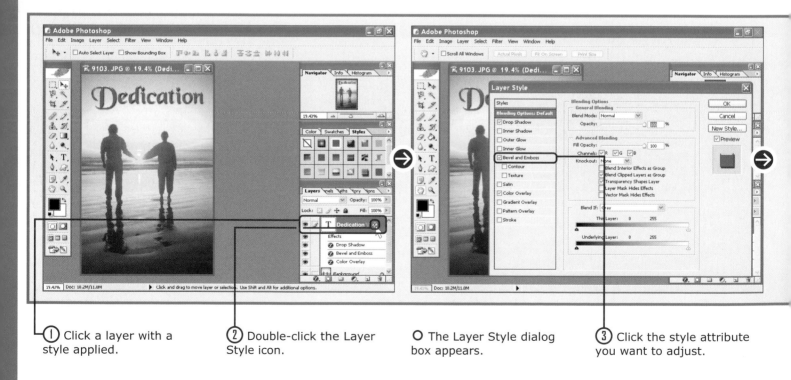

① Click a layer with a style applied.

② Double-click the Layer Style icon.

○ The Layer Style dialog box appears.

③ Click the style attribute you want to adjust.

Did You Know? ☀

You can also add new attributes
to your style by using another
method. Simply click any unused attribute,
and the check box automatically activates.
Set the attributes you want and click OK to apply
them. You can also clear the check box (☑ changes
to ☐) to temporarily turn off the attribute.

Did You Know? ☀

You can double-click a single listed effect in the Layers palette
to open the Layer Style dialog box to that attribute. You can then
make changes to that specific attribute. To view the individual
effects for a layer that has a layer style applied to it, click the ▶
next to the 🗗 on the layer.

Did You Know? ☀

You can right-click a layer and choose the Clear Layer Style option
from the menu that appears. Photoshop automatically removes all
layer styles from that layer. Although you can undo this action by
clicking Edit, and then Undo, you should still use it with caution.

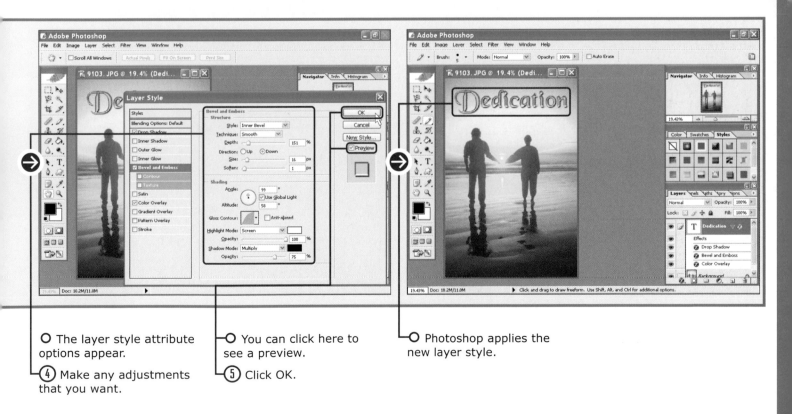

O The layer style attribute
options appear.

④ Make any adjustments
that you want.

O You can click here to
see a preview.

⑤ Click OK.

O Photoshop applies the
new layer style.

IMPORT NEW LAYER STYLES
to use in Photoshop

You can use the many layer styles in Photoshop for all of your custom work. There are, however, other layer styles available online that you can import into Photoshop to expand your available tools and enhance your creativity.

You can visit many sites online that have available layer styles that you can use in Photoshop. Adobe Studio Exchange, hosted by Adobe, has hundreds of styles available from which you can choose, and all work within Photoshop. There are dozens of personal Web sites by Photoshop experts that have hundreds of layer styles available. Do a search for

Photoshop layer styles in a search engine, and you will be amazed at how many results you find.

You can expand your creativity with outside styles. You can download and save these files for use in Photoshop. You can save them to the Photoshop Styles folder, and when you restart Photoshop, the program automatically loads the styles into the available styles menu.

With the incredible array of different effects and combinations of designs, you can learn new ways to create your own layer styles.

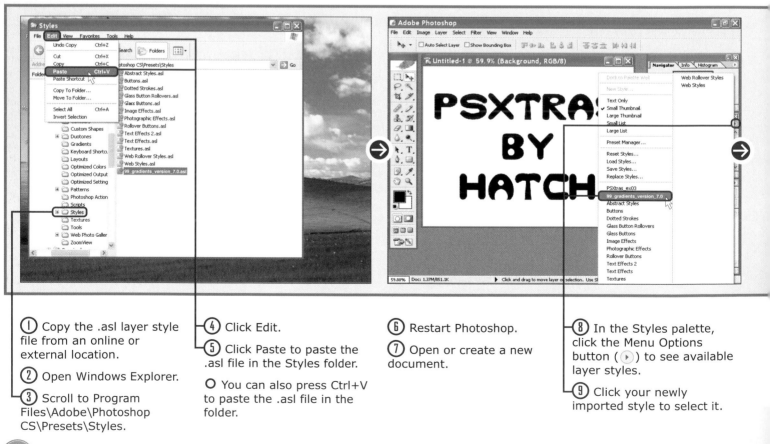

① Copy the .asl layer style file from an online or external location.

② Open Windows Explorer.

③ Scroll to Program Files\Adobe\Photoshop CS\Presets\Styles.

④ Click Edit.

⑤ Click Paste to paste the .asl file in the Styles folder.

○ You can also press Ctrl+V to paste the .asl file in the folder.

⑥ Restart Photoshop.

⑦ Open or create a new document.

⑧ In the Styles palette, click the Menu Options button (⊙) to see available layer styles.

⑨ Click your newly imported style to select it.

6

DIFFICULTY LEVEL

Apply It! ☀

In the Styles palette, as well
as the Styles area in the Layer
Style dialog box, click ☑, and choose
Save Styles. You can save the styles that
appear in your Styles palette as a custom
file. You can create your own custom sets of
styles for specific projects, or to share online
and with friends.

Check It Out! ☀

There are many places online with layer styles
that you can use. You can go to http://share.
studio.adobe.com, which is the open exchange
forum of Adobe for their graphics programs.
The layer styles used in this example are from
F. Hatcher at www.psxtras.com. Another good
site is www.ActionFx.com. You can also use an
Internet search engine to find other great links.

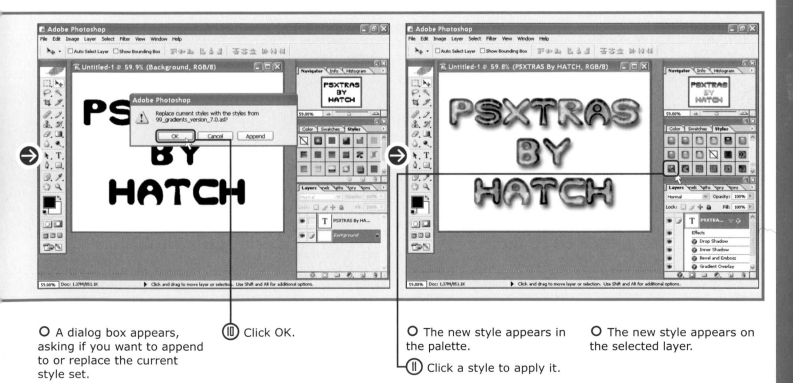

O A dialog box appears,
asking if you want to append
to or replace the current
style set.

⑩ Click OK.

O The new style appears in
the palette.

⑪ Click a style to apply it.

O The new style appears on
the selected layer.

Work with
BLENDING MODES
to blend layers

You can use the Photoshop blending modes to create special effects on your layers. Blending modes cause the pixels of a layer to interact with the pixels of another layer. There are several groups of blending modes from which you can choose. Each group has a particular area of modification, changing highlights, midtones, shadows, or colors of the affected lower layers. Highlight-based filters ignore midtones and shadows, and adjust only the lighter-colored pixels. Shadow and midtone blending modes modify dark tones and the middle range of tones,

respectively. The color modes change only the hue, saturation, and color blends of the layer they modify, leaving the contrast and tones alone.

It is a good idea to experiment with each blending mode, because each image has a particular range of tones and color, and there is no way to predict how each blending mode changes the other layers. You can even experiment with the effect that one blended layer has upon another blended layer. The creative combinations are endless.

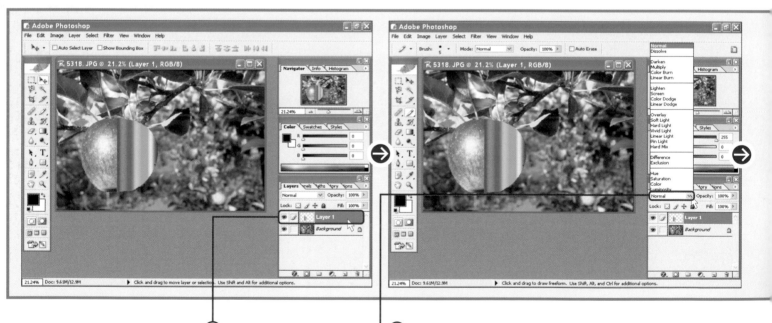

Note: This example has a spectrum gradient applied to better show the final result.

① In the Layers palette, click the layer that you want to blend.

② Click here to open the Blending Modes menu.

Did You Know? ※

You can reset and adjust
blending modes at any time. The
blending modes are not permanent
effects. However, they do affect all layers
below the layer with the blending modes.
You can adjust the layer opacity to lessen and
lighten the effects that the blending modes apply.

Did You Know? ※

You can use multiple layers for different effects.
Blending modes are cumulative, meaning that they
build upon and modify each other as you apply them.
For example, if you have three layers, and the middle
layer has one blending mode, then only the bottom
layer is affected. If the top layer also has a blending
mode applied to it, then this blending mode affects
both the middle and the bottom layer, compounding,
or adding to, the effect the middle layer is creating.

#7

DIFFICULTY LEVEL

③ Click a blend mode.

○ Photoshop blends the
layers you select with the
layers below it.

LINK LAYERS
to keep objects together

You can do many different things to affect layers and the objects that they contain. For example, you can have a layer that changes the color of another layer, or two objects on separate layers that overlap for a 3D effect. However, when you need to move these objects on multiple layers, it can be difficult to realign them individually. This is where linking the layers can help.

When you link layers, you essentially lock multiple layers together as if they were one individual layer. A small chain icon appears next to each layer that you link. Now, when you move one layer object, any

linked layer objects move together with the object you are moving. You can also transform and scale the layers simultaneously when they are linked.

You can find this feature useful with projects for Web sites and montage photo layouts. By linking the layer objects together, you maintain their original layout, and any changes you make to the layout affect the group as a whole, saving time and reducing error. You can even link layers to the background, which is extremely useful, because the background cannot be moved or altered.

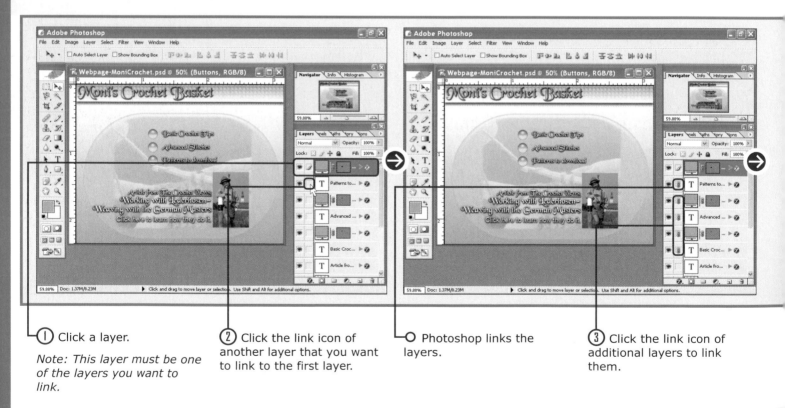

① Click a layer.

Note: This layer must be one of the layers you want to link.

② Click the link icon of another layer that you want to link to the first layer.

○ Photoshop links the layers.

③ Click the link icon of additional layers to link them.

Customize It! ※

You can use the Link feature to align and distribute objects. After you link the layers, click the Move tool (⊞). In the Options bar, the alignment buttons appear. With these buttons, you can align linked layers, respective to horizontal and vertical points of the layer objects. The selected layer is considered the base, and all other linked layers align to the selected focal point of the layer. The alignment buttons are listed in the table below.

DIFFICULTY LEVEL

Alignment Buttons	Distribution Buttons
Align Top Edges	Distribute Top Edges
Align Vertical Centers	Distribute Vertical Centers
Align Bottom Edges	Distribute Bottom Edges
Align Left Edges	Distribute Left Edges
Align Right Edges	Distribute Horizontal Centers
Align Horizontal Centers	Distribute Right Edges

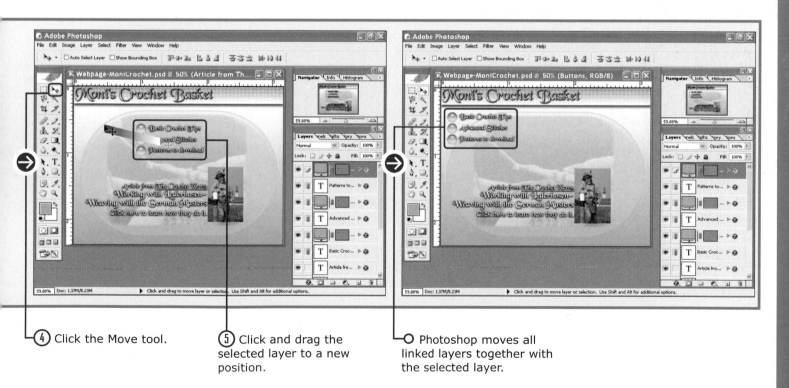

④ Click the Move tool.

⑤ Click and drag the selected layer to a new position.

◯ Photoshop moves all linked layers together with the selected layer.

Get organized with
LAYER SETS AND NESTED LAYER SETS

You can sometimes lose track of layers in a complicated image. To prevent this, you can use the layer sets feature to keep track of complex or numerous groupings of layers.

Layer sets are essentially folders inside the Layers palette that you can use for grouping together related layers. For example, when designing Web buttons, you can easily have four layers dedicated to each button. By placing these button layers into layer sets, you can more easily identify them, and clean up the clutter in the Layers palette. You can

even alter layer sets with blending modes, opacity changes, and several other select layer modifiers.

You can also use nested layer sets — layer sets within layer sets — up to five levels deep. This is especially handy with Web design, where you can have the same background with several different button sets or object layouts. You can place each page design in a separate nested layer set, and toggle their visibility to turn off or on all related layers at once, instead of each individually.

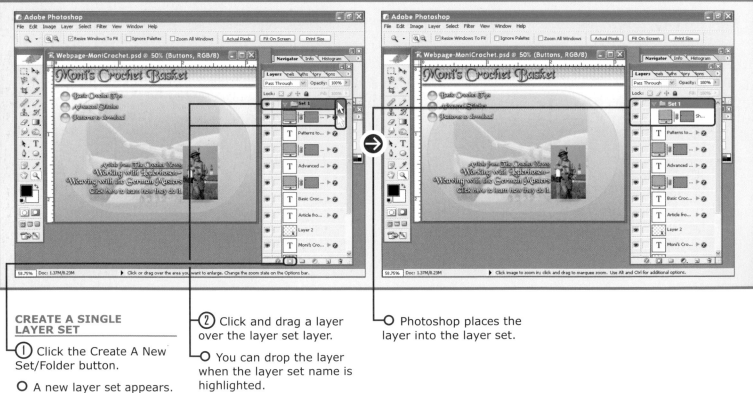

CREATE A SINGLE LAYER SET

① Click the Create A New Set/Folder button.

○ A new layer set appears.

○ This example uses the default layer set name, Set 1.

② Click and drag a layer over the layer set layer.

○ You can drop the layer when the layer set name is highlighted.

○ Photoshop places the layer into the layer set.

Did You Know? ※

You can apply blending modes, opacity, and other layer set modifiers to nested layer sets as well. When Photoshop begins rendering the image for screen, it applies the Inside-Out rule. Photoshop applies all blends, styles, modes, and adjustment layers from the innermost layer set first. Then the program treats that composite layer set as a flat image and applies the next outer level of modifiers, and so on until no more levels exist.

Did You Know? ※

You can apply opacity, blending modes, certain Transform tools, and any adjustment layer types to layer sets. This allows for some sophisticated design work that you can do with complex images. You cannot apply filters or layer styles to layer sets.

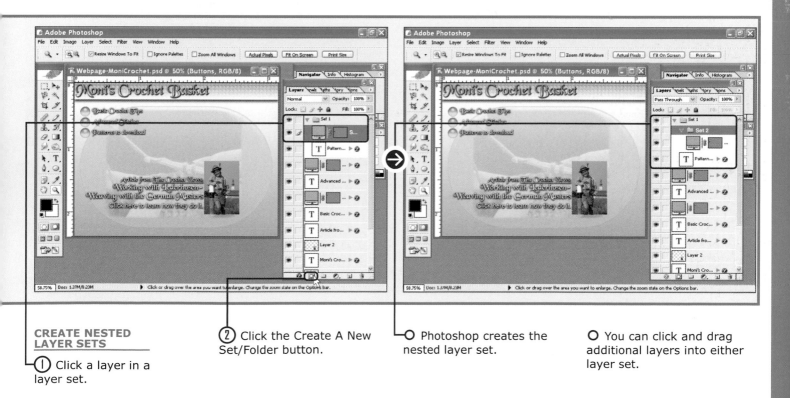

CREATE NESTED LAYER SETS

① Click a layer in a layer set.

② Click the Create A New Set/Folder button.

O Photoshop creates the nested layer set.

O You can click and drag additional layers into either layer set.

Capture versions of your work with
LAYER COMPS

You can take advantage of a great new feature in Photoshop called layer comps. Layer comps use the layout settings of your image, including layer object placement, styles, opacities, and blending modes, to create a composite file containing that information. After creating a layer comp, you can change the visibility, position, and appearance of the available layers and create a different layer comp. You can recall any saved layer comp that is available in the layer comp palette, and all layer changes automatically return to that state.

You can save multiple layer comps within each image. When you save the image in the .psd file format, Photoshop saves the comps with the image, so that you can return to the document and re-use the comps. Layer comps allow you to toggle the layer comp state on or off, which enables you to move back and forth through the different comps.

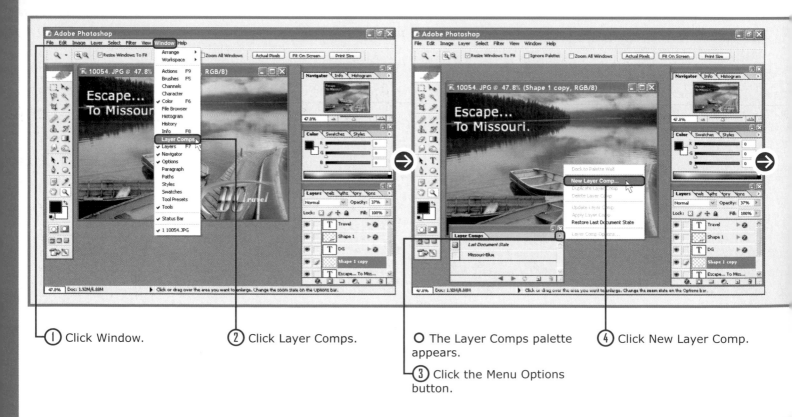

① Click Window.

② Click Layer Comps.

○ The Layer Comps palette appears.

③ Click the Menu Options button.

④ Click New Layer Comp.

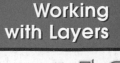

DIFFICULTY LEVEL

Caution! ※

When you delete a layer from
a layer comp, this deletion causes
that comp to become incomplete,
and an alert icon (⚠️) appears in the
palette. Any other layers within that layer
comp will change as normal when the comp
is recalled, but the missing layer will no longer
be there for you to modify.

Did You Know? ※

The Layer Comps palette contains an Update Layer
Comp button (🔄). You can make changes to your
saved comp, and then click this button to update
your selected layer comp in the palette. You should
be careful not to overwrite the wrong layer comp,
although, if you do, you can always undo it.

Apply It! ※

When creating your layer comps, you can save time by
giving each comp a name that describes the contents
of the comp. Each name should reflect the contents of
that comp clearly.

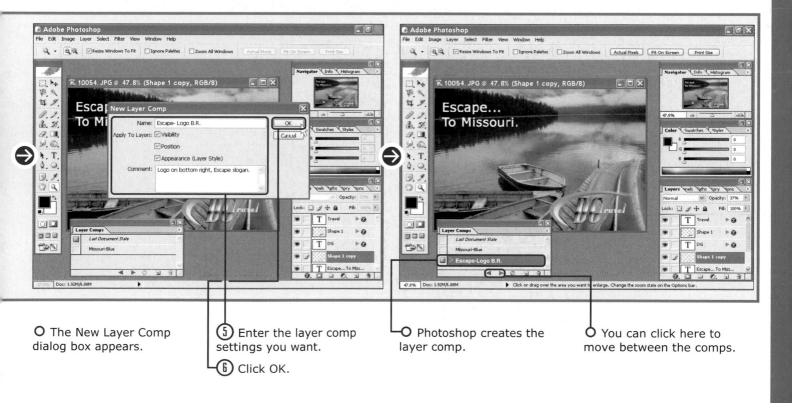

○ The New Layer Comp
dialog box appears.

⑤ Enter the layer comp
settings you want.

⑥ Click OK.

○ Photoshop creates the
layer comp.

○ You can click here to
move between the comps.

CHAPTER 2

Working with Drawing Tools

You can do much more in Photoshop than just photo manipulation. Photoshop has a wide range of tools, filters, and utilities that allow you to perform an incredible number of graphics-related tasks. Some of the most versatile tools you can use are text, brushes, and shapes.

You can insert text to create a Web page, add a caption to an advertisement, or label a photograph. You can enliven your text with patterns, styles, and special effects, such as beveling and drop shadows.

Text is not the only special tool at your disposal. Photoshop offers a wide variety of brushes, and you can also create your own custom brushes. Whatever your artistic skill,

you can make your work more creative with the Photoshop brushes.

You can add shapes, from simple geometric to complex custom shapes. You can then add these shapes to your photographs, or to the buttons on your Web page. Just as you can add patterns, styles, and special effects to text, you can modify your shapes in the same way. You can also design and save your own custom shapes.

Photoshop also adds new features, like typing text on a path, and brush groups, a feature that joins different brush tips into an individual brush. These new features give you even more ways to design fantastic graphics.

TOP 100

Write with
PARAGRAPH TYPE

You can place text in your image using a paragraph type. Normally, you insert text by clicking anywhere in the image with the Type tool. You type the text you want, and when you want to continue on a new line, you must press the Enter key. Otherwise, your text continues off the screen. However, with the paragraph type feature, you can specify the text area you want, and Photoshop wraps the text to fit those dimensions. Photoshop automatically moves text to the next line down when the text reaches the side boundary of the bounding box.

Creating paragraph type is easy. You simply select the Type tool, and then click and drag the cursor. A bounding box appears to help you specify the text area. You can then release the mouse button, and begin typing inside the text box. You can edit, format, and delete text within the box by clicking the Type tool and then clicking inside the text box.

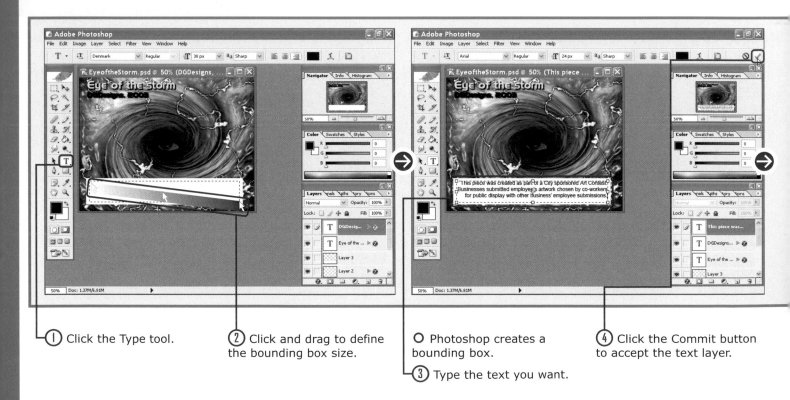

① Click the Type tool.

② Click and drag to define the bounding box size.

O Photoshop creates a bounding box.

③ Type the text you want.

④ Click the Commit button to accept the text layer.

Did You Know? ☀

You can change the attributes of your text block without selecting the actual text. In the Layers palette, click your text layer. Click the Type tool (T.), and then make any changes you want to the text format in the Options bar. If you need to edit the text, you can click inside the text box to change, delete, and format the text.

Customize It! ☀

You can resize the dimensions of your text box. Click the Type tool, and then click anywhere in the text box; the bounding box appears around the text. When you move your mouse over the bounding box corners, the cursor becomes a double arrow (↖ changes to ✛). Click and drag your text box to the dimensions you want.

DIFFICULTY LEVEL

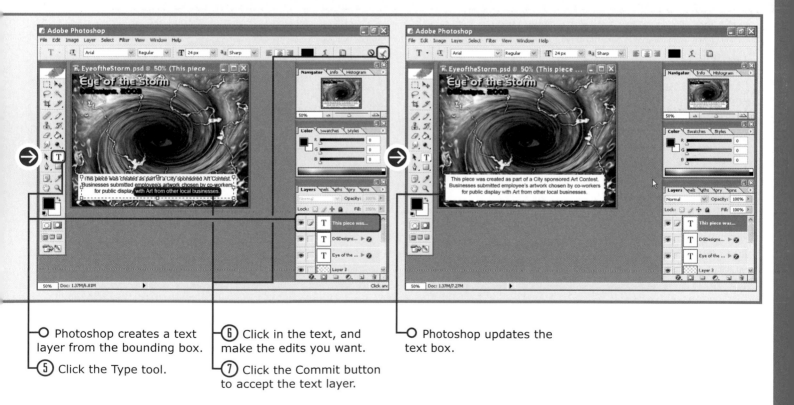

─○ Photoshop creates a text layer from the bounding box.

⑤ Click the Type tool.

⑥ Click in the text, and make the edits you want.

⑦ Click the Commit button to accept the text layer.

─○ Photoshop updates the text box.

WARP YOUR TEXT
for special effects

You can make ordinary text dramatically stand out by using the Warp Text tool. When an ornate font or a layer style that you apply to your text does not give you the effect you want, you can use the Warp Text tool to create a wide variety of different text shape effects. From a Fish to a Bulge to an Arch, you can create lively shapes for your text. You can even adjust the amounts of horizontal and vertical warping that occur when you apply this effect.

One of the best aspects of this feature is that you can still fully edit the text with the regular Type tool options. This gives you a great deal of flexibility when using the Warp tool. You can create your text shape effect, and edit and replace text if necessary, while keeping the original shape you created. This is a powerful feature, because it allows you to make corrections quickly without having to retype your text and reapply your effects from the beginning.

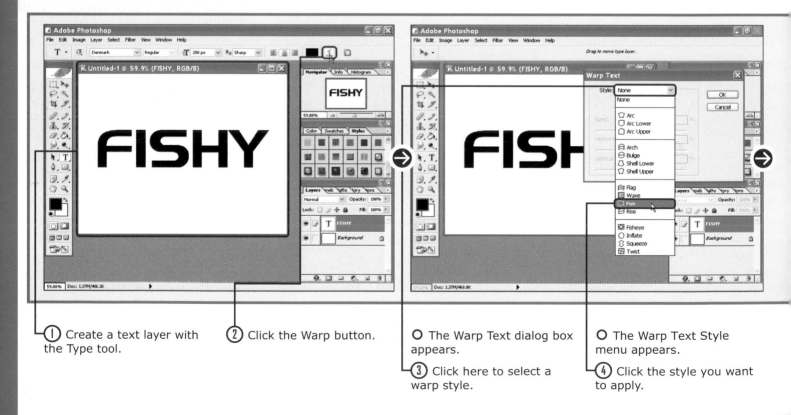

① Create a text layer with the Type tool.

② Click the Warp button.

O The Warp Text dialog box appears.

③ Click here to select a warp style.

O The Warp Text Style menu appears.

④ Click the style you want to apply.

Did You Know? ※

You can also use layer styles to make your text more exciting. The Warp Text feature allows you to use the layer style effects to enhance the appearance of warped text.

Did You Know? ※

You can use the Warp Text tool on vector-based type, but you cannot use the Warp Text tool on rasterized text. Vector type is mathematics-based, and can be warped, with the math automatically calculated by Photoshop. However, you can create similar styles on rasterized text when you use the Liquefy Filter in the Filters menu.

DIFFICULTY LEVEL

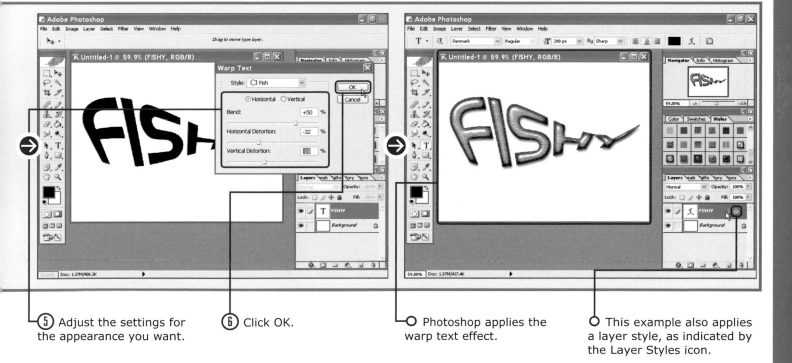

⑤ Adjust the settings for the appearance you want.

⑥ Click OK.

○ Photoshop applies the warp text effect.

○ This example also applies a layer style, as indicated by the Layer Styles icon.

TYPE TEXT
on a path

The Text tool is very versatile. You can combine text boxes with the warp feature for many creative options. A new text feature allows you to place text on a customized path. You can create wide, curvy lines of text, or design text that follows along a corner. Because type tools are vector-based, the text remains fully editable and resizable. Keep in mind that if you rasterize the text, then you cannot edit it.

You can easily create text on a customized path. Using the Pen tools, you can draw the path you want the text to follow. Then you can use the Type tool anywhere on that path; the text that you type follows the direction of the path. See tasks #11 and #12 for more information.

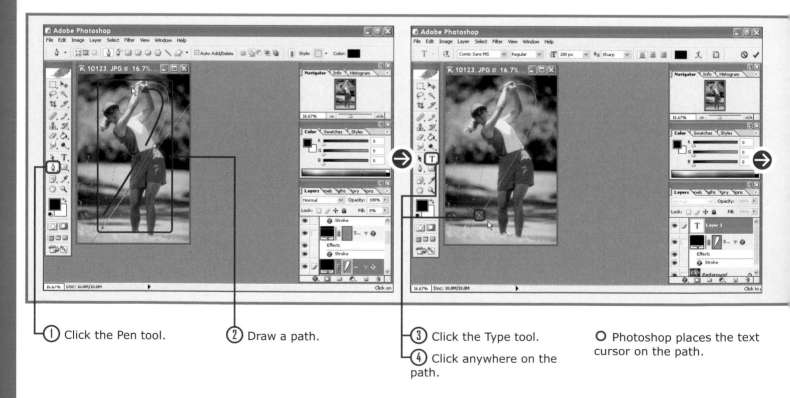

① Click the Pen tool.　② Draw a path.　③ Click the Type tool.

④ Click anywhere on the path.

○ Photoshop places the text cursor on the path.

Did You Know? ※

You can also apply both the layer styles and the warp text effects to text that is on a path. Simply apply the effects as you normally would to regular text. With these combined features, you can create incredible text and type designs.

Did You Know? ※

You can use the Direct Select tool ( ) to reverse the text. Click the Direct Select tool, and then click your text and drag the tool across the path to the opposite side. The text is now reversed.

DIFFICULTY LEVEL

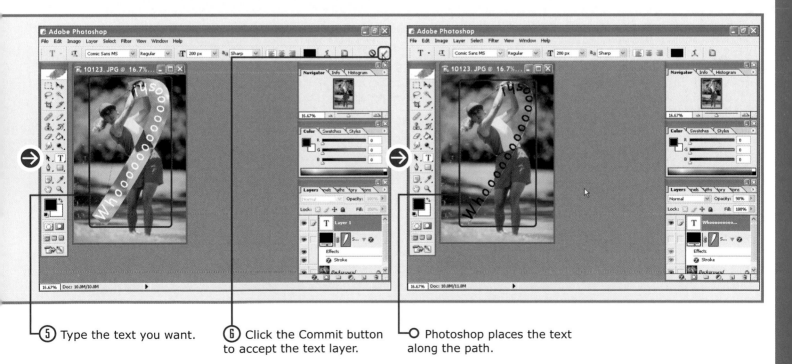

⑤ Type the text you want.

⑥ Click the Commit button to accept the text layer.

○ Photoshop places the text along the path.

Design your own
CUSTOM BRUSHES

In Photoshop, you can choose from hundreds of brushes to create your artwork and graphic designs. You can access these brushes through the Brushes palette. In addition to these regular brushes, Photoshop allows you to create custom brushes for your specific designs. You can specify the size, feather, and angle of your brush.

You can also define any portion of an image or an object as a custom brush. For example, you can convert a cutout of a face into a custom brush. You

can resize the cutout, and turn it into a brush. You can then save it with your current brush set or a custom set. Then when you want to use the brush you created, you can access it in the Brushes palette, just like all of the other brushes.

You can also use special options that allow you to change the spacing and fade-out points, create dotted lines instead of solid, and add color jitter, which changes the color and placement of your brush dots.

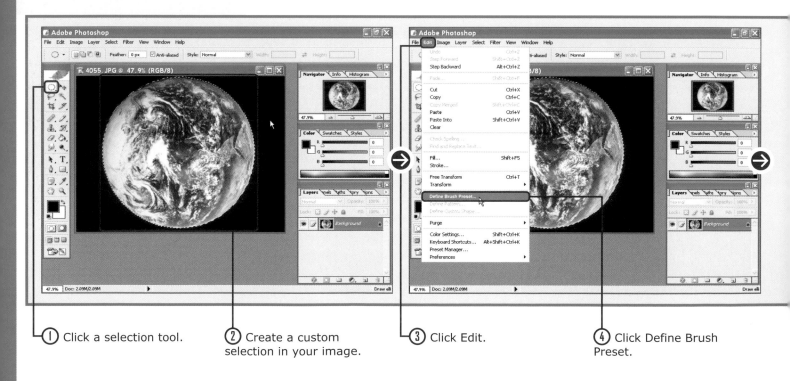

① Click a selection tool.

② Create a custom selection in your image.

③ Click Edit.

④ Click Define Brush Preset.

Customize It! ※

You can change the shape
of your cursor to the shape of
the brush you are using. Open the
Preferences dialog box and select Display
& Cursors from the drop-down menu. In the
Printing Cursors area of the dialog box, click
the Standard option (○ changes to ⦿) and then
press Enter.

Did You Know? ※

You can draw perfectly straight lines. With your brush,
click where you want your line to begin, move the cursor to
your end point, and then press Shift while you click. A straight
line appears between the two points using the current brush.

Customize It! ※

You can resize your brush from inside your image. Simply move
your brush cursor over your image, and right-click. A dialog box
appears with options to adjust both the brush diameter and the
hardness of the outer edge.

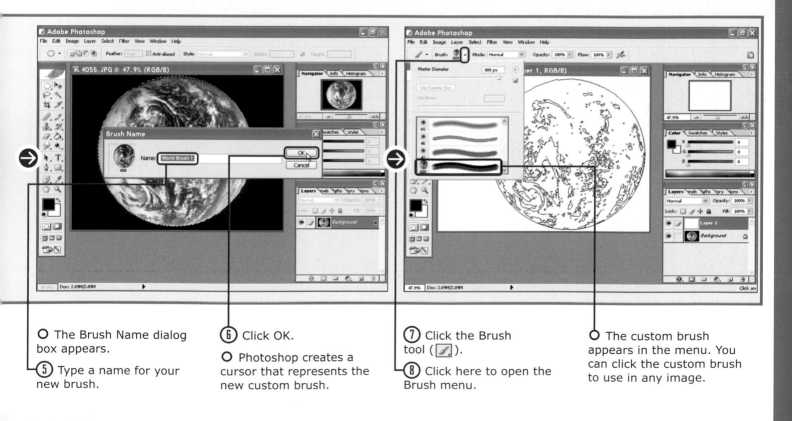

○ The Brush Name dialog
box appears.

⑤ Type a name for your
new brush.

⑥ Click OK.

○ Photoshop creates a
cursor that represents the
new custom brush.

⑦ Click the Brush
tool ( ).

⑧ Click here to open the
Brush menu.

○ The custom brush
appears in the menu. You
can click the custom brush
to use in any image.

Work with
SHAPES

You can use the Shape tools to create geometric shapes. Photoshop has a library of simple geometric shapes, and custom shape sets, from animals to fancy ornamental shapes. You can select your shape from the menu, and then click and drag your cursor to the size and dimensions of the shape you want.

You have six different Shape tools in Photoshop: Rectangle, Rounded Rectangle, Ellipse, Polygon, Line, and the Custom Shape tool. The first five

Shape tools are your basic geometric shapes. The Custom Shape tool has specialty shapes for other uses.

The five basic geometric shapes are shapes that may be difficult to draw freehand. You can create a hexagonal shape, but it could take time to create six equilateral lines for that shape. The Shapes tool is a shortcut that you can use to create simple shapes quickly and easily in Photoshop.

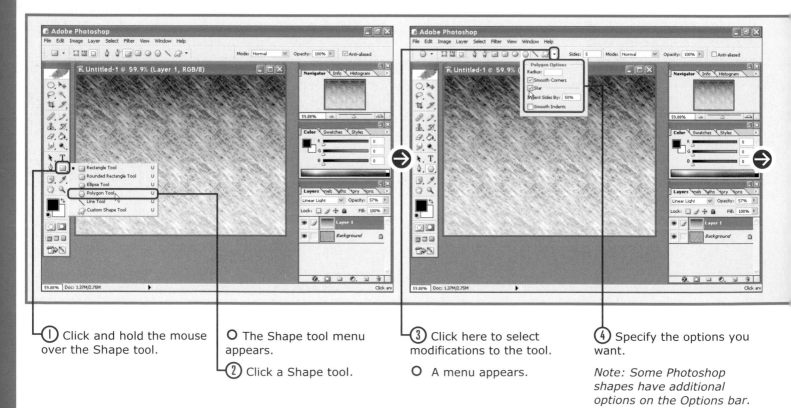

① Click and hold the mouse over the Shape tool.

○ The Shape tool menu appears.

② Click a Shape tool.

③ Click here to select modifications to the tool.

○ A menu appears.

④ Specify the options you want.

Note: Some Photoshop shapes have additional options on the Options bar.

Customize It! ※

The shape you create is filled with the same color that you select as your foreground color. If you decide that you want to change this color, click the Color box in the Options bar, and specify a new color in the Color Picker. You can also set your foreground color before drawing with the Shape tool.

15

DIFFICULTY LEVEL

Did You Know? ※

Several of the available geometric shapes offer additional options in the Options bar. For example, when you click the Rounded Rectangle shape tool (▢), you can set the radius of your rounded corners. The Polygon shape tool (⬡) allows you to determine the number of sides for your shape. You can specify from 3 to 100 sides.

⑤ Click Layer.
⑥ Click New.
⑦ Click Layer.

○ A New Layer dialog box appears.
⑧ Type a name for the layer.
⑨ Click OK.

○ Photoshop creates a new layer.
⑩ Click and drag the tool to create the shape you want.

○ To constrain proportions, you can press and hold the Shift key while creating the new shape. Constraining shapes to equal proportions creates squares and perfect circles.

○ The shape appears.

ADD LAYER STYLES
to shapes

You can use layer styles to creatively enhance the appearance of your shapes. The Layer Styles palette has different style categories that produce a wide range of effects. You can apply these styles to any shape, text, or design you create, and then you can add depth and pizzazz by applying bevels, shadows, and glows to your graphics.

With Photoshop, you can also add complex layer styles that give character to your shapes, such as chrome, glass, and even texture patterns. These styles are useful to provide character to shapes,

even more so than the basic bevels and shadows mentioned above. You can create dynamic graphics with the large selection of layer style options by clicking Layer, Layer Styles, and then selecting one of the available categories.

After you apply a style to a layer, you can click the Layer Styles icon for that layer, and modify the options in the Layer Style dialog box that appears. This is very useful when you want to adjust the scale of your styles to fit different sized shapes.

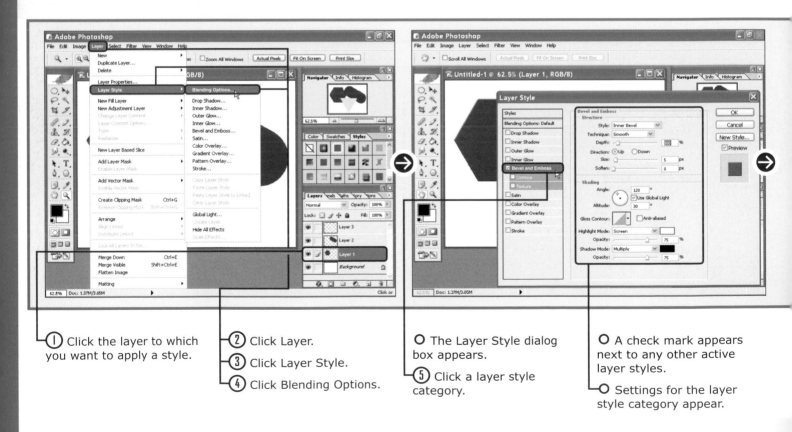

① Click the layer to which you want to apply a style.

② Click Layer.

③ Click Layer Style.

④ Click Blending Options.

O The Layer Style dialog box appears.

⑤ Click a layer style category.

O A check mark appears next to any other active layer styles.

O Settings for the layer style category appear.

Customize It! ※

You can transform your shapes after you apply a layer style. Transforming a shape adds perspective or resizes the shape to fit your needs. Click the shape layer and then click Image, Transform Shape, and then click a transform command. Click and drag the bounding box handles to transform and scale your shape. Press Enter when you are done.

Did You Know? ※

You can apply any of the preset layer styles found in the Styles palette to any shape. To do this click the shape layer, and then click the style you want from the Styles palette. The preset styles automatically apply the style category settings to create a viewable thumbnail of the style in the palette. To view the Layer Styles palette, click Window and then Styles.

#16

DIFFICULTY LEVEL

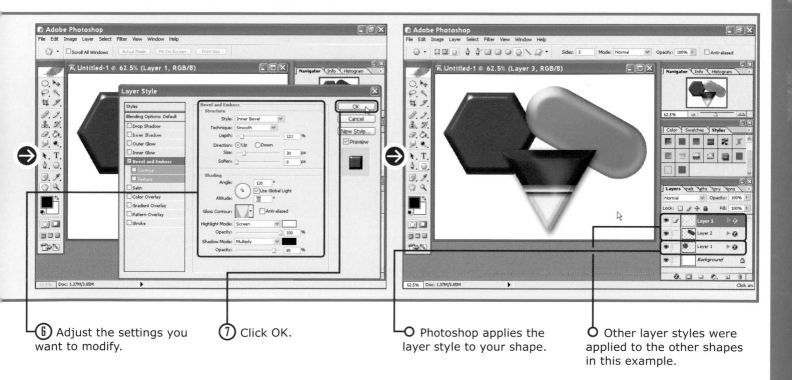

⑥ Adjust the settings you want to modify.

⑦ Click OK.

○ Photoshop applies the layer style to your shape.

○ Other layer styles were applied to the other shapes in this example.

Design your own
CUSTOM SHAPES

You can do more than use the preset shape sets that are in Photoshop. By following a few simple steps, you can create your own custom shapes out of everything from images to custom graphics. Photoshop allows you to define a shape you want to change into a vector-based image. When creating vector graphics, Photoshop calculates the outer edge, or path, of a shape. Photoshop then fills this outline with the default color, defined by your foreground color. Because of this color limitation,

there is not a method to convert the shapes using multiple colors, and as a result, Photoshop discards the colors, and creates a monotone shape.

You can use a photo as a base by reducing the amount of detail in the image, using tools and filters. When you have the image you want, you can define your shape as a work path, smooth out any jagged edges, and define it as a Custom Shape. This is an excellent way to store shapes that you use on a regular basis.

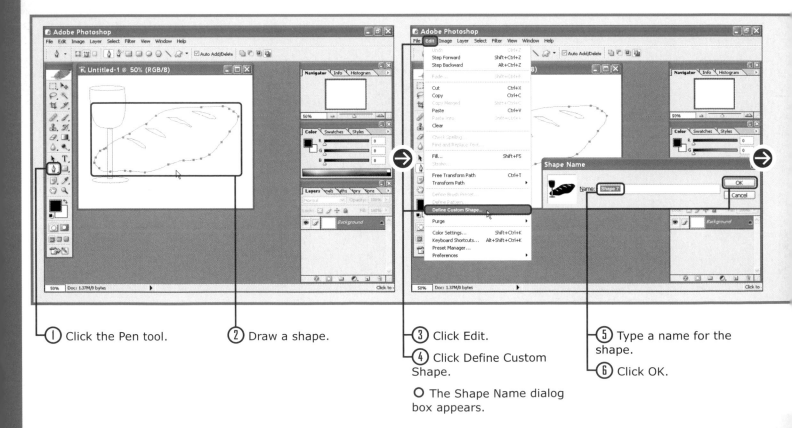

① Click the Pen tool.

② Draw a shape.

③ Click Edit.

④ Click Define Custom Shape.

O The Shape Name dialog box appears.

⑤ Type a name for the shape.

⑥ Click OK.

#17

Did You Know? ※

You can also create Custom Shapes from any defined selection. Create your selection and then click the Paths palette. Click ▶, and click Make Work Path from the menu that appears. Enter a tolerance level in the Make Work Path dialog box that appears, and then click OK. You can now follow steps **3** to **11** below to convert this new path into a custom shape.

Did You Know? ※

You can save your custom shapes in a separate file. Click the Shape ⬝ in the Options bar to open the Custom Shape picker. Click ▶, and click Save Shapes from the menu that appears. All the shapes that appear in the Custom Shape picker are saved in individual CSH files. You can share these files with other users, and store custom shapes for future use.

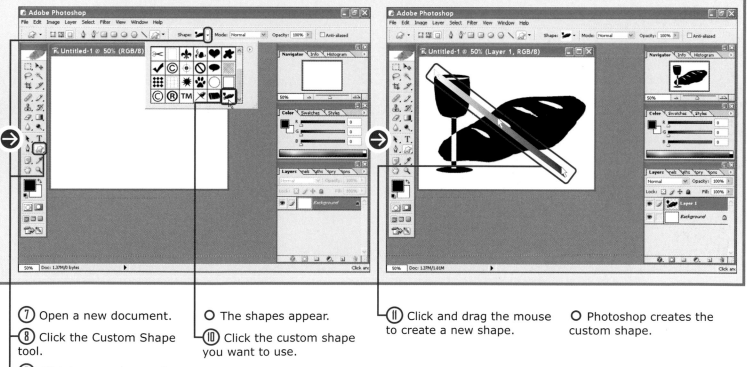

⑦ Open a new document.

⑧ Click the Custom Shape tool.

⑨ Click here to choose the new shape.

○ The shapes appear.

⑩ Click the custom shape you want to use.

⑪ Click and drag the mouse to create a new shape.

○ Photoshop creates the custom shape.

CONVERT TYPE
to shapes

You can take advantage of the tools in Photoshop to create custom shapes from characters in the fonts on your system. For example, you may have used stylized fonts, such as Wingdings, or unusual shapes available in other fonts, but these are not available as shapes that you can manipulate. Because unrasterized type is in a vector-based format, Photoshop can convert this type to a custom shape very easily.

You can use type in your image, and apply the same layer styles and filters to it as you would for shapes.

However, you gain an advantage when you convert an unusual character into a shape. When you use a stylized font such as Wingdings, you have to specify the font, size, and other characteristics. You must also search for the appropriate keystroke to produce the Wingding. By converting the character to a shape, you can easily locate the symbol in the Custom Shape palette, and then simply resize it by dragging it to the size you want. You can save time with this feature, especially with uncommon wingdings.

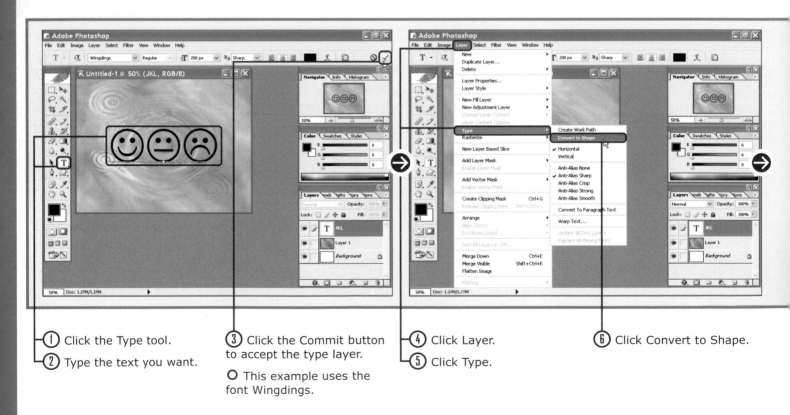

① Click the Type tool.

② Type the text you want.

③ Click the Commit button to accept the type layer.

○ This example uses the font Wingdings.

④ Click Layer.

⑤ Click Type.

⑥ Click Convert to Shape.

#18

Customize It! ☀

You can easily create your
own custom shape sets. In the
Custom Shape Picker dialog box, you
can right-click any shape and choose
between renaming and deleting the shape.
You can open up a shape set, delete the
unnecessary shapes, add your own custom
designs, and save them as CSH files. See the tip
section in task #17 for more information on saving
shape sets.

Caution! ☀

You can convert almost any character in a font into a shape.
However, some fonts do not include the outline data that
Photoshop needs to create a vector-based shape. Shapes are
based on an outline determined by mathematical formulae. Fonts
that do not have outline data cannot convert into a vector-based
shape because Photoshop cannot generate the needed math
formula for the shape. Bitmap fonts are an example of fonts that
Photoshop cannot convert.

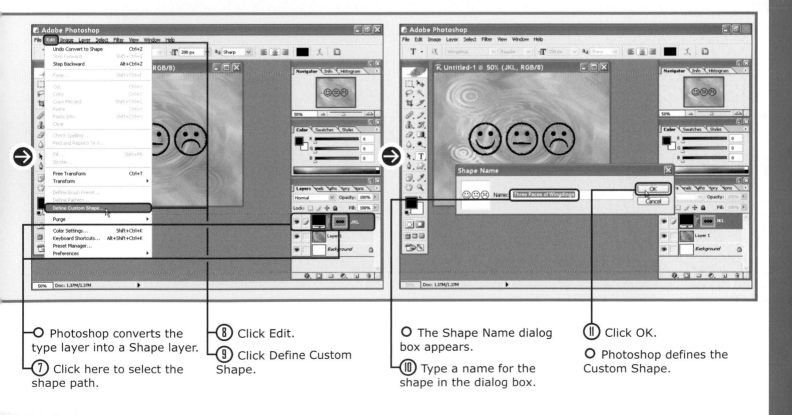

○ Photoshop converts the
type layer into a Shape layer.

⑦ Click here to select the
shape path.

⑧ Click Edit.

⑨ Click Define Custom
Shape.

○ The Shape Name dialog
box appears.

⑩ Type a name for the
shape in the dialog box.

⑪ Click OK.

○ Photoshop defines the
Custom Shape.

Import
ADDITIONAL BRUSHES AND SHAPES

You can import brushes and shapes from outside of Photoshop for use inside the program. Many Web sites offer custom brushes and shapes that you can use in Photoshop. This is a great way to add to your collection of designs and shapes.

You can import custom sets by copying the files onto your computer in the appropriate directory. When you start Photoshop, the program automatically loads the brushes, shapes, and other presets that it finds within the default folders. Next, click the Shape selection options menu to load your new set, or click Load Brushes in the Brush selection menu options.

Brush files have the .abr extension, and Shape files have the .csh extension. You can tell that you are using the correct folders by the similar file extensions within them. By default, you can find both Brushes and Custom Shapes folders in: C:\Program Files\Adobe\Photoshop CS\Presets.

You can find incredible brushes and shapes available at many different locations online. For more information about online resources, see Chapter 10.

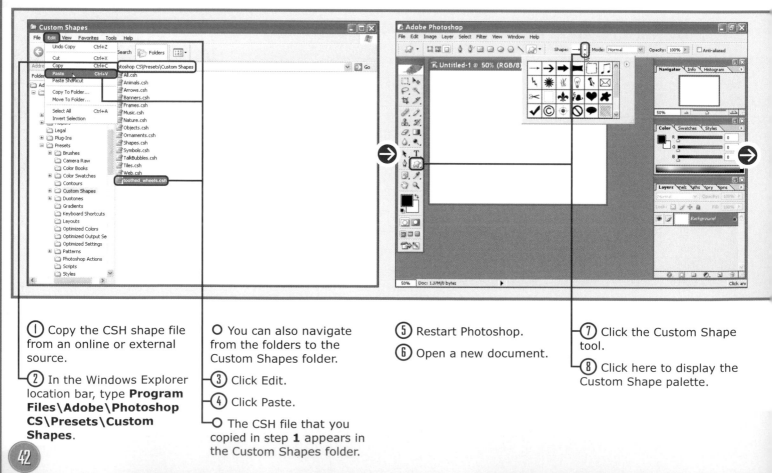

① Copy the CSH shape file from an online or external source.

② In the Windows Explorer location bar, type **Program Files\Adobe\Photoshop CS\Presets\Custom Shapes**.

○ You can also navigate from the folders to the Custom Shapes folder.

③ Click Edit.

④ Click Paste.

○ The CSH file that you copied in step **1** appears in the Custom Shapes folder.

⑤ Restart Photoshop.

⑥ Open a new document.

⑦ Click the Custom Shape tool.

⑧ Click here to display the Custom Shape palette.

#19

DIFFICULTY LEVEL

Did You Know? ☀

You can easily install your imported brushes. Paste your ABR file into the Preset/Brushes folder. Restart Photoshop, click the Brush ⊡, the ⊙, and then Load Brushes from the menu that appears. You can open the brush file from the selection that appears in the resulting Open dialog box by clicking the file and then OK. You can now use your new brush set by clicking the Brush selection drop-down menu.

Did You Know? ☀

You can always return to your original brush and shape sets. In the Brush selection drop-down menu is the Reset Brushes option. In the Shape selection drop-down menu is a Default shapes setting. Clicking either of these two choices resets to the corresponding default sets.

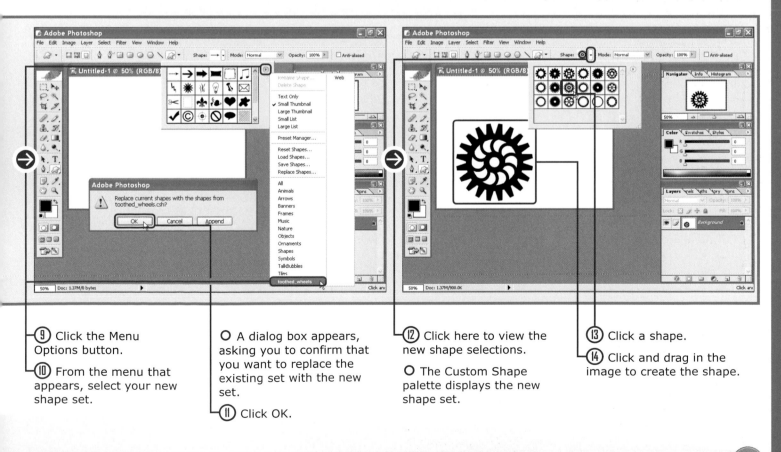

⑨ Click the Menu Options button.

⑩ From the menu that appears, select your new shape set.

O A dialog box appears, asking you to confirm that you want to replace the existing set with the new set.

⑪ Click OK.

⑫ Click here to view the new shape selections.

O The Custom Shape palette displays the new shape set.

⑬ Click a shape.

⑭ Click and drag in the image to create the shape.

Alter objects with the
TRANSFORM COMMAND

You can transform the basic design of your images, text, and shapes with the Transform command. The Transform command allows you to alter the shape and dimensions of a selected object, by stretching or scaling the object in several ways.

The Transform tool is located in the Edit menu. You can use it to size, stretch, and adjust the position of a selected object, allowing for a wide array of different pasted or layer objects to be placed and adapted to your base image.

This command is invaluable for graphic design, because you can adjust the scale, or size, of an object to fit better with your design. For example, you can skew the object to horizontally or vertically shift one side of the object, causing it to look as if it is slanted or leaning. You can also rotate the object into another angle, distort individual parts of the object, or change the perspective of it.

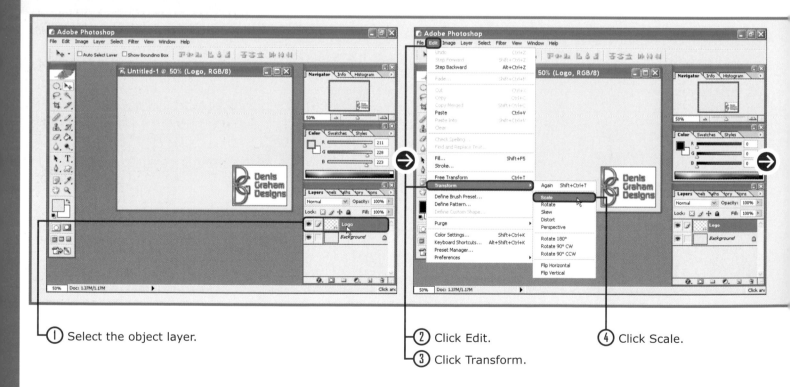

(1) Select the object layer.

(2) Click Edit.

(3) Click Transform.

(4) Click Scale.

#20

DIFFICULTY LEVEL

Did You Know? ※

You can transform an object in different ways. Holding the Shift key constrains proportions and resizes in the direction you drag the mouse. When you hold the Alt and Shift keys together, the object scales proportionately, from the center point in all directions. Holding the Ctrl key changes the current tool to the Distort Transform tool, allowing single bounding box points to be dragged out, distorting the object.

Did You Know? ※

You can transform more than one object at the same time. When you link two layers together, you can use the Transform command to scale, rotate, distort, skew, and change the perspective of the linked objects as if they were a single object. The center point Photoshop uses is the center point between the two linked layers.

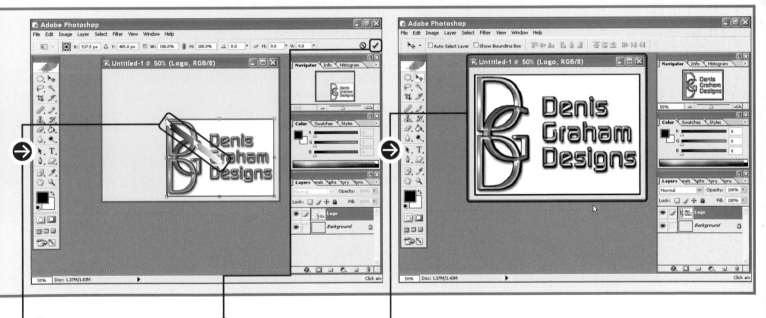

⑤ Press the Shift key, and click and drag away from the center of the object.

○ Holding the Shift key constrains the command to scale the object proportionately.

⑥ Click the Commit button to accept the transformation.

○ Photoshop transforms the object.

CHAPTER 3

Creating Selections, Masks, and Paths

You can use the Photoshop selection tools, masks, and paths to define areas of an image that you can modify for different graphic and photo design projects.

The selection tools in Photoshop define specific areas of the image by dashed blinking lines, or "marching ants," to outline selections in an image that you want to modify; only pixels within those boundaries are affected. The selection boundary display is called a marquee.

There are two different types of masks in Photoshop, Layer Masks and Quick Masks. A Layer Mask allows you to define areas of the image that are visible or transparent. Layer Masks do not delete pixels: they hide them. A Quick Mask is a temporary mask that allows you to see protected areas as a red overlay.

You can use paths to define the boundaries of a vector-based shape or area. They are often used to create precise selections of subjects in bitmap images. Typically, you use the Pen tool to create a path, allowing for flowing and creative shapes. A path appears as a thin gray line, with anchor points placed along the length, defining the path shape.

Each of these three features can overlap the function of the others. You can use selections to create a mask, convert the mask into a path, and use paths to define selections and masks. However you use them, the Selection, Mask, and Path tools are indispensable tools for your graphic design projects.

TOP 100

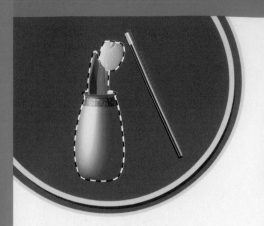

Work with the
LASSO TOOL

The Lasso tools allow you to create selections that have irregular borders. You can make both custom and complex selections with the Lasso tools. There are three types of Lasso tools — the regular Lasso, the Polygonal Lasso, and the Magnetic Lasso.

The Lasso tool is a good choice when you want to make quick freehand selections, but because the selection is automatically completed when you release the mouse button, it is not the best choice when you want to create long, complicated selections.

The Polygonal Lasso tool allows you to create only selections with straight lines. The Polygonal Lasso

tool has an advantage over the regular Lasso tool: With the Polygonal Lasso tool, you can stop and release the mouse button without the selection being closed. You can switch back and forth between the regular Lasso tool and the Polygonal Lasso tool while creating a selection by pressing the Alt key.

You can use the Magnetic Lasso tool for a selection around very complex objects. The Magnetic Lasso tool follows the boundary of contrasting pixels in an image, placing anchor points at regular distances from each other, or as placed by you. The Magnetic Lasso is the most detailed selection tool, and so it can also be the most time-consuming to use.

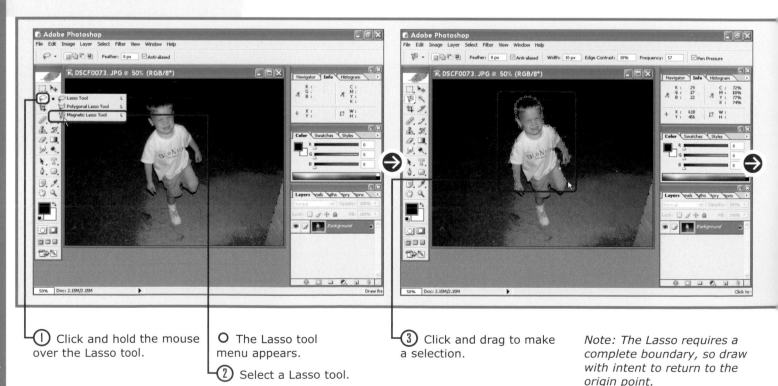

① Click and hold the mouse over the Lasso tool.

Ⓞ The Lasso tool menu appears.

② Select a Lasso tool.

③ Click and drag to make a selection.

Note: The Lasso requires a complete boundary, so draw with intent to return to the origin point.

Did You Know? ※

You can choose to feather the
edges of your selection before
you use the Lasso tools. In the
Options bar, you can enter a value
into the Feather box. This value feathers
the edges of your selection, creating a
semitransparent, blurred edge. When you use
your Lasso tool, Photoshop blurs or feathers the
selection based on the value you enter.

DIFFICULTY LEVEL

Customize It! ※

You can add to or remove from a selection
after you complete it. Press and hold the Shift
key while making a selection to add to the current
selection. Press and hold the Alt key while making
a selection to erase from the current selection.
Whatever areas you select using these options,
Photoshop adds to or erases the new selection you
create from your existing selection.

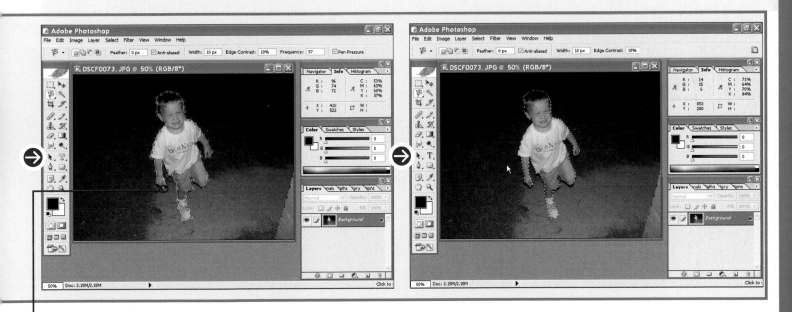

④ Drag the cursor back to
the origin point, and release
the mouse button.

○ A small letter *o* appears
by the cursor when you
reach the origin point.

○ Photoshop generates a
selection based on the
boundaries you drew.

CONTRACT AND EXPAND
your selections

You can make additional adjustments to selections in your image after completing the original adjustments. These modifications affect the size, structure, and edges of the selection. Two of the most commonly used are Contract and Expand. They are both excellent for working with complex shapes.

You can use these commands to modify the size of your selections. The Contract modification reduces the total scale of your selection. You can enter a value to specify the number of pixels you want the selection to contract inward. Photoshop constrains the contraction, so that it is equal in all directions

towards the point that Photoshop considers to be the center of the selection — which may or may not be the actual center. This is useful if you want to create an inner edge on an object.

The Expand modification is similar to Contract, except that it expands the pixel size outwards. You can use the Expand modification to create an outline or to ensure that what you delete from an image leaves no lingering pixels. Both commands allow you to make adjustments, but excessive adjustments can cause the selection to lose clarity and detail.

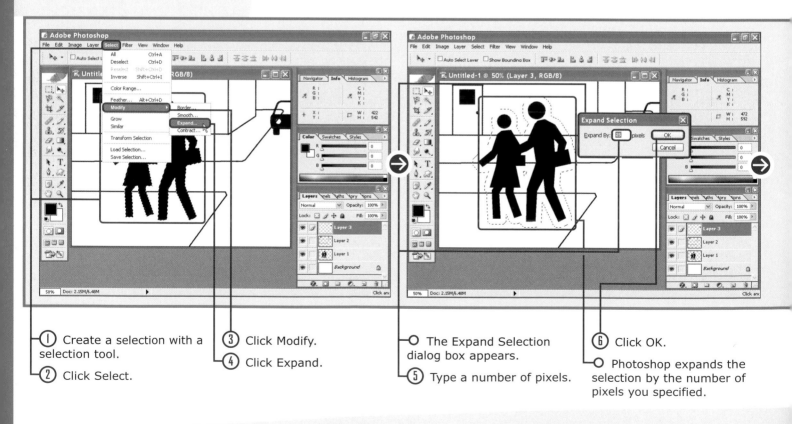

① Create a selection with a selection tool.

② Click Select.

③ Click Modify.

④ Click Expand.

─○ The Expand Selection dialog box appears.

⑤ Type a number of pixels.

⑥ Click OK.

─○ Photoshop expands the selection by the number of pixels you specified.

Customize It! ☀

You can easily make an outline around any object. First, make a selection outlining your subject. Click Edit and then Stroke. The Stroke dialog box appears. In the Location area, click Outside (○ changes to ◉), and choose a color from the Stroke area. When you click OK, Photoshop applies a stroke according to the options you chose.

Caution! ☀

When you create an outline around a selection, you should create the outline on a new layer. This way, if you later apply a Fill or use the Delete command they do not affect your original image. If you place a stroke around a selection on a layer that contains an image, the stroke becomes a part of the image, similar to drawing an outline with the Brush tool (), or other painting tool.

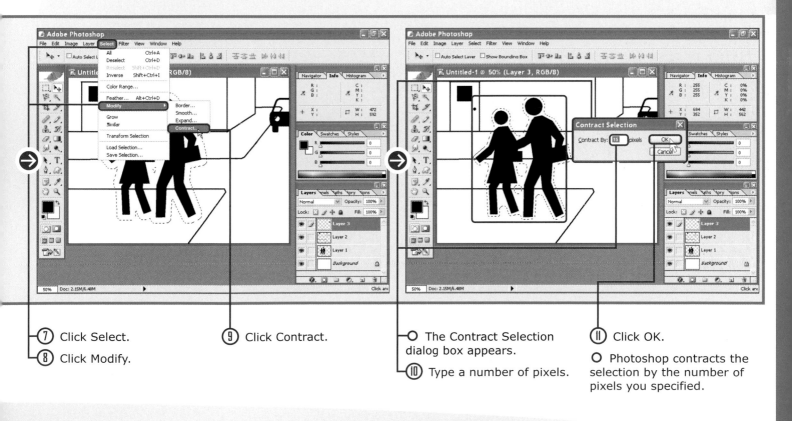

⑦ Click Select.

⑧ Click Modify.

⑨ Click Contract.

○ The Contract Selection dialog box appears.

⑩ Type a number of pixels.

⑪ Click OK.

○ Photoshop contracts the selection by the number of pixels you specified.

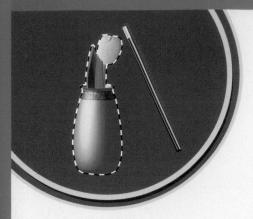

Remove elements in a photo with the
EXTRACT COMMAND

When you use the Extract command to create selections, you can draw and fill in your selections in the dialog box, preview the results, and make adjustments before applying them. Unlike the other selection tools, the Extract command enables you to isolate a foreground subject from its background. Even objects with indefinite edges like hair can be easily clipped from their backgrounds. When finished, you can extract the selected subject from the original image and place it seamlessly into another image.

In the Extract dialog box, you can use the Edge Highlighter tool to define the boundaries of the desired subject in green, the default color. You can

use the Edge Highlighter tool where the edge of your object fades into the background. Photoshop analyzes the highlighted areas to determine which should be kept and which deleted. Then, you can use the Fill tool to create the selection with the default color blue.

The Edge Highlighter tool may not create a smooth edge every time: the pixel selection can be choppy. When this occurs, you can use the Cleanup tool and the Edge Touchup tool. These tools help to rebuild or erase the selection edges. When using these tools, you are specifying which parts of the elements you want to remove from the image; by pressing the Alt key, you can add parts of an element to the selection.

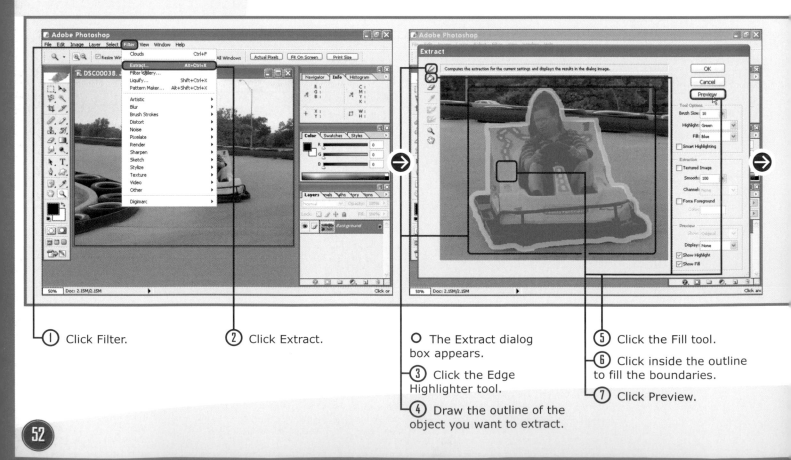

① Click Filter.

② Click Extract.

○ The Extract dialog box appears.

③ Click the Edge Highlighter tool.

④ Draw the outline of the object you want to extract.

⑤ Click the Fill tool.

⑥ Click inside the outline to fill the boundaries.

⑦ Click Preview.

23

DIFFICULTY LEVEL

Did You Know? ※

When using the Edge Cleanup tool ([icon]) or the Edge Touchup tool ([icon]), you can change the pressure of the brush, increasing the amount of effect each tool delivers. The settings range from 1 to 9, and 0, with 1 the weakest pressure, and 0 the strongest pressure. Simply click the tool you want to use, and press a number key to set the pressure.

Did You Know? ※

You can edit the edges of the extraction after the filter is applied and you have returned to the regular Photoshop window. By using the Art History brush ([icon]), you can restore missing or choppy edges. You can use the Eraser tool ([icon]) to smooth and remove unwanted pixels.

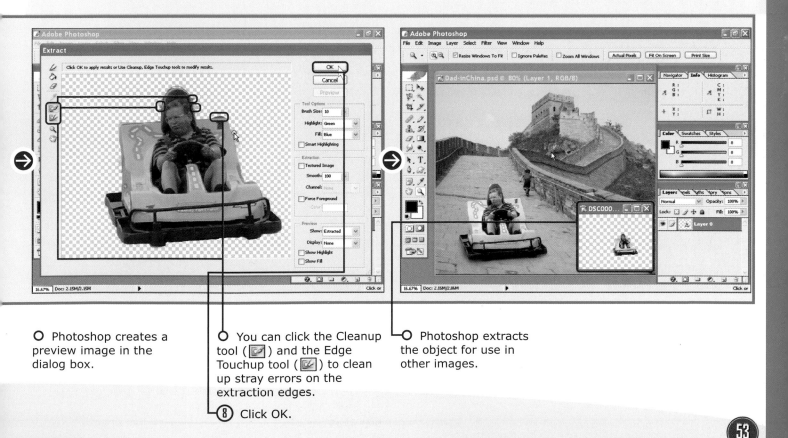

O Photoshop creates a preview image in the dialog box.

O You can click the Cleanup tool ([icon]) and the Edge Touchup tool ([icon]) to clean up stray errors on the extraction edges.

O Photoshop extracts the object for use in other images.

⑧ Click OK.

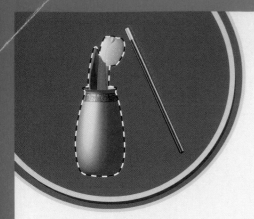

APPLY A QUICK MASK
for selections and effects

In Photoshop, a selection protects part of an image by masking the unselected area to prevent change. You can edit a selection with one of the selection tools. A Quick Mask is a temporary mask that you can edit using a brush tool.

A Quick Mask shows the protected areas that you do not want to edit with a translucent red overlay. When you click a button in the toolbox, the Quick Mask is turned off, and the edited selection appears as a normal selection.

If you save the selection as an alpha channel, you can return to your Photoshop file and edit the selection later. You can use regular selection tools to edit the selection, or use the Quick Mask feature to edit it using the brush tools.

With the Quick Mask tool, you can quickly add the areas you want to incorporate into the mask with any brush tool. The mask appears onscreen as a translucent red color over the image. When you finish defining your Quick Mask, Photoshop makes your mask an active selection.

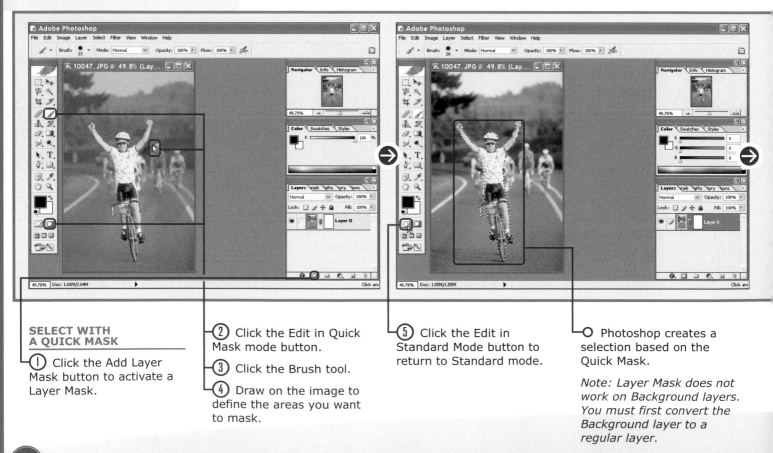

SELECT WITH A QUICK MASK

① Click the Add Layer Mask button to activate a Layer Mask.

② Click the Edit in Quick Mask mode button.

③ Click the Brush tool.

④ Draw on the image to define the areas you want to mask.

⑤ Click the Edit in Standard Mode button to return to Standard mode.

○ Photoshop creates a selection based on the Quick Mask.

Note: Layer Mask does not work on Background layers. You must first convert the Background layer to a regular layer.

24

DIFFICULTY LEVEL

Did You Know? ☀

A Quick Mask is an excellent
tool for creating or modifying an
existing selection because it shows
an accurate representation of where the
edges of the selection are. The "marching
ants" marquee display can only give an
approximation of the edge of a selection. With the
Quick Mask enabled, you can see the edge of your
selection and easily modify it using a brush tool.

Did You Know? ☀

You may want to change the color of your
Quick Mask overlay when you work on an image
that contains the same colors as the overlay. To
change the color of your Quick Mask overlay,
double-click the Quick Mask Enable button (⬛).
When the Quick Mask Options dialog box appears,
click the Color box to open the Color Picker, and
choose a different color.

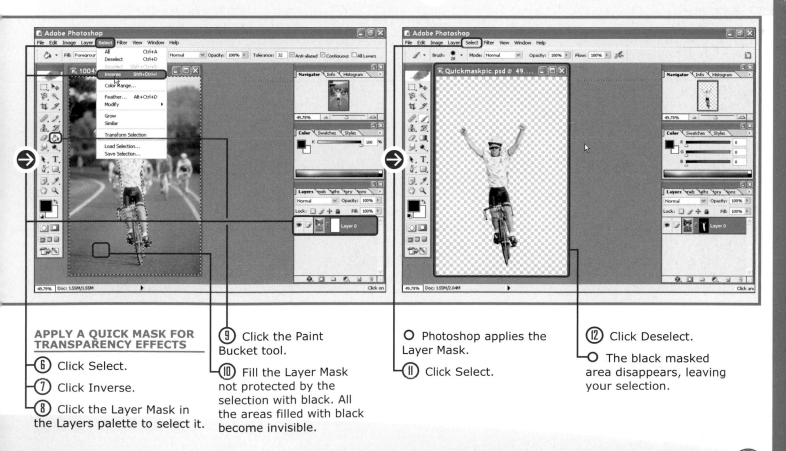

APPLY A QUICK MASK FOR TRANSPARENCY EFFECTS

⑥ Click Select.

⑦ Click Inverse.

⑧ Click the Layer Mask in the Layers palette to select it.

⑨ Click the Paint Bucket tool.

⑩ Fill the Layer Mask not protected by the selection with black. All the areas filled with black become invisible.

○ Photoshop applies the Layer Mask.

⑪ Click Select.

⑫ Click Deselect.

○ The black masked area disappears, leaving your selection.

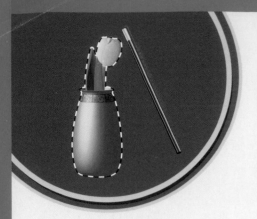

Blend two pictures together with MASKS

You can create a graphic layout design using masks. Blending two different pictures into one image is a popular layout technique for ads and graphic art. You can create this with masks, by overlapping your two images on separate layers, one atop the other, and masking out the boundary between the two images.

Applying black to the Layer Mask hides the pixels of the image it is masking, and white reveals the underlying image. You can also use shades of gray to create a semi-transparent effect. You can use black-to-white gradients to merge images together. The merge creates a smooth change in the overlap of the images.

You can use other brush and paint tools to make adjustments to the Layer Mask, to customize the appearance of the image. When you blend two images together, you can be as creative as you want with the brush tools and not damage the original images.

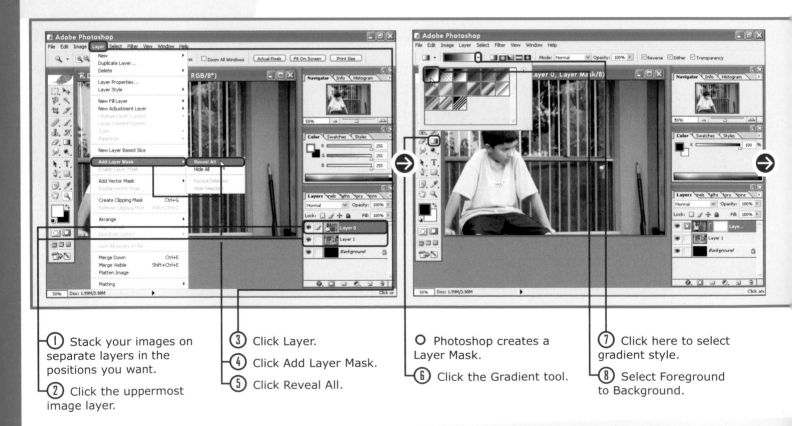

① Stack your images on separate layers in the positions you want.

② Click the uppermost image layer.

③ Click Layer.

④ Click Add Layer Mask.

⑤ Click Reveal All.

O Photoshop creates a Layer Mask.

⑥ Click the Gradient tool.

⑦ Click here to select gradient style.

⑧ Select Foreground to Background.

Customize It! ☀

You can use the Radial
Gradient option to create
vignette-like effects in your images.
Use white as your foreground color, and
black as your background color, and create
a radial gradient beginning from the center
of the object you want to reveal. The distance
you drag the mouse determines the length of the
gradient blend, and therefore the amount of transition
between the images.

#25

DIFFICULTY LEVEL

Did You Know? ☀

You can use the Airbrush option (✍) of the
brush tool to reduce the opacity and flow of the
brush when you paint on your masks. This allows
you to create easy and quick transparency effects.
Using the Fade option in the Brush palette, you can
add the subtle effect to the mask of the transparency
or opacity fading away with the brush.

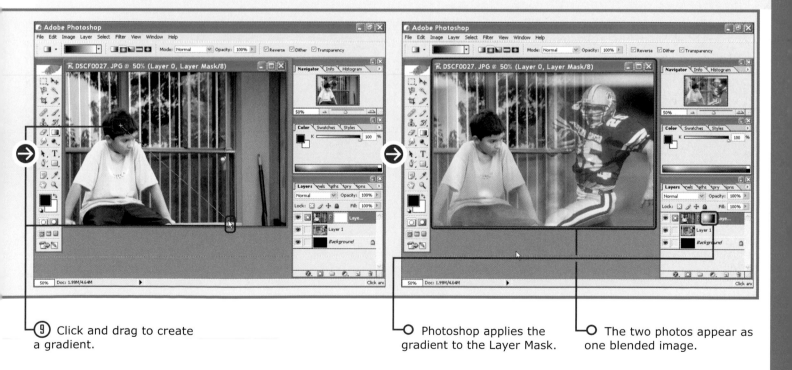

⑨ Click and drag to create
a gradient.

○ Photoshop applies the
gradient to the Layer Mask.

○ The two photos appear as
one blended image.

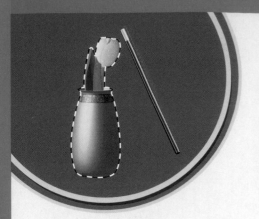

Create images within type with
MASKS

You can use a mask in Photoshop to hide part of an image. Text masking is a feature that allows you to add special effects and overlays to your text layers. For example, you can use text to mask an image, where the mask functions like a stencil, allowing the photo to appear where the text cuts through the mask.

There are two components with this type of mask: the text, which you create, and the overlay, which can be any image you want to put on a layer. When you put the two layers together with a mask, the overlay shows only where the text is.

Layer Masks work by defining visible and hidden areas in an image layer. The area of a layer that is white on the Layer Mask is visible on-screen. If the area is not visible on-screen, then the mask is filled with black in that area. The actual image is not erased.

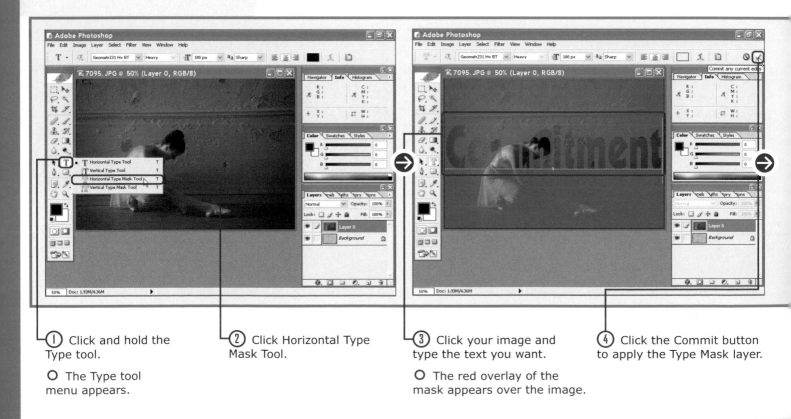

① Click and hold the Type tool.

O The Type tool menu appears.

② Click Horizontal Type Mask Tool.

③ Click your image and type the text you want.

O The red overlay of the mask appears over the image.

④ Click the Commit button to apply the Type Mask layer.

Did You Know? ☀

You can create the previously described effect using shapes just as easily as using text. Create a selection of any shape or geometric pattern on a layer above the image you want to mask. Then repeat steps **5** to **7** below. This technique enables you to turn any shape or selection into a mask to create many kinds of photo effects.

Did You Know? ☀

You can apply the Stroke command to a text mask to create the illusion of a neon sign. Begin with a dark background and create a text mask using a sans serif typeface such as Arial. Click Edit and then Stroke. In the Stroke dialog box, type a value in the Width text field to apply a border through the middle of the text mask selection. The stroke width should be wide enough to look like a neon tube. Click the Color box, and choose the darkest shade of the color you want to use. The secret of the effect is to apply additional stroke commands to the same text mask using progressively smaller and lighter strokes.

#26

DIFFICULTY LEVEL

○ Photoshop creates a text selection.

⑤ Click Layer.

⑥ Click Add Layer Mask.

⑦ Click Reveal Selection.

○ Photoshop creates a Text Mask.

○ This example uses a textured background and adds a shape to the mask.

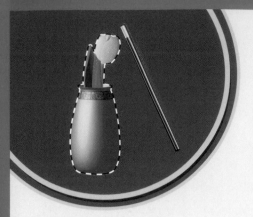

CREATE A STROKE PATH
with the Pen tool

You can create highly detailed and accurate selections with the Pen tool. The Pen tool works similarly to most of the brush or selection tools, but because the Pen tool is a vector-based tool, it operates on an independent layer, allowing you to edit the path until you are ready to apply it to a selection or other path option. Paths have several options available to them, including creating a filled shape, a selection, or a stroke outline. These options are available from the Paths palette when you right-click a path.

You can easily create the outlines of an object with the Stroke Path option. By utilizing the Pen tool to create the outline of your image, you can apply a stroke directly to the path. This method is very effective when working with highly detailed selections that you want to outline. For more information on creating a selection from a path, see task #29.

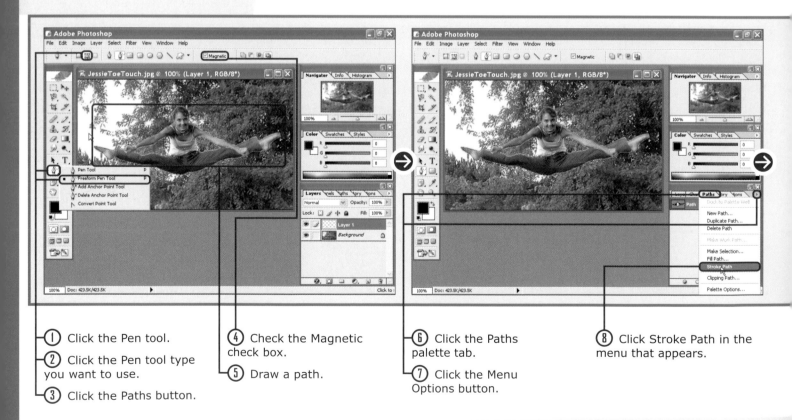

① Click the Pen tool.

② Click the Pen tool type you want to use.

③ Click the Paths button.

④ Check the Magnetic check box.

⑤ Draw a path.

⑥ Click the Paths palette tab.

⑦ Click the Menu Options button.

⑧ Click Stroke Path in the menu that appears.

Did You Know? ※

When you apply the Stroke
path, you select the tool type that
you want the stroke to resemble.
These tools retain the setting from the
last time they were used. You can set your
tool options before using the Stroke path, to
customize your final result.

DIFFICULTY LEVEL

Did You Know? ※

You can save the paths within the image only
when you save it as a PSD file. This is a very
useful feature when you are working with a project
that may require returning to an image repeatedly.
Because you can resize paths without losing clarity,
you can also use them for projects where you want
to scale an image, such as a logo.

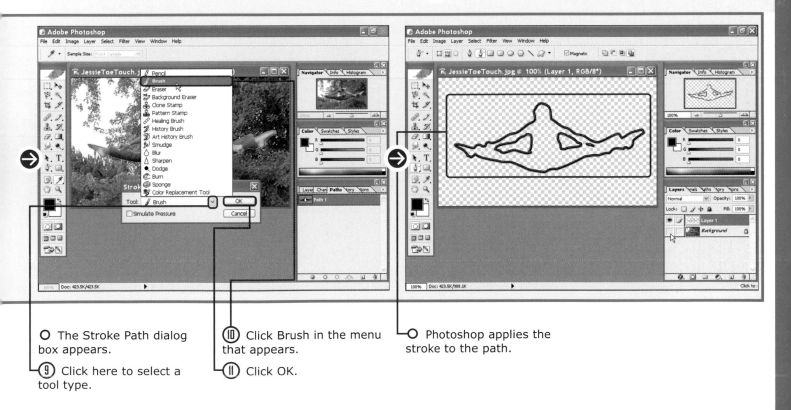

○ The Stroke Path dialog
box appears.

⑨ Click here to select a
tool type.

⑩ Click Brush in the menu
that appears.

⑪ Click OK.

○ Photoshop applies the
stroke to the path.

61

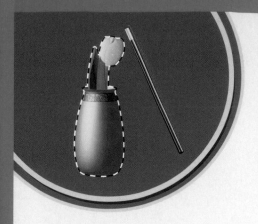

Create a
CUSTOM
SHAPE PATH

When you are drawing and editing paths for use in your image, you can save a lot of time and energy by using custom shapes. You can take any custom shape and draw it as a path, instead of a shape.

When you click the Pen tool, you can click the custom shapes in the Options bar and use the preset shapes to create a path in the selected shape. This allows you to create selections based on any custom shape available in Photoshop, or even to import new

shapes to edit and use with the Pen tool to make selections. For more information on importing custom shapes, see task #19.

You can easily scale your paths. When you click the Show Bounding Box option in the Options bar, a bounding box surrounds the path you select. You can now drag any of the box points to stretch or scale your paths into the shape you want.

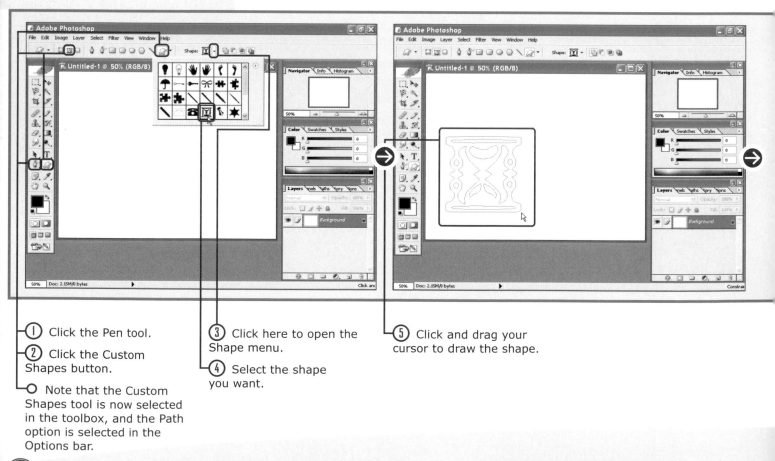

① Click the Pen tool.

② Click the Custom Shapes button.

O Note that the Custom Shapes tool is now selected in the toolbox, and the Path option is selected in the Options bar.

③ Click here to open the Shape menu.

④ Select the shape you want.

⑤ Click and drag your cursor to draw the shape.

#28

DIFFICULTY LEVEL

Did You Know? ※

After you create your shape, you can create a selection from it, and then make a Stroke Path, or create a filled shape, just as with drawn paths. The main difference is that Photoshop places all the points and draws the curves for you, simplifying the process considerably.

Did You Know? ※

You can also alter a path after you create it. Click the Direct Select tool (▸.), and click the path. The anchor points on the path appear. You can move these points to change the shape of the path. You can also add and delete anchor points using other Pen tools from the toolbox.

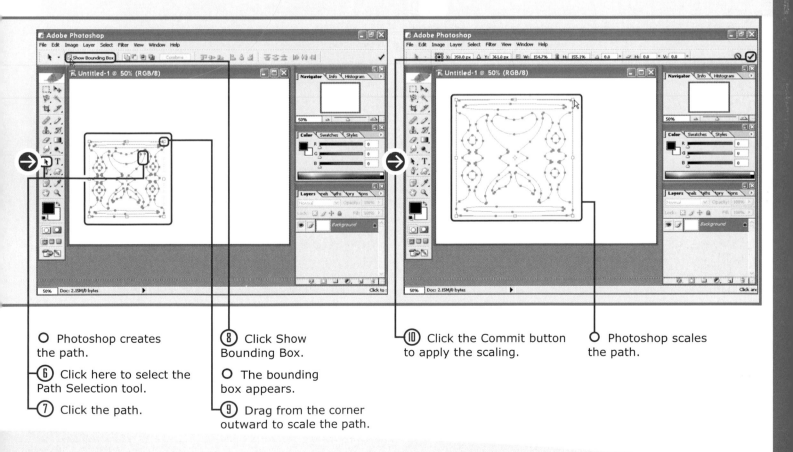

○ Photoshop creates the path.

⑥ Click here to select the Path Selection tool.

⑦ Click the path.

⑧ Click Show Bounding Box.

○ The bounding box appears.

⑨ Drag from the corner outward to scale the path.

⑩ Click the Commit button to apply the scaling.

○ Photoshop scales the path.

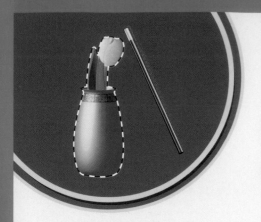

CONVERT A PATH
into a selection

One of the most popular uses for a path is to create accurate selections. You can create a detailed path, convert the path into a selection, and edit the selected pixels.

To convert a path into a selection, you begin by drawing your path with the Path design tools. Next, in the Paths palette, you can click the path layer, the Menu Options button, and then the Make Selection command. Your selection becomes active, and thus ready to be edited like any other selection. Your path remains in the Paths palette, allowing you to return and reselect the same shape to make more changes.

Because paths save with the image, you can reopen the file later, and recall the path to generate a new selection. This is a useful timesaver for repeat selections.

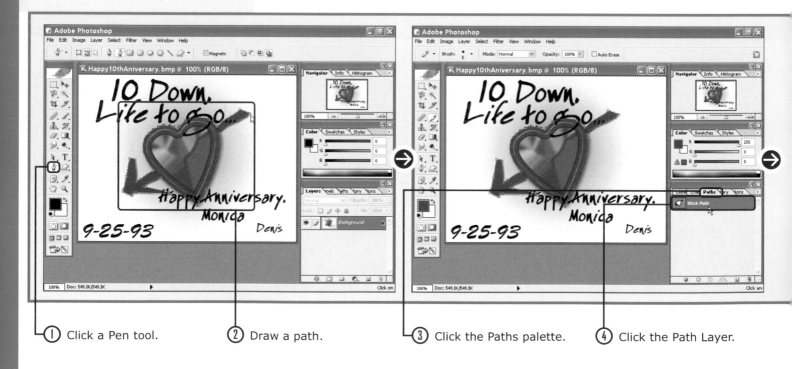

① Click a Pen tool.　　② Draw a path.　　③ Click the Paths palette.　　④ Click the Path Layer.

Did You Know? ☀

You can also fill your path by choosing the Fill Path option in the Paths palette menu, which is similar to the Fill command under the Edit menu. The Fill Path dialog box appears, allowing you to select the Fill options you want. The path appears as a filled shape on your active image layer. You can also click the Fill Path with Foreground Color icon (⬤) at the bottom of the Paths palette to automatically fill your path with the foreground color. Another option in the Fill Path dialog box is Feather. When you enter a value for feathering, your Fill Path blurs the edges of the fill, similar to that of a feathered selection.

29

DIFFICULTY LEVEL

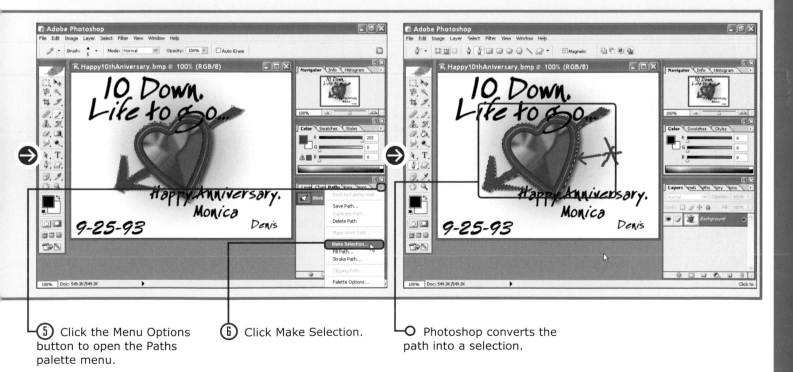

⑤ Click the Menu Options button to open the Paths palette menu.

⑥ Click Make Selection.

○ Photoshop converts the path into a selection.

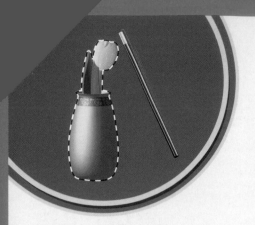

SAVE
selections

You can create selections with many different tools in Photoshop. However, when you finish with a selection, you must re-create it to use it again, a very tedious and time-consuming process. However, Photoshop allows you to save your selections, which you can recall later. This is an excellent time saver, especially if you work with repetitious, uniform selections in a project, like a yearbook, or a contact page for photos. You can keep complex and difficult-to-replace selections as well.

You can save your selection by clicking the Select menu. At the bottom of the menu is the Save Selection command. Create a selection and go to the Save Selection command, and type a name for your selection.

After you save your selection, reloading it is just as easy. In the Selection menu is another command, Load Selection. You can choose from all the saved selections, including the default layer transparency, which selects the outline of floating objects on the active layer. Click OK to load your selection.

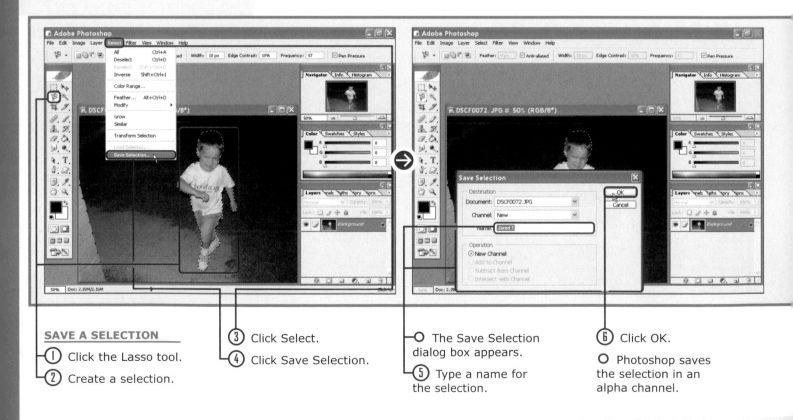

SAVE A SELECTION

① Click the Lasso tool.

② Create a selection.

③ Click Select.

④ Click Save Selection.

○ The Save Selection dialog box appears.

⑤ Type a name for the selection.

⑥ Click OK.

○ Photoshop saves the selection in an alpha channel.

Did You Know? ※

When you save a selection it becomes part of the image and is called an alpha channel. When you save the image in either Photoshop (.psd) or TIFF (.tif) format, the alpha channel information is saved with the file. If you open a photo that contains a selection, you can click Select and then Load Selection. In the Load Selection dialog box, you can choose any selection stored in the image from the Channel ☑. Many stock photography houses that sell photos include a selection in the alpha channel. To ensure that you get any selection information with the file, you must use the PSD or TIFF format because JPEG files do not support alpha channels.

#30

DIFFICULTY LEVEL

Customize It! ※

You can save more than one selection in an image, especially in a larger or detailed project. Be sure to use a descriptive name for your selections to distinguish the selections from each other. For example, if you have multiple, similarly shaped selections, then accidentally choosing the wrong shape can ruin an image.

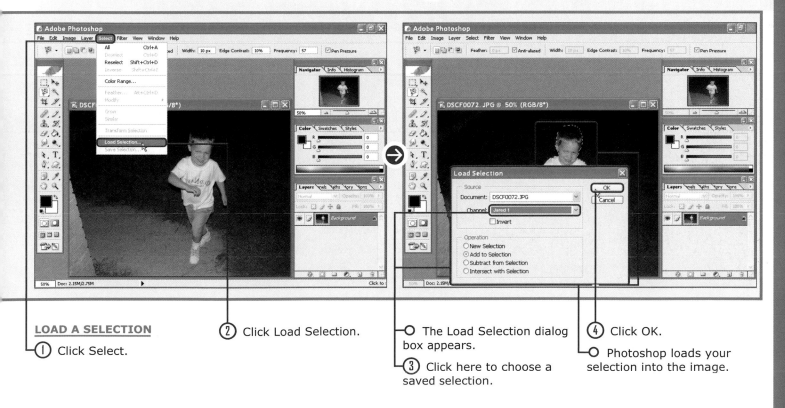

LOAD A SELECTION

① Click Select.

② Click Load Selection.

○ The Load Selection dialog box appears.

③ Click here to choose a saved selection.

④ Click OK.

○ Photoshop loads your selection into the image.

Applying Drawing and Adjustment Tools

Photoshop tools offer amazing ways to manipulate a photo. The most popular tools include the brush, the selection, and the custom shape tools. However, there are many other useful tools, including the History Brush and the Magic Eraser that, while not used as frequently, can accomplish results that are equally impressive. Specifically, this group of tools allows you to manipulate and correct your images.

Often, when you look at a photograph, you can see minor mistakes or flaws in the image. This chapter can show you how to correct some of these problems. Photoshop offers a wide range of tools with which you can adjust or correct these flaws, from removing wrinkles to erasing entire objects from an image.

You can also apply effects that give an image texture or patterns, and even change their color. You can erase a background and restore it, draw an outline, and create custom shapes. You can use the techniques and tools in this chapter for new ways to create graphics and correct images that you design or edit. The only limit on what you can do with the drawing tools in Photoshop is imagination.

TOP 100

Correct flaws with the
HEALING BRUSH TOOL

Everyone has a photograph that contains smudges, artifacts, or dust, and normally, these imperfections do not affect our enjoyment of the image. Occasionally, a more serious problem, such as a burr on the film that cuts across a crucial area of the image, requires attention. With Photoshop, you can use several tools to correct this problem.

However, with some of these tools, the final result seems artificial, or inconsistent with the areas surrounding the fix. Photoshop has developed the

Healing Brush tool to make this type of correction easier. All the cloning tools, including the Healing Brush, use a sampled area of an image to brush over the target area.

The key difference with the Healing Brush tool is that it not only brushes the target area with the sampled source area, it also matches the texture, lighting, and shading of the sampled pixels to those of the target pixels. This brush creates a smoother and more seamless repair of the unwanted pixels.

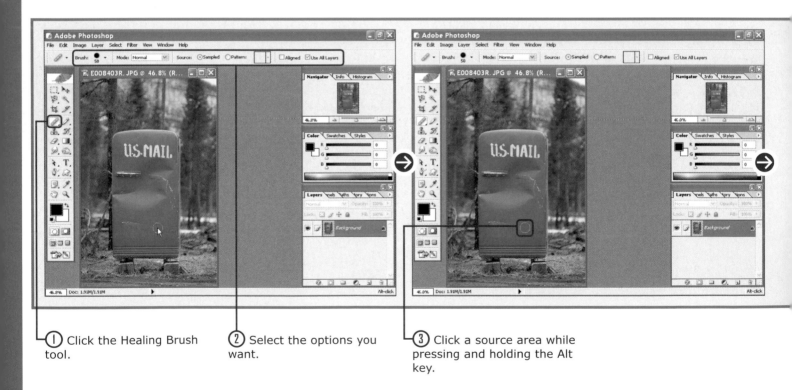

① Click the Healing Brush tool.

② Select the options you want.

③ Click a source area while pressing and holding the Alt key.

DIFFICULTY LEVEL

Did You Know?

You can get much better results by using selected areas close to the flaw you are trying to correct. This makes the texture, lighting, and shading of the final result more consistent with the surrounding area. Use smaller brushes and sample frequently. You may spend more time using this method, but the results are better.

Caution!

You can avoid duplicating work by making smaller, more frequent brush strokes rather than larger, continuous strokes. When you make a correction with a large stroke, and use the Undo command, you must redo all the work up to the error for that stroke. It is best to use smaller strokes, and to click often if you want to make a successful repair. This way, if you use the Undo command, there is less make-up work to return to your point of error.

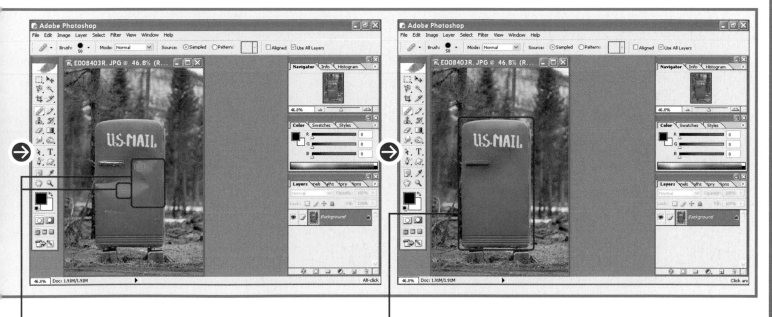

④ Apply the brush to the area you want to correct.

O The source point moves in alignment with the brush tip.

O The Healing Brush tool repairs the area with source pixels.

O The Healing Brush tool corrects the flaw.

Cover unwanted elements with the
CLONE STAMP TOOL

You can use the Clone Stamp tool on your photographs to remove blemishes commonly found on photos, such as dust, scratches, watermarks, and other unwanted elements. With the Clone Stamp tool, you can cover these artifacts by copying an unblemished area of your image and placing it over the blemish. Depending on the area, you can use opacity settings with the tool to create a more subtle coverup effect.

You can use the Clone Stamp tool quickly and easily. Simply select the area you want to borrow, or

sample from, and move the brush-shaped cursor to the area you want to cover. You can then use the Clone Stamp tool with the brush option, applying the selected source area to your stroke instead of a color.

Depending on the image, you may have seamless results, or more obvious coverups. Try to keep clicking new source areas close to the artifact if the covered object is larger. This helps by keeping the pixel colors, tones, and textures more closely blended with the background behind the object.

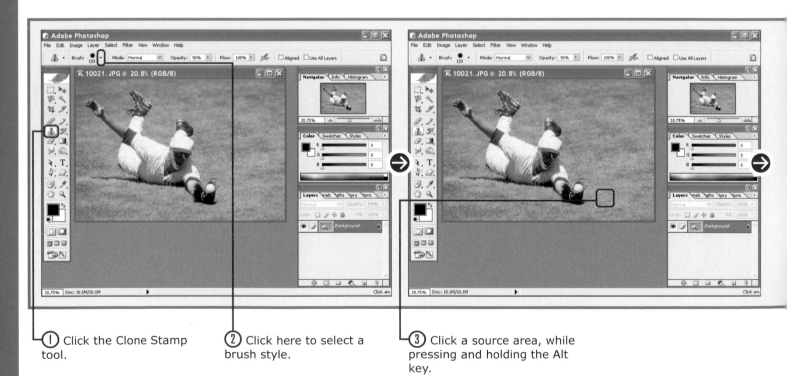

① Click the Clone Stamp tool.

② Click here to select a brush style.

③ Click a source area, while pressing and holding the Alt key.

Customize It!

In a perfect photo, the surrounding scenery provides abundant areas to use as source pixels, and the scenery has consistent color and lighting. However, if the only scenery available is of a slightly different color or shading, you can use the opacity setting of the Clone Stamp tool (🔖) to your advantage. By adjusting the setting to less than 100 percent, you can clone semitransparent copies of different areas of the scenery to make up for areas that do not exactly match.

Customize It!

It can be useful to first constrain the area around the unwanted object with a selection tool before applying the Clone Stamp. This way, the tool does not affect scenery near the unwanted object. The best tool for this purpose is the Lasso tool (🔖), which makes it easy to select objects with curved or soft edges.

④ Click and drag the source area over the unwanted objects.

○ The source point moves in alignment with the brush tip.

○ The Clone Stamp tool covers the area with source pixels.

⑤ Repeat steps **3** and **4** until the unwanted objects are covered up.

○ The Clone Stamp tool covers the object.

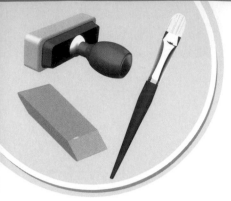

PATCH TOOL

You may sometimes have to correct an image that contains a very large error, or a large unwanted object. The best tool for large areas is the Patch tool. With the Patch tool you can copy a selected area of an image and use it to cover up the unwanted area or object.

Like other cloning tools, the Patch tool brushes pixels from the source area to repair or cover up pixels in the destination area. The Patch tool also matches the texture, lighting, and shading of the

sampled pixels to those of the target pixels, blending it in seamlessly over the covered area.

When you check the Source check box in the Options bar, you can click and drag the area you want to repair over to the part of the image that you want to use to replace it. Alternatively, when you choose the Destination option, you can click and drag the area you want to use as the replacement over to the area you want to repair. Both options work equally well.

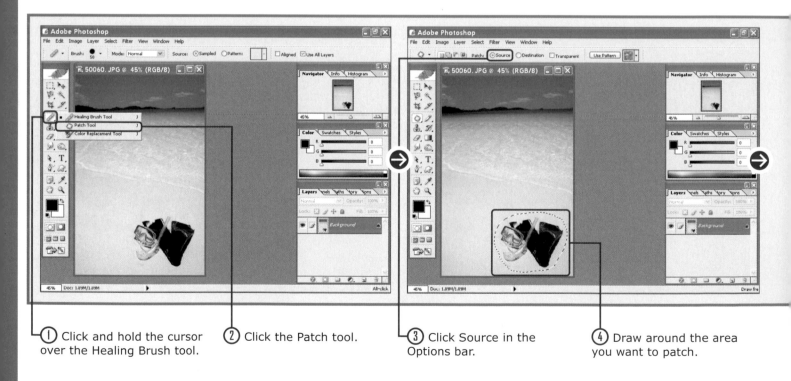

① Click and hold the cursor over the Healing Brush tool.

② Click the Patch tool.

③ Click Source in the Options bar.

④ Draw around the area you want to patch.

Did You Know?

Probably the most common use for the Healing Brush tool ( ) and the Patch tool ( ) is to remove the time date stamp that appears in the corners of photos taken by digital cameras and by some film cameras as well.

Caution!

When you use the Patch tool or the Healing Brush to remove items from a photograph, be careful when applying either tool near an area of contrasting colors because the tools will attempt to blend those colors into the final results. For example, if you are removing a defect from a blue sky that is near a dark building, the Patch tool may read the pixels in the dark building, and you end up with a cloud of darker pixels in the sky near the building. In such situations, you should use the traditional Clone Stamp ( ) tool to remove the defect. See task #32 for more about the Clone Stamp tool.

DIFFICULTY LEVEL

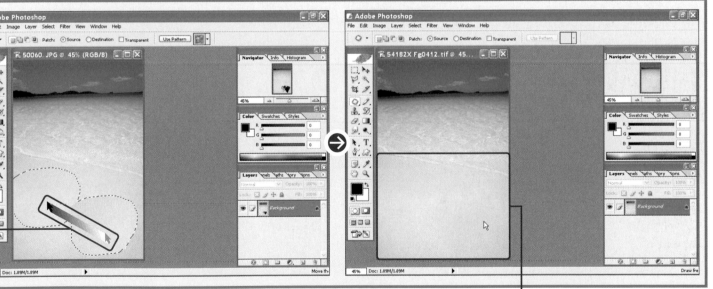

⑤ Drag the selection to an area of the image containing the pixels you want to use for replacement.

○ Photoshop applies the patch.

Note: If you have high contrast between the source and destination pixels, then you may need to repeat step 5.

⑥ Deselect the area.

○ The unwanted object no longer appears in the image.

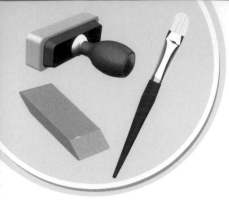

Create outlines with the
STROKE
COMMAND

At times, you may want to paint an outline along an irregular edge using a brush tool to emphasize an object or other element in a photo. Painting accurately with your mouse is not possible and using a stylus, if you even own one, is not much easier. Photoshop has a solution for these situations. You can use the Stroke command to paint a colored border around selections, layers, or paths. Photoshop reads the outer edges of your selection, and paints a border all the way around the item. The advantage of this approach is that you can make a very precise path using the Pen tool, and then you can use the Stroke command to make a brush tool paint along the path

or selection. Although you can use a Stroke layer style to perform this task, the Stroke command, found under the Edit menu, allows a softer-edged border.

You can control the size and color of the stroke in the Stroke dialog box, creating strong, bold outlines, or thin, crisp outlines.

Options for the Stroke command include choosing placement of the stroke inside, outside, or centered on the selection, as well as the opacity of the stroke. You can also use the layer blending modes to affect the results.

① Click a selection tool. ② Create a selection. ③ Click Edit. ④ Click Stroke.

#34

Customize It!

You can create a feathered or faded stroke by applying the Stoke command to a feathered selection. Either enter a Feather value in the Options bar before you make the selection, or after you make your selection by clicking Select, Modify, and then Feather. When you click Edit, and then Stroke, your stroke applies a border according to the amount of feathering in a selection. The higher the feather value, the larger the faded stroke effect appears.

Caution!

Where you choose to place your stroke can affect your image. If you have a full-sized image that you are giving a border, do not choose Outside in the Stroke dialog box, because the stroke pixels will not be visible. Choose Inside (○ changes to ◉), and the stroke will appear inside the image boundary, creating your border. If loss of detail occurs, then increase the canvas size, located in the Image menu.

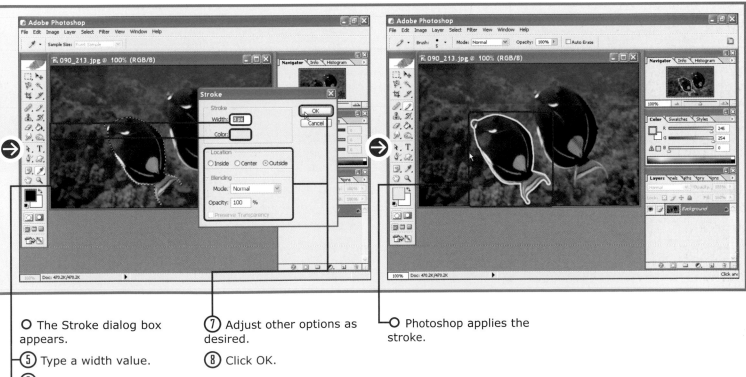

○ The Stroke dialog box appears.

⑤ Type a width value.

⑥ Click here to choose a color with the Color Picker.

⑦ Adjust other options as desired.

⑧ Click OK.

○ Photoshop applies the stroke.

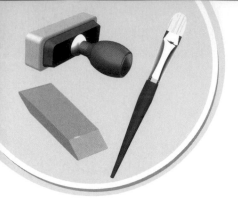

Restore your image with the
HISTORY BRUSH TOOL

You can restore your image to a prior state by using the History Brush tool. The History Brush tool allows you to select a prior state in the History palette and restore portions or your entire image by painting with the brush. You can use the History Brush tool just like a regular paint brush tool; however, instead of applying a color, the brushed area reverts back to the selected prior history state. This can be very helpful if you are creating a before-and-after comparison, or only want to revert a portion of your image to the prior state. As many other users do, you may want to use this tool after you have applied

an effect to an entire image. You can then choose the History Brush tool and selectively undo part of the effect.

One advantage with the History Brush tool is that you can use all the same options and adjustments as with a normal brush. Opacity, flow, and blending modes are all adjustable, as with a regular brush, enabling you to perform some unusual effects. You can also choose from any available brush in your Brush palette, which opens even more design possibilities.

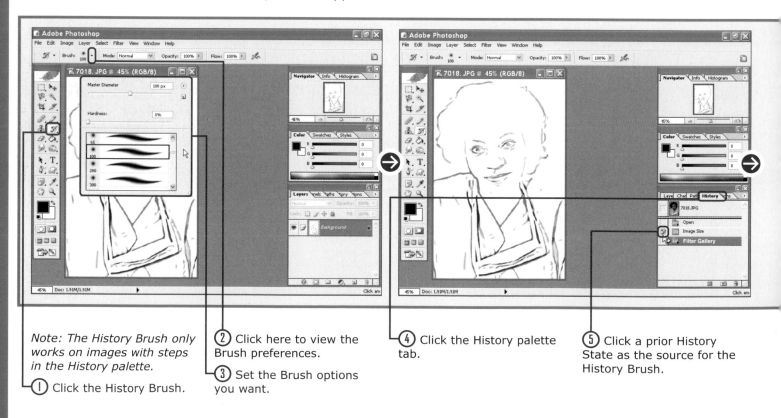

Note: The History Brush only works on images with steps in the History palette.

① Click the History Brush.

② Click here to view the Brush preferences.

③ Set the Brush options you want.

④ Click the History palette tab.

⑤ Click a prior History State as the source for the History Brush.

Apply It!

Imagine a black-and-white image of a circus, with a full-color clown or other circus performer. You can design this eye-catching effect with the History Brush tool (🖌). Open your image, and click Image, Adjustments, and then Desaturate. This decreases the color intensity in your image. Click the History Brush tool, and in the History palette, click the full-color state of the image. Now, when you use the History Brush tool, you can restore portions of the image to full color.

Did You Know?

You can also use the Art History Brush tool (🖌), which also paints on a prior History State, but with a difference. The Art History Brush tool reverts to the prior state with a displacement effect that you can select, creating an Impressionist art effect.

⑥ Brush areas that you want to revert to the prior History State.

○ Photoshop replaces areas that you brush with the prior History State.

BACKGROUND ERASER TOOL

You can erase a portion of a background image by using the Background Eraser tool. The Background Eraser tool samples the color of the pixels you select, and erases only that color. There is a small crosshair inside the center of the brush tip of the Background Eraser tool, and Photoshop only samples the color under the crosshair. You can erase all the sample colored pixels inside the brush tip. You can erase near the edge of an object and not affect it unless the crosshair actually moves over the object, which causes the Eraser tool to sample the object colors instead.

There are several options for the Background Eraser tool. One option is the Sampling rate. You can choose Continuous, to resample the colors under the cursor each time you move the cursor, or you can choose Once, which sets the first sampled color as the only color to be removed for each stroke. Other options include affecting Limits, which erases only the pixels under the Eraser tool, and all the pixels in the image of that color, regardless of location.

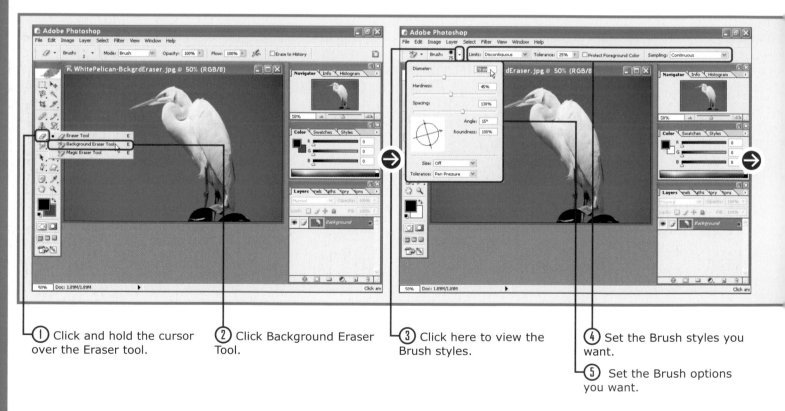

① Click and hold the cursor over the Eraser tool.

② Click Background Eraser Tool.

③ Click here to view the Brush styles.

④ Set the Brush styles you want.

⑤ Set the Brush options you want.

Did You Know?

If your subject has colors similar to those of the background, then you should change the Tolerance setting in the Options bar. The Tolerance setting specifies how close to the sampled color the neighboring pixels can be before the Background Eraser tool (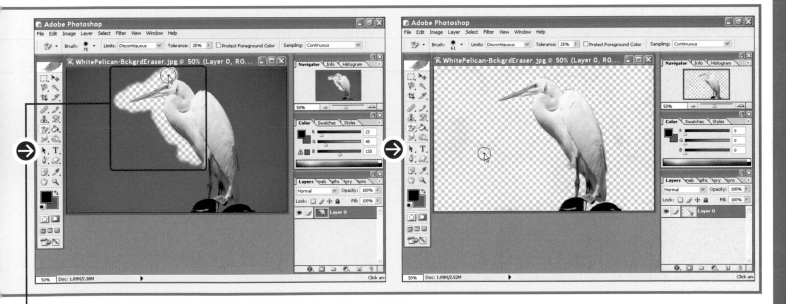) removes the pixels. A higher Tolerance setting can accidentally erase adjacent pixels in your subject that are within the brush area, even if you do not place the crosshairs (+) over your object.

Did You Know?

You cannot use the Background Eraser tool on layers that are locked. Locking a layer protects all pixels on that layer from accidental erasure and movement. If you try to erase a locked layer, then a dialog box appears, telling you that the layer is locked. The Background layer, while considered locked for many other filters and tools, automatically converts to a regular layer when you apply the Background Eraser tool.

⑥ Brush along the edges of an object.

Note: Do not allow the crosshair in the brush to move over the object.

O The Background Eraser removes background pixels.

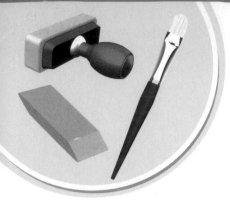

Design
CUSTOM GRADIENTS

You can use the Gradient tool to create many kinds of graphical effects. From shading an object to creating a metallic appearance, gradients enhance many aspects of design. You can access many different gradients in the default Gradient tool presets, or, if you prefer, you can design your own custom gradients.

You can access the Gradient Editor by clicking inside the gradient sample in the Options bar. The Gradient Editor allows you to edit and save an original gradient to add to the preset sets. You can create

and edit gradients by adding opacity stops and color stops to the gradient bar. The opacity stops allow you to make sections of a gradient semi-transparent. The color stops indicate the colors that you want to blend together in your gradient. By sliding the color stops along the gradient bar, you can affect the way in which two colors blend. The farther apart the colors are, the smoother and longer the blend. By double-clicking the color stop, you can change the color placed there.

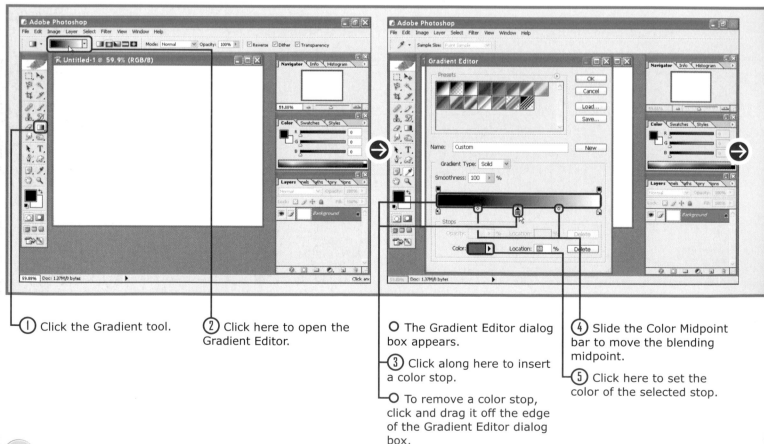

① Click the Gradient tool.

② Click here to open the Gradient Editor.

O The Gradient Editor dialog box appears.

③ Click along here to insert a color stop.

O To remove a color stop, click and drag it off the edge of the Gradient Editor dialog box.

④ Slide the Color Midpoint bar to move the blending midpoint.

⑤ Click here to set the color of the selected stop.

Customize It!

You can create a Noise gradient using the Gradient Editor by choosing Noise from the Gradient Type ⌄ in the Gradient Editor dialog box. Noise gradients have nothing to do with noise, but are called that because Photoshop uses random noise to calculate the dozens of colors that appear in the resulting gradient. The Roughness setting in the dialog box controls whether the adjacent colors in the gradient are blurred or sharply defined.

DIFFICULTY LEVEL

Did You Know?

You can save and share gradient files. After you create your new gradients, you can save them by clicking the Save button in the Gradient Editor. Photoshop prompts you to name the gradient, and to browse to the file location where you want to save It. By default, you can find gradient files in the Adobe\Photoshop CS\Presets\Gradients folder.

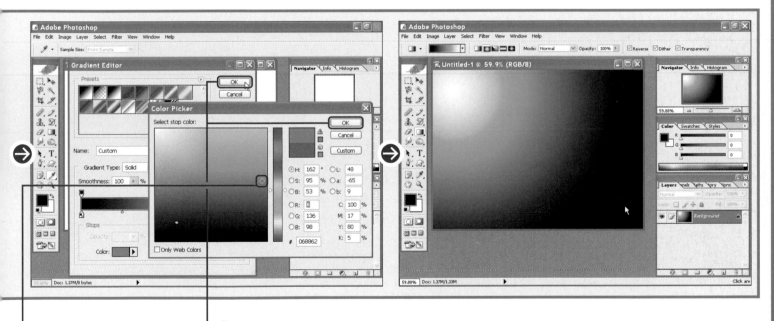

○ The Color Picker dialog box appears.

ⓖ Select the color you want.

⑦ Click OK.

⑧ In the Gradient Editor dialog box, click OK.

○ Photoshop creates the custom gradient.

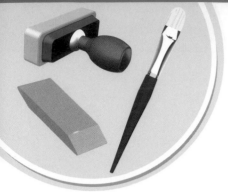

Make a
CUSTOM SHAPE
from a photo

You can use Custom Shapes for many purposes in your design work. Photoshop gives you dozens of preset groups of Shapes to choose from, and you can also create your own Custom Shapes. You can easily create new shapes from Selections and Paths.

You can also create Custom Shapes from a photograph, and save them for later use. You can use almost any photo, but the larger the photo, the better the detail in the final result. It is also easier

to reduce the image to two-color black and white so that the edges of the shape you want are more easily defined for when you convert it to a custom shape.

After you create a shape, Photoshop places it in the current Custom Shape preset group. See task #17 for more information on making shapes from Selections and Paths.

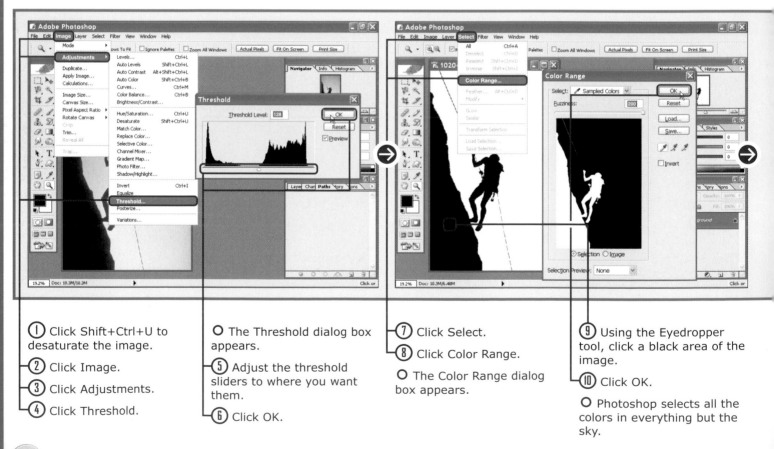

① Click Shift+Ctrl+U to desaturate the image.

② Click Image.

③ Click Adjustments.

④ Click Threshold.

○ The Threshold dialog box appears.

⑤ Adjust the threshold sliders to where you want them.

⑥ Click OK.

⑦ Click Select.

⑧ Click Color Range.

○ The Color Range dialog box appears.

⑨ Using the Eyedropper tool, click a black area of the image.

⑩ Click OK.

○ Photoshop selects all the colors in everything but the sky.

#38

DIFFICULTY LEVEL

Customize It!

You can create smoother edges to your shapes. Repeat steps **1** to **6** below, and then click Filter, Blur, and Gaussian Blur. The Gaussian Blur filter makes the selection smoother when you use the Color Select command, resulting in a smoother work path and shape. You can lose detail when you use this filter, so keep the Gaussian Blur settings low.

Did You Know?

You get better results when you create a Custom Shape from a large image. Your images should be at least 1500 to 2000 pixels wide, which is a typical high-resolution digital camera width. Smaller images also work, but with less detail and harsher edges. When you use larger images, you can apply a higher Gaussian Blur setting for smoother edges with less detail loss.

⑪ Click the Paths palette tab.

⑫ Click here to open the palette menu.

⑬ Click Make Work Path.

○ The Make Work Path dialog box appears.

⑭ Type a tolerance value.

⑮ Click OK.

⑯ Click Edit.

⑰ Click Define Custom Shape.

○ The Shape Name dialog box appears.

⑱ Type the name you want for the new shape.

⑲ Click OK.

○ Photoshop defines the new shape, and places it in the Custom Shapes selection menu.

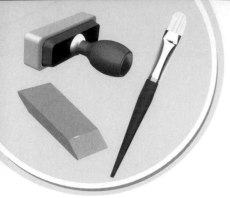

FILL COMMAND

You can quickly create a colored or textured selection by using the Fill command. The Fill command can use any selection or layer, and fill it completely with colors or gradients. You can also fill your layer or selection with a pattern.

The Fill command is located in the Edit menu. When you select the Fill command, a dialog box appears, displaying different fill options. You can choose foreground and background colors, preset colors — such as black, white, and 50% gray — or select your

own with the Color Picker. You can also choose Pattern, which lets you select from any of the Photoshop patterns available.

The Fill tool also allows you to apply all the layer blending modes to the fill. You can use this option on pattern fills as well, enabling you to create unusual designs or add texture without affecting colors. In the Fill dialog box you also have the option to specify the opacity of the fill.

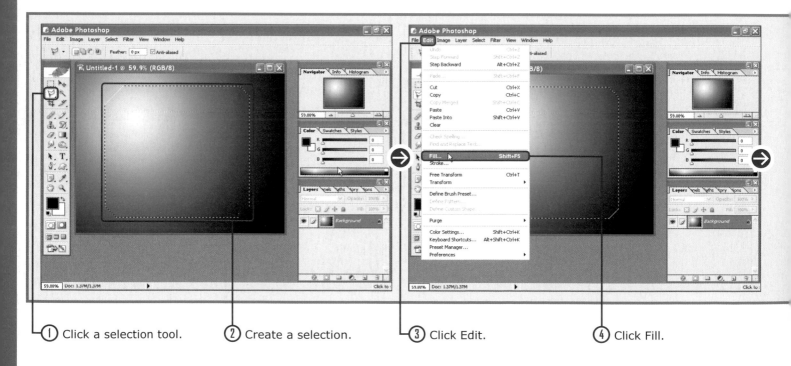

① Click a selection tool. ② Create a selection. ③ Click Edit. ④ Click Fill.

#39

DIFFICULTY LEVEL

Did You Know?

You can quickly create your
own patterns to use with the Fill
command and other Photoshop tools.
To create a Pattern, select part or all of
an image, click Edit, and then click Define
Pattern. Photoshop prompts you to name your
pattern, and saves it to the pattern preset group.

Did You Know?

You can use the Preserve Transparency
radio button in the Fill dialog box to preserve
transparent areas in a layer. When you click this
option (○ changes to ◉), Photoshop fills only
the pixels in that layer that contain a color, and
leaves transparent areas unfilled. You can use this
option with any of the Fill commands. This is very
useful for filling complex objects on a layer without
having to make a selection.

O The Fill dialog box
appears.

⑤ Click here and select
Pattern.

⑥ Click here to view
pattern styles.

⑦ Click a style.

⑧ Click OK.

O Photoshop fills the
selection with the Pattern
you want.

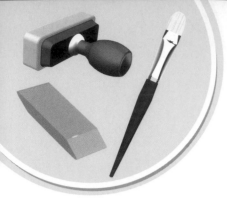

Modify a photo with the
BURN AND DODGE TOOLS

You can use the Photoshop Burn and Dodge tools to modify the tone of an image or photo. The Burn and Dodge tools are based on the traditional darkroom techniques of altering exposure time for different parts of an image during processing in the darkroom. Photoshop has made this process much easier and more predictable than the traditional method.

The Burn tool adjusts the tone of an image by darkening the pixels. When you click and drag the Burn tool brush across an image, Photoshop darkens the affected pixels based on the settings you

entered. The Dodge tool has the opposite effect of the Burn tool, making the image lighter where you apply the brush.

When you use the Burn and Dodge tools, you can apply your changes with all the available brushes in the Brush Presets, increasing the uses for the tool. You can also choose between adjusting the highlights, the midtones, and the shadows of your image. You can also control the exposure, or intensity, of the change.

USE THE BURN TOOL

① Click here to select the Burn tool.

② Click here and select your brush.

③ Brush over your image where you want to darken the tone.

O The Burn tool darkens your image where you apply the brush.

#40

DIFFICULTY LEVEL

Did You Know?

You can quickly add shading and highlighting to an object with the Burn and Dodge tools (🔥 and 🔍). First, type a low number for the Exposure setting in the Options bar. Next, decide on a light direction, and brush the areas with the Burn tool that would be shaded based on the light direction. Then, use the Dodge tool to brush the areas where the highlights would be.

Did You Know?

You can use the Burn and Dodge tools to bring out detail in an image. If an area is too dark or too bright, you can apply a few brush strokes with a Burn or Dodge tool at a low opacity setting to accentuate details in the image.

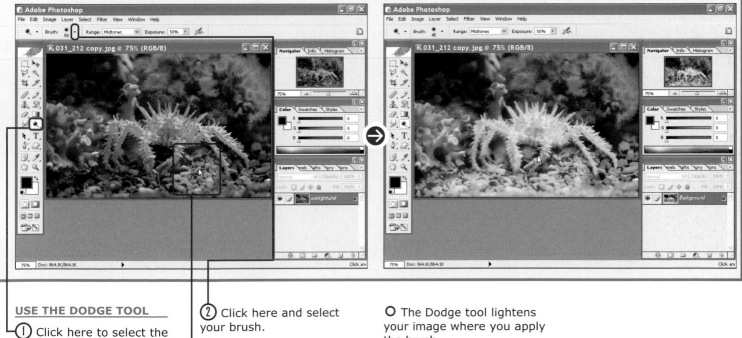

USE THE DODGE TOOL

① Click here to select the Dodge tool.

② Click here and select your brush.

③ Brush over your image where you want to lighten the tone.

O The Dodge tool lightens your image where you apply the brush.

CHAPTER 5

Adjusting Photos

Whether you use a digital camera or scan in photographs with a scanner, you will often want to make minor corrections and adjustments to the images so that they appear their best.

You can correct mild over and underexposures with the Levels command, or correct undesirable color casts with the Auto Color command. You can use the Auto Contrast command to make your photos appear to jump out of the screen.

A new set of filters in the form of traditional photographic filters offers familiar tools to adjust the color and contrast of images in ways that previously were not possible on a computer.

An often-overlooked aspect of photography is composition. Using

the Crop tool you can improve the composition of any photo to direct the viewer's attention to the subject in the most flattering way.

Viewing the world with two eyes gives us a panoramic view that most cameras cannot capture. Using some simple photographic techniques, you can create a panoramic image when you stitch together photos with the Photomerge command. The limitation of cameras to capture what we see also includes areas of extreme shadow and light. You can use the shadow and highlight correction to recover detail that is lost in the shadows without overexposing the rest of the photograph.

Finally, you can use Photoshop to easily create a slide show that friends and family can play on their own computers.

TOP 100

USE THE MEASURE TOOL
to straighten photos

When you scan a photo, you may end up with a slightly, or sometimes not so slightly, crooked photo in your Photoshop image, no matter how carefully you place the photo on a scanner. Or, you may have a crooked shot from a camera. Regardless of why, Photoshop has a tool, called the Measure tool, which allows you to straighten photos, almost perfectly.

Located in the Eyedropper menu, the Measure tool resembles a little ruler. Photoshop measures the distance between your origin and end points to calculate the angle of the line, and shows the X and Y coordinates of the point of origin for the line in the

Options bar. You can measure the angle of a line by holding down the Alt key while you drag the line. The resulting angle appears in the Options bar.

You can use the Measure tool to measure the angle of a side of a crooked image, and apply that measurement to the Rotate command in the Transform menu, under the Edit menu. Based on this measurement, you can adjust the angle in the Options bar of the Rotate command, and rotate the image so that the measured side is fully horizontal or vertical.

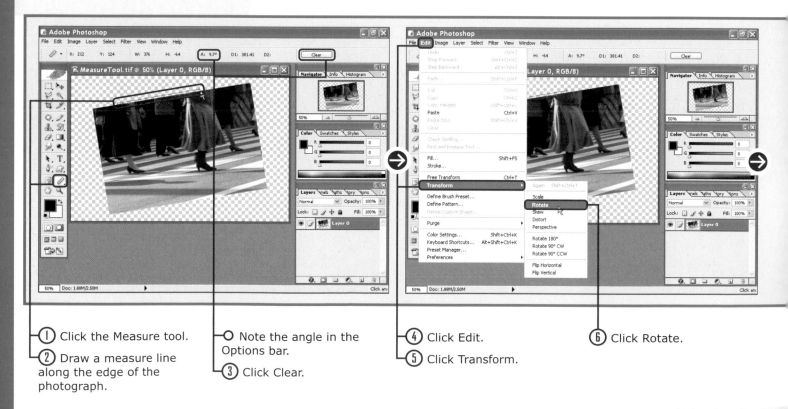

① Click the Measure tool.

② Draw a measure line along the edge of the photograph.

○ Note the angle in the Options bar.

③ Click Clear.

④ Click Edit.

⑤ Click Transform.

⑥ Click Rotate.

41

DIFFICULTY LEVEL

Did You Know? ※

You can use the Measure tool
🖉 to rotate an entire canvas
containing an image instead of just
a layer object, such as a photo. Simply
draw a line with the Measure tool, click
Image, Rotate Canvas, and then Arbitrary.
Photoshop automatically enters the angle of the
line you draw with the Measure tool into the Angle
value, and when you click OK, your canvas rotates to
this angle. This is an excellent tool for straightening a
picture where the edges of the photo are straight, but the
subject is at an angle.

Customize It! ※

Even though there are no visible options, the Options bar
now contains all of the information that the Info palette
displays, including the protractor data for measuring your
defined angles. You can change how this information displays
by clicking the Info palette menu and selecting a different
measurement type.

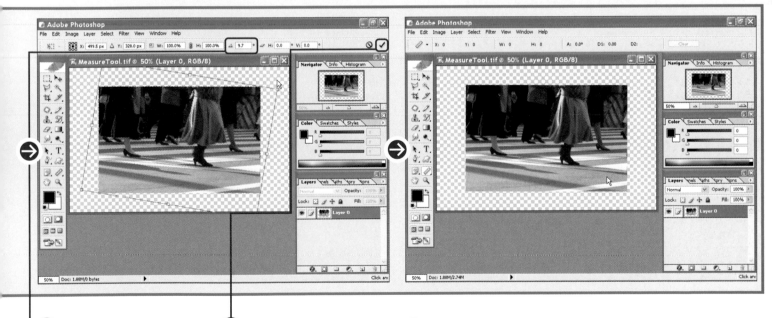

⑦ In the Options bar, type
the angle you noted.

⑧ Click here to apply the
transformation.

O Photoshop rotates the
image to the angle you
specified in step **7**.

Give photographs a new look with the
PHOTO FILTER

You can create professional effects with the new Photo Filter in Photoshop. These adjustment layers apply a color overlay to the image similar to the color filters that professional photographers use. You can select from eighteen different preset photo filters.

While a photographer uses an actual filter over the lens during the exposure of the photo, you apply the Photo Filters to images after the photo is taken. The names of the 18 Photoshop filters match those of standard lens filters that have been used by photographers for years. Many of the filters were designed to change the characteristics of the light

exposing the film. Adobe offers descriptions of these filters in their on-line user's guide, but to get more detailed information about the purpose of each type of lens filter, you can check the Web sites of the two major filter manufacturers, Tiffen, www.tiffen.com, and Hoya, www.hoya.com.

You can apply the Photo Filter to a full image or to an individual layer or object. If you want to apply a Photo Filter to an entire image that contains layers, then you must merge the layers, or apply separate Photo Filters to each layer.

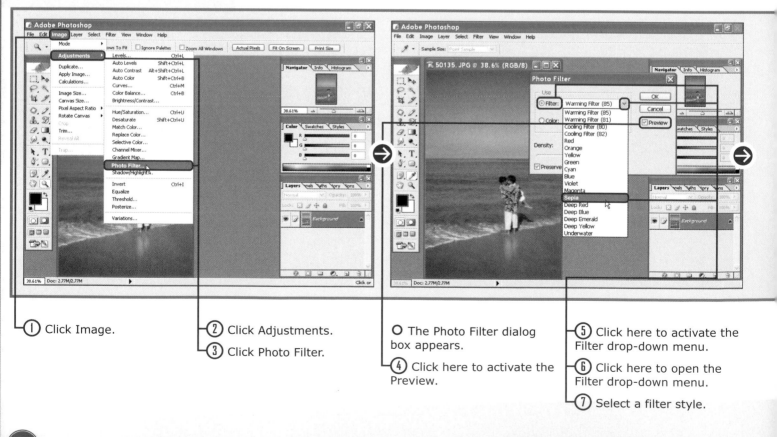

① Click Image.

② Click Adjustments.

③ Click Photo Filter.

⊙ The Photo Filter dialog box appears.

④ Click here to activate the Preview.

⑤ Click here to activate the Filter drop-down menu.

⑥ Click here to open the Filter drop-down menu.

⑦ Select a filter style.

#42

Caution! ☀

The Photo Filter adjustments affect the image directly, unlike adjustment layers for hue and saturation. After you apply a Photo Filter, your image is permanently changed, unless you use the Undo command. Be sure to test it out on a copy of the image or layer prior to applying the filter.

DIFFICULTY LEVEL

Did You Know! ☀

The lens filters that Photoshop re-creates in the Photo Filter set were designed to affect film. If you read about how the filters work, remember that even though the Photo Filters have the same names and colors as the original lens filters, how the Photo Filters affect an image may differ from how the lens filter was designed to affect a photo shot using film.

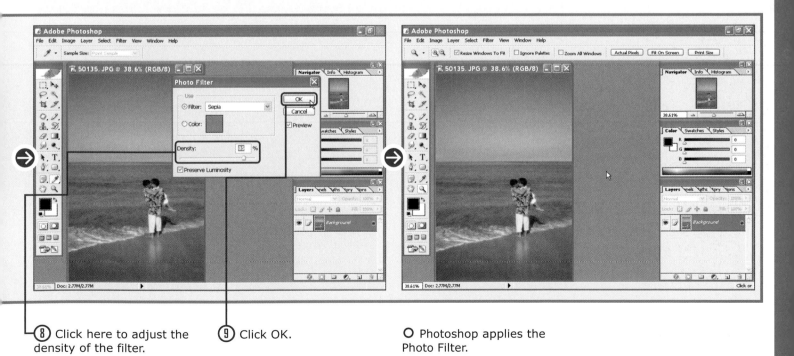

⑧ Click here to adjust the density of the filter.

⑨ Click OK.

O Photoshop applies the Photo Filter.

ADJUST LEVELS
to correct your photo

You can easily increase the contrast and color accuracy of a photograph by using the Levels command. The Levels command allows you to make individual adjustments to the highlights, midtones, and shadows of an image. When you open the Levels command, you see a histogram of the image that represents the density of pixels in the shadow, midtone, and highlight regions of an image. Underneath the histogram are three sliders that you can use to redistribute the pixels. Below these sliders is another set of sliders called the Output Levels sliders. You can use these sliders to reduce the range of shadow and highlight details when an image is being printed by a commercial printer.

When the channel is set to RGB or CMYK, moving the slider redistributes the pixels in all three (RGB) or four (CMYK) channels, controlling how dark and light the pixels in the image appear. You can also select individual color channels to correct color casts when the Auto Color command does not produce the results you want.

With the Levels command, you can change a dull, low contrast photograph into a clearer and more colorful image, drawing out details you may otherwise miss.

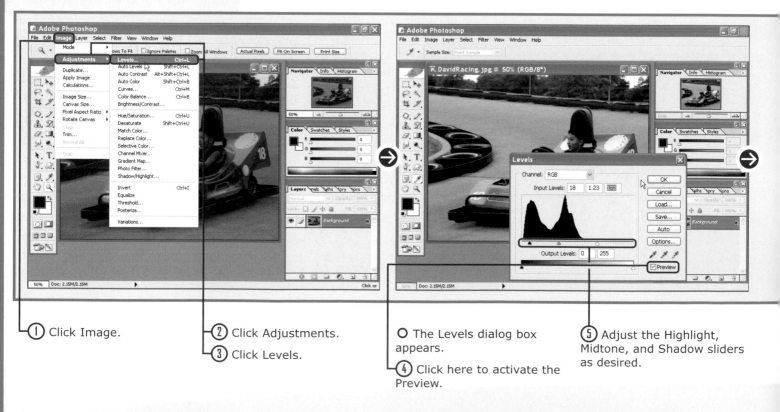

① Click Image.

② Click Adjustments.

③ Click Levels.

○ The Levels dialog box appears.

④ Click here to activate the Preview.

⑤ Adjust the Highlight, Midtone, and Shadow sliders as desired.

Did You Know? ※

You can use the Auto Levels function to automatically redistribute the pixels in the image. Redistributing the pixels can change the color or contrast of an image, although the change may not be an improvement. Click Image, Adjustments, and then Auto Levels. Photoshop calculates and then applies a Levels adjustment to the image. This feature, at times, is handy for fast and minor corrections to an image. Complex changes may require the Levels function instead of Auto Levels.

Customize It! ※

You can save your Levels corrections for use at another time. In the Levels dialog box, click the Save button. The Save dialog box appears, and you can give the settings a name. You can click the Load button to reload your saved settings into the Levels dialog box, and apply them to your image.

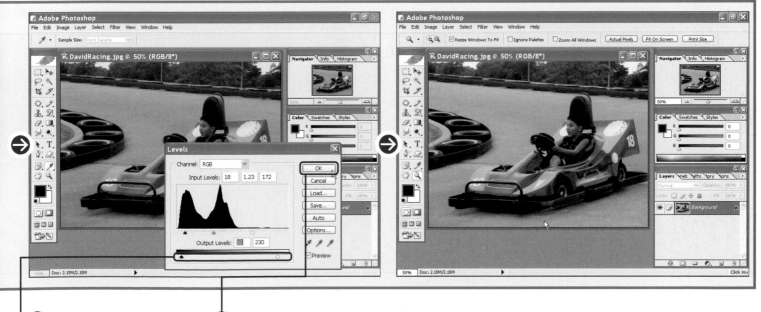

⑥ Adjust the Brightness and Contrast sliders as desired.

⑦ Click OK.

○ Photoshop applies the Levels adjustments to the image.

Fix colors in your photo with the
AUTO COLOR COMMAND

DIFFICULTY LEVEL

You can use the Auto Color command to make quick and easy color corrections to a photograph. Auto Color reads the colors of your image and automatically attempts to correct the colors by removing any color casts.

The challenge facing the Auto Color command is that there are no foolproof ways of determining which colors in the image are correct or what color cast is dominant in a photo. Using a complex process, Auto Color reads the pixels in all three color channels and attempts to balance the colors.

You can find the Auto Color command in the Adjustments menu, which is under the Image menu. The Auto Color command does not require you to select any options or settings. Sometimes, as with most Auto functions, it does not produce the change you expect. If this happens, you can choose the Undo command and make the color adjustments with other correction tools, such as Levels or Curves to get the results you want.

① Click Image.

② Click Adjustments.

③ Click Auto Color.

○ Photoshop applies the Auto Color command.

Sharpen it up with
AUTO CONTRAST

DIFFICULTY LEVEL

You can use Auto Contrast to change a dull, lifeless photo into a vivid one with a simple mouse click. Auto Contrast increases the differences between lighter and darker pixels in an image, which increases the contrast of the image.

Auto Contrast does not alter the colors of an image, as Auto Levels does, because it affects the composite image as opposed to affecting individual color channels one at a time. By not specifying a channel, Auto Contrast affects all colors equally, preserving color tone and hue.

The Auto Contrast command strengthens the definition of edges around contrasting colors, bringing out detail, and defining shapes in the image.

The Auto Contrast feature, located in the Adjustments menu, under the Image menu, does not require you to select any options or settings. As with any Auto command, you can get varying results based on the original image. You may need to make further adjustments afterward.

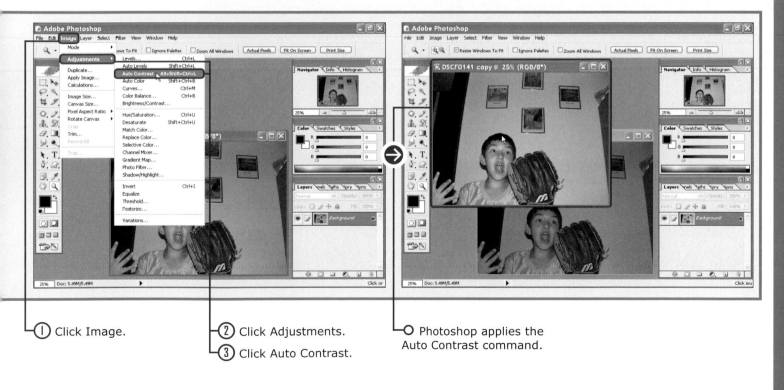

① Click Image.

② Click Adjustments.

③ Click Auto Contrast.

⦿ Photoshop applies the Auto Contrast command.

REMOVE ELEMENTS
for use in another photo

You can copy an object out of one image and paste it into another. This is a common practice that is easy to do. You can use this technique to create a surreal background for an object, create a photo collage, or even place a person in a fun location.

You can use any of the selection tools to outline an area or object, copy it, and then drag it to the new location, or paste it from the menu.

When adding an object from one photo into another, you should attempt to match color hue and brightness.

For example, you can easily mix together a daytime beach scene with a person in another daytime scene, but taking a dark silhouette of a tree and placing it on the same beach would contrast too starkly. If the elements seem different, yet you still want to place them together, you can use your image-correction tools, including Levels, Hue and Saturation, and Brightness and Contrast, to match the added object to the new background.

① Click and hold the Lasso tool.

② Select a Lasso Tool.

③ Create a selection.

④ Click Edit.

⑤ Click Copy.

#46

DIFFICULTY LEVEL

Customize It! ⁂

You can paste your image
and automatically create a Layer
Mask. To do this, create a selection
with the Marquee tool and use the Paste
Into shortcut, Shift+Ctrl+V. Photoshop
pastes a copy of the image with a mask that
reveals only the inside of the selection. If you
press Shift+Alt+Ctrl+V, then Photoshop pastes your
copied selection with a mask that reveals everything
except for the area within the selection.

Did You Know? ⁂

You can achieve a smoother transition of the
copied object by using the Feather option. After
you create your selection, click Select, Feather, and
then enter a value. This causes the edges of the
selection to be less harsh and conspicuous in the new
image. Some selection tools also have a Feather option
in the Options bar, so you can preset the feather before
you make your selections.

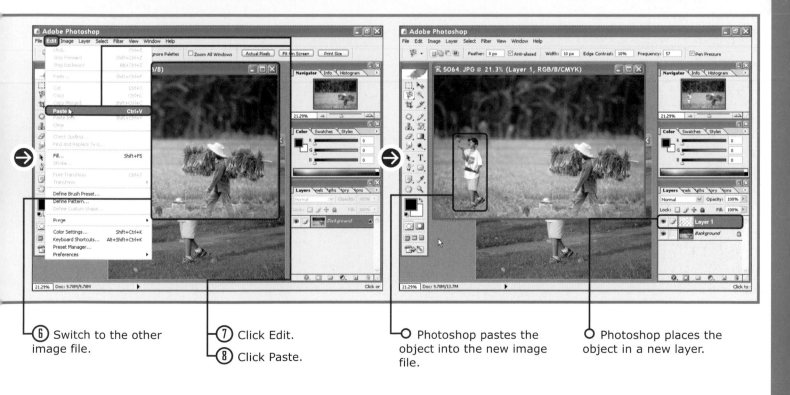

⑥ Switch to the other
image file.

⑦ Click Edit.

⑧ Click Paste.

○ Photoshop pastes the
object into the new image
file.

○ Photoshop places the
object in a new layer.

USE THE CROP TOOL
for more dynamic photos

You can use the Crop tool to make a normal, ordinary photograph more dynamic and appealing. The Crop tool allows you to select a portion of the image, and trim off the rest of the image outside that selection. Photoshop automatically resizes the image to the same width and height dimensions as the selection.

You can use the Crop tool to select a subject of an image and crop around it to improve the overall composition of the image, or simply to remove unwanted space around your subject. Cropping is also a good way to reduce the file size.

The Crop tool has several options in the Options bar. You can enter the dimensions or alter the resolution of the area you want to crop. When you enter values for dimensions, the crop constrains to those values by scale, meaning the height and width scale together as you crop.

Exercise caution when cropping for print. If you crop a section out of a photo for printing and need to size the section up, you can lose enough pixel detail to cause your photo to be grainy or poor quality. Also, allow enough space on the edges of the photo for bleed, so that you do not cut off part of your image when printing.

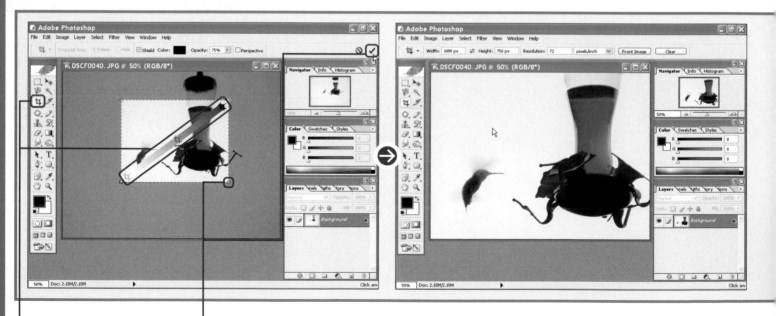

CHANGE THE FOCUS OF A PHOTO

① Click the Crop tool.

② Click and drag inside the photo to define the boundary you want to crop.

③ Click and drag the crop handles to adjust the boundary you want to crop.

④ Click here to apply the crop.

○ Photoshop crops the photo.

Did You Know? ※

You can perform a crop using any selection tool. First, use the selection tool to create a selection of the area you want to crop. Click Image and then click Crop. Photoshop crops to the boundaries based on the width and height of the selected pixels. Odd-shaped selections, such as an object in an image, crop to the proportions of the selection.

Caution! ※

Cropping an image affects all the layers of the image, even those not currently visible. It is also permanent unless you click the Hide option (○ changes to ◉) in the Options bar after you make your selection. This option places removed pixels invisibly outside the selected area. To reveal them again, click Image and then Reveal All, and Photoshop reveals the hidden pixels in the image window.

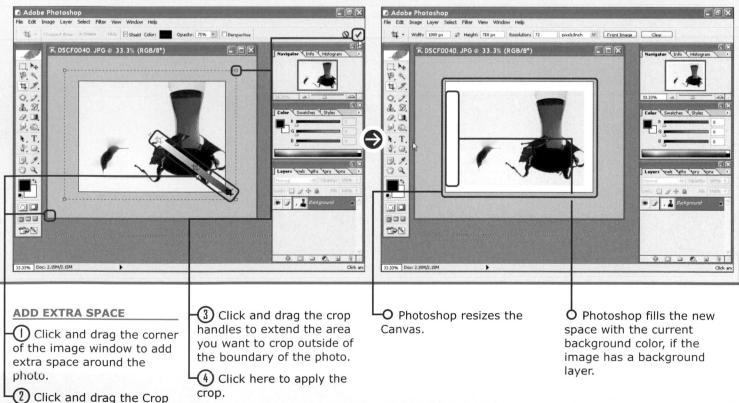

ADD EXTRA SPACE

① Click and drag the corner of the image window to add extra space around the photo.

② Click and drag the Crop tool to define the area you want to crop.

③ Click and drag the crop handles to extend the area you want to crop outside of the boundary of the photo.

④ Click here to apply the crop.

○ Photoshop resizes the Canvas.

○ Photoshop fills the new space with the current background color, if the image has a background layer.

Create a
PANORAMIC PHOTO

You can use the Photomerge feature to place several images together into a single, panoramic image. Panoramic images are wide photographs that encompass an area that an individual photo cannot cover. Panoramas allow you to display more scenery in a single image than is usually possible in a normal-sized photograph. You usually need a special camera to shoot a panoramic view, but Photoshop's Photomerge feature now allows you to create them by combining multiple photos into one wide photo.

When you set up a Photomerge composition, you identify your source photos, and then Photoshop

attempts to automatically create the panorama for you. After Photoshop places the images, you can make changes to the placement of the individual source photos to correct the alignment mishaps that can occur during the merge process.

The Photomerge dialog box includes tools for manipulating the source photos, a lightbox for organizing source images that are not in use, and a work area for assembling the panorama. There are also settings for adjusting perspective in the final image.

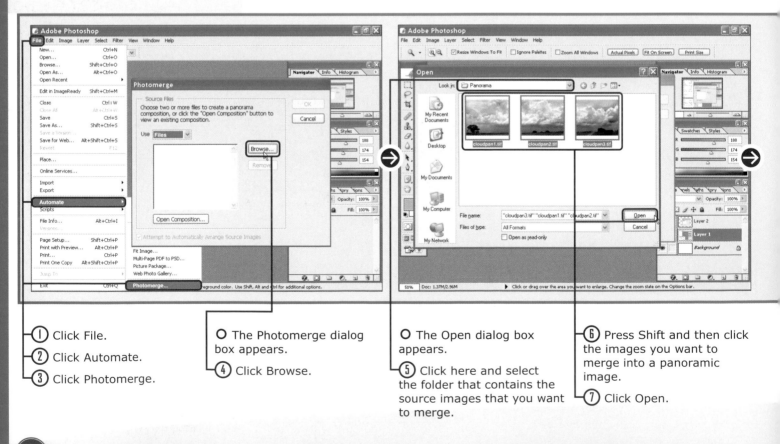

① Click File.

② Click Automate.

③ Click Photomerge.

● The Photomerge dialog box appears.

④ Click Browse.

● The Open dialog box appears.

⑤ Click here and select the folder that contains the source images that you want to merge.

⑥ Press Shift and then click the images you want to merge into a panoramic image.

⑦ Click Open.

#48

DIFFICULTY LEVEL

Did You Know? ※

Wide-angle lenses can help you maximize the field of view attained in your source photographs, as well as your resulting panorama. However, fisheye lenses should be avoided when creating panoramas, because they can distort your photographs, making it harder for Photoshop to combine your images with one another.

Did You Know? ※

Consistent exposure throughout your set of source photos is important when creating a panorama. For example, using flash in some of the photos but not in others can make blending them together difficult; it can also create a panorama with odd light shifts across the picture. You may want to apply some photo adjustments to correct minor differences in color, tone, or contrast.

CONTINUED ▶

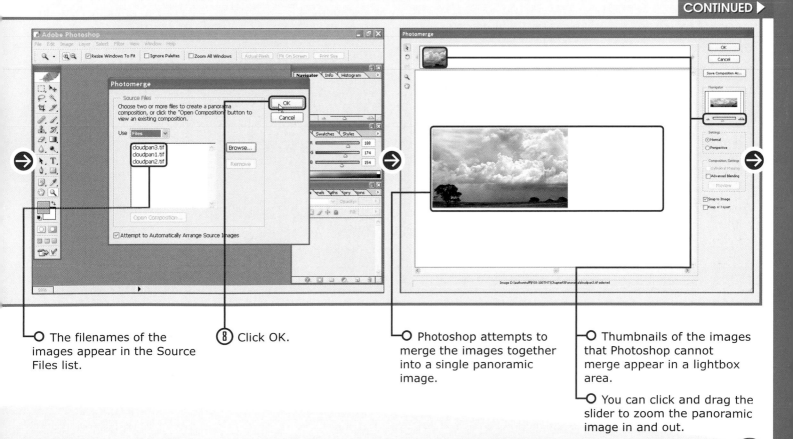

─O The filenames of the images appear in the Source Files list.

⑧ Click OK.

─O Photoshop attempts to merge the images together into a single panoramic image.

─O Thumbnails of the images that Photoshop cannot merge appear in a lightbox area.

─O You can click and drag the slider to zoom the panoramic image in and out.

Create a
PANORAMIC
PHOTO

While you create your panorama, you may need to reposition or rotate an individual source file in your composition in order to achieve smoother blending of the pictures. You can use the Photomerge dialog box editing tools to help you work with your panorama. The Zoom tool helps you to more accurately see the alignment of each file when you are making manual adjustments.

You can save time and reduce manual adjustments by using source photos that have the right amount of overlap. For best results, source photos should

overlap one another approximately 15 to 40 percent. If the overlap is less than 15 percent, then Photomerge may not be able to automatically assemble the panorama, and you may need to manually place the picture layout.

After your panorama is complete, you can edit and make adjustments to it like any other Photoshop image. For example, you may want to make exposure adjustments to the seams where the source photos are combined.

CONTINUED ▶

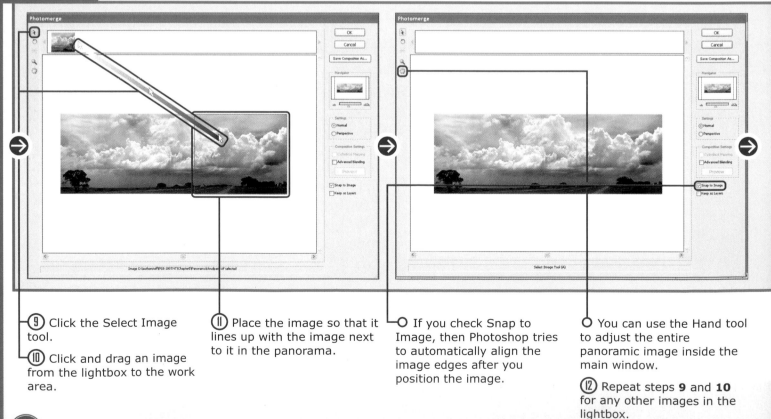

⑨ Click the Select Image tool.

⑩ Click and drag an image from the lightbox to the work area.

⑪ Place the image so that it lines up with the image next to it in the panorama.

○ If you check Snap to Image, then Photoshop tries to automatically align the image edges after you position the image.

○ You can use the Hand tool to adjust the entire panoramic image inside the main window.

⑫ Repeat steps **9** and **10** for any other images in the lightbox.

#48
CONTINUED

Did You Know? ※

When Photomerge blends your images together, it uses similar blending methods to those used by the Healing tool and the Patch tool. Photomerge determines the best placement of pixels for the overlap and then blends the overlapped areas together seamlessly. Similar to the Healing and Patch tools, Photomerge matches the texture, lighting, and shading of the pixels of one image to those of the pixels of the overlapping image.

Did You Know? ※

While most of your panoramas may be a horizontal arrangement of photos, you can also use Photoshop to create a vertical panorama. To create a vertical panorama, first rotate your source photos 90 degrees. This allows you to merge them together as if they were a horizontal panorama. Rotate the resulting panorama 90 degrees in the opposite direction for a vertical panorama.

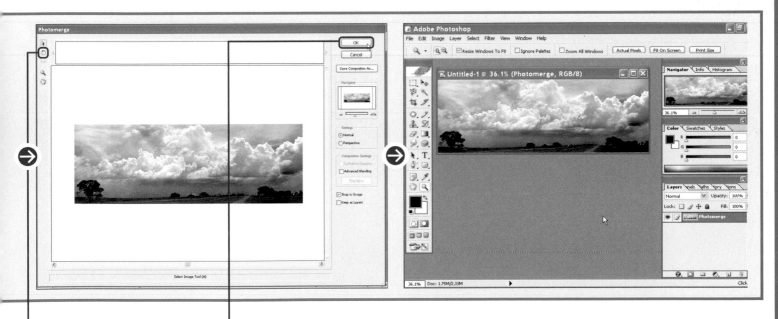

○ You can click the Rotate Image tool, and then click and drag one of the images to align image seams that are not level with one another.

⑬ Click OK.

○ You can click the repeat Undo shortcut, Alt+Ctrl+Z, to undo your Photomerge commands one at a time.

○ Photoshop merges the images and opens the new panorama in a new image window.

Correct exposure problems with the
SHADOW/ HIGHLIGHT COMMAND

You can correct the part of a backlit photo that is underexposed or the overexposed area produced by a flash using the Shadow/Highlight correction command.

When a subject is backlit, the subject is typically underexposed and the background is a little overexposed. The details that are lost in the shadows can usually be recovered, while the details lost in overexposed areas are more likely to be unrecoverable. Conversely, when the subject is too close to the camera when the camera flash fires, the subject tends to be washed out.

While all of these conditions can be corrected with traditional Photoshop tools, the process is greatly simplified using the Shadow/Highlight command. Without this command, it would be necessary to carefully select the affected area and apply the necessary tonal adjustment. The Shadow/Highlight command analyzes the photo for darker and lighter pixels and selectively applies correction to either the darker or lighter parts of the photo.

The Shadow/Highlight command allows the correction of both the overexposed and the underexposed parts by moving sliders in the dialog box and watching the preview.

① Click Image.

② Click Adjustments.

③ Click Shadow/ Highlight.

O The Shadow/ Highlight dialog box appears.

④ Click here to activate the Preview.

#49

DIFFICULTY LEVEL

Did You Know? ☼

You can click the Show More Options check box (☐ changes to ☑) to expand the Shadow/Highlight dialog box. By doing this, your editing options include not only Shadows and Highlights, but also more advanced options. The operation of these controls is described in great detail in the user manual.

Did You Know? ☼

You can create a collection of preset Shadow/Highlight settings. Clicking the Save button in the Shadow Highlight dialog box allows you to save the current settings as a custom configuration. You can reload any time by clicking the Load button, browsing to your saved custom .shh file, and clicking Load. This is a great help for regularly used or favorite settings.

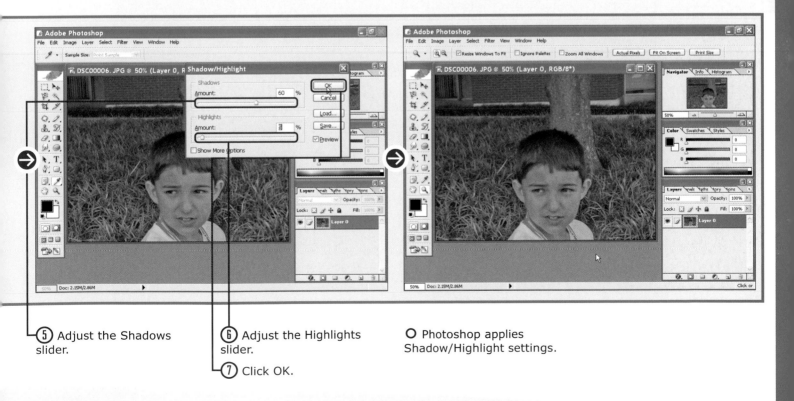

⑤ Adjust the Shadows slider.

⑥ Adjust the Highlights slider.

⑦ Click OK.

O Photoshop applies Shadow/Highlight settings.

Design a
PDF SLIDESHOW

You can use your digital pictures to create a fun and useful presentation or slideshow. Photoshop has a new tool, called PDF Presentation, which can help you organize and share your images.

You can now import a number of photos that Photoshop then compiles into a PDF-format slideshow. This utility imports files from a location that you specify, and then lays them out like rotating slides, saved in a PDF format. You simply choose the images, and Photoshop does the rest. Photoshop

also gives you transition timers and special effect options to make it even more exciting. The process is quick and simple.

The PDF Slideshow is a useful way to store and share your photos. To read the PDF, you need Adobe Reader, which is free and easy to download, making the PDF format widely accepted. You can send family members the slideshows they always avoid when they come to visit, or you can send business partners a set of presentations.

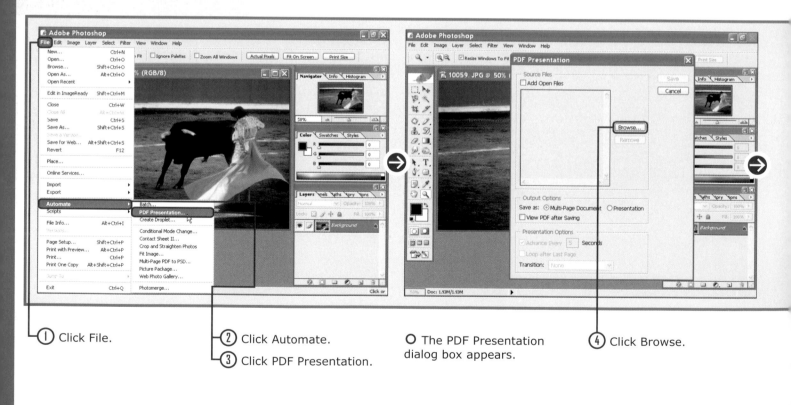

1 Click File.

2 Click Automate.

3 Click PDF Presentation.

O The PDF Presentation dialog box appears.

4 Click Browse.

Customize It! ☀

After you create the PDF file you can share it with friends and family in several ways. Depending on the size of the PDF file, you can attach it to an e-mail. Another option is to burn it to a CD or DVD, both of which can be played on another computer. Be aware that to get the best playback the computer should have the most current version of Adobe Reader, which can be downloaded for free from www.adobe.com.

Customize It! ☀

You can choose images from more than one source folder by selecting from one folder, and then clicking Browse again to select from other folders. You also have the option to delete files contained within the slideshow before you save it, by highlighting the images you want to delete, and then clicking Remove.

CONTINUED ▶

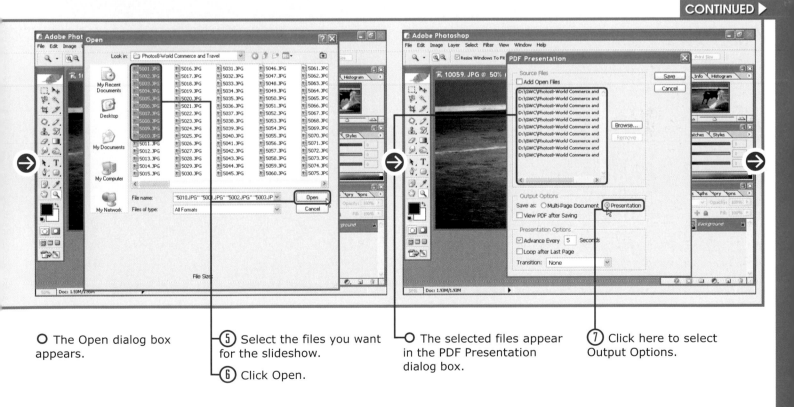

○ The Open dialog box appears.

⑤ Select the files you want for the slideshow.

⑥ Click Open.

─○ The selected files appear in the PDF Presentation dialog box.

⑦ Click here to select Output Options.

Design a
PDF SLIDESHOW

You can set the available Slideshow options in a variety of ways. How you set these options can make a difference in your slideshow's overall appearance. You can use all of the options in different combinations to create a wide variety of slideshows. This added flexibility makes PDF Slideshow a great tool.

You can affect the speed in which the slides rotate with the Advance Every X Seconds option. For example, works of art may benefit from longer pauses, whereas very similar and repetitive slides may benefit from a shorter pause.

You can select the Loop after Last Page option to have the slides roll continuously through the sequences. If you leave Loop unchecked, then the slideshow plays once and stops on the last image. For example, a running presentation for a tradeshow would use the continuous Loop option.

There is also a wide variety of transition selections available to make your slideshow stand out, such as Split Vertical Out and Dissolve. Transitions enable you to move smoothly from slide to slide.

CONTINUED ▶

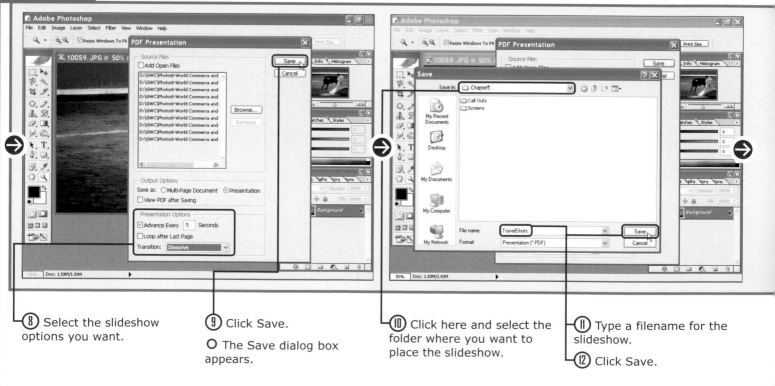

⑧ Select the slideshow options you want.

⑨ Click Save.

O The Save dialog box appears.

⑩ Click here and select the folder where you want to place the slideshow.

⑪ Type a filename for the slideshow.

⑫ Click Save.

#50
CONTINUED

Did You Know? ※

You can rearrange the order of your slides as you create the slideshow. You can click and drag an image thumbnail from one position to another, for an improved transitional order. In addition, you have the option to delete a slide if it does not belong in the slideshow.

Caution! ※

You can quickly make slideshows that are extremely large. Each image that you place inside the PDF Slideshow adds to the total size of the final file. To keep the size of the slideshow down, you can either reduce the size of the images before you add them to the slideshow, increase the compression in the Encoding area of the PDF Options dialog box, or both. You can have high quality images in there as well, but it is recommended that you keep the total image count low. By limiting file size or count, you can create a great slideshow without making it enormous in file size.

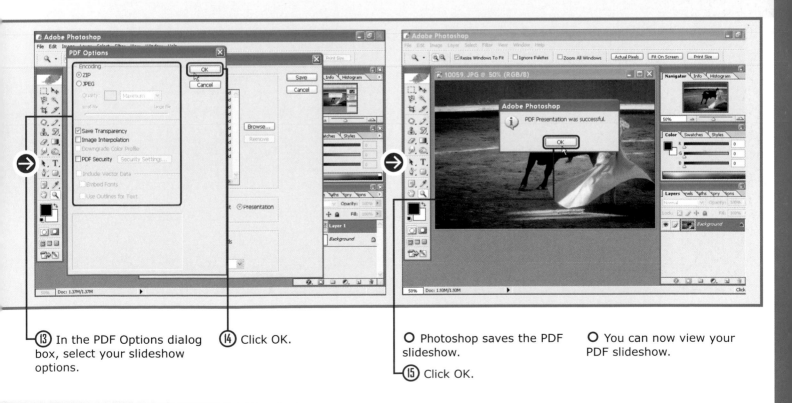

⑬ In the PDF Options dialog box, select your slideshow options.

⑭ Click OK.

◯ Photoshop saves the PDF slideshow.

⑮ Click OK.

◯ You can now view your PDF slideshow.

CHAPTER 6

Working with Color Tools

Accurate, vibrant color is crucial to every successful digital photography project. Therefore, it should come as no surprise that many of the more powerful tools in Photoshop are dedicated to the adjustment and optimization of color.

With the Color Variations tool, Photoshop offers a powerful but user-friendly way to adjust the overall color balance of your digital photographs. The Color Cast tool gives you the ability, with a single mouse click, to remove unnatural tints that can permeate an image. With these two tools, Photoshop makes correcting the colors in your digital photographs a snap.

Photoshop also offers tools to precisely change specific colors in your image. Using the Replace Color command, you can quickly and easily

select all instances of a given color, and then shift that color to a different hue or change its brightness or intensity. By combining various Photoshop selection tools with the color adjustment tools, you can pinpoint objects in your image and customize their colors, as well as remove color from them altogether.

If you want to apply a specific color to your image, then the Swatches palette offers you an easy way to pick colors from across the spectrum, or pick only from colors that show up accurately on all Web browsers.

You can also change the colors in your image by using fill and adjustment layers. Fill layers let you quickly add color, pattern, and gradient elements to an image, while adjustment layers let you make color and tonal changes.

TOP 100

Color coordinate two images with the MATCH COLOR COMMAND

You can take two images with different colors and adjust one image to match the other one using the Match Color command. The Match Color command can help adjust the brightness, color balance, and saturation of an image, based on the same information from another source image. This is useful when you are working with extracted elements from different photos and you want to make them similar in appearance.

When you define your source image and your target image, Photoshop assigns the colors from your source image and matches them to the target

image. You can then make adjustments to the luminance and color intensity to increase the brightness and saturation of the target image. You can also click the Neutralize check box to eliminate color casts in the target image, thereby matching the colors more closely. You have the option to use the source file or any of the component layers in this file from which to make your color matching. You can also create a selection in either image from which to work. You can use selections to define the color areas you want to match or change.

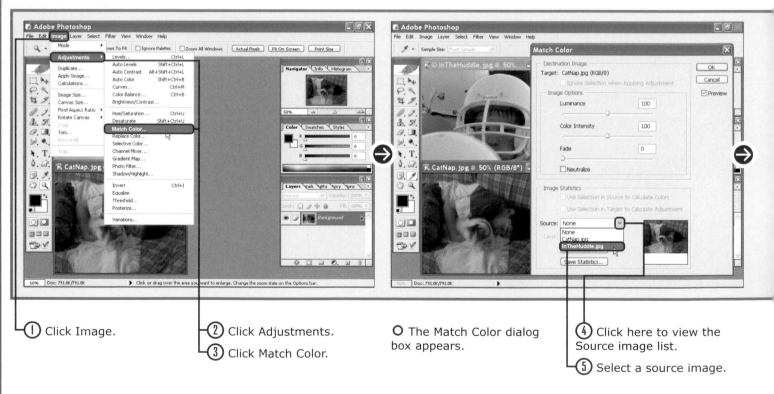

① Click Image.

② Click Adjustments.

③ Click Match Color.

● The Match Color dialog box appears.

④ Click here to view the Source image list.

⑤ Select a source image.

Did You Know? ※

You can use the Match Color command to remove color casts from within an image. In the Match Color dialog box, click the ∨ and set the Source image to None. Click the Neutralize check box (☐ changes to ☑), and Photoshop removes the predominant color cast. You can also use the Image Options sliders to make further adjustments.

Did You Know? ※

You can use one layer in an image to match colors on another layer within the same image. Select the layer you want to correct, and open the Match Color dialog box. Click ∨ and set the Target image as the Source image. Then select a layer from the Layer ∨. Photoshop uses this layer as the Source Image. Adjust your Image Options, and click OK.

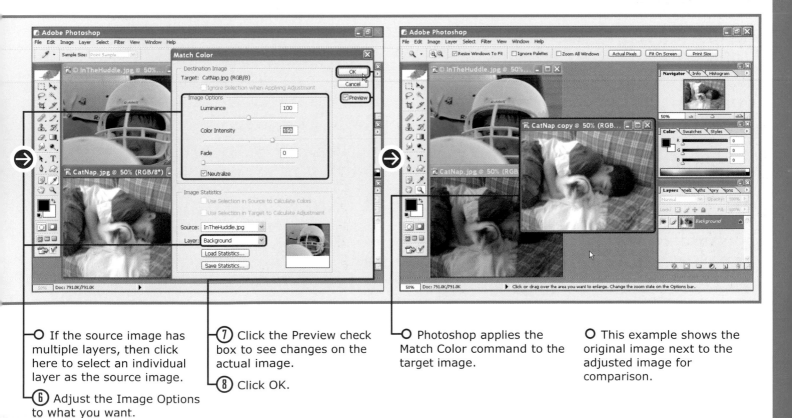

─O If the source image has multiple layers, then click here to select an individual layer as the source image.

⑥ Adjust the Image Options to what you want.

⑦ Click the Preview check box to see changes on the actual image.

⑧ Click OK.

─O Photoshop applies the Match Color command to the target image.

O This example shows the original image next to the adjusted image for comparison.

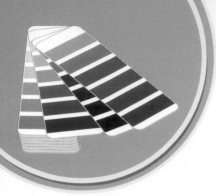

REDUCE AND REMOVE COLOR
selectively

You can selectively reduce or remove color from your images. This is a great way to decrease the dominance of a single color, or to create a more subtle color cast in an image. You can do this using the Sponge tool, a brush-based color adjuster that increases or decreases the saturation level of the colors you brush over. When you use the Desaturate mode, the Sponge tool can lower the color saturation down to zero percent, or grayscale. You can set the Flow setting to increase or decrease the amount of desaturation that occurs each time you

brush over an area, so you can easily create subtle color reductions, or desaturate to black and white. Even if you desaturate a color image to zero percent, the image remains in the same color mode as the original image.

If the area you remove color from is a complex shape, then you can create a selection with any of the Selection tools, and Photoshop only desaturates within the boundaries of the selection. This allows you to control the color change without making unwanted changes in adjacent areas of the image.

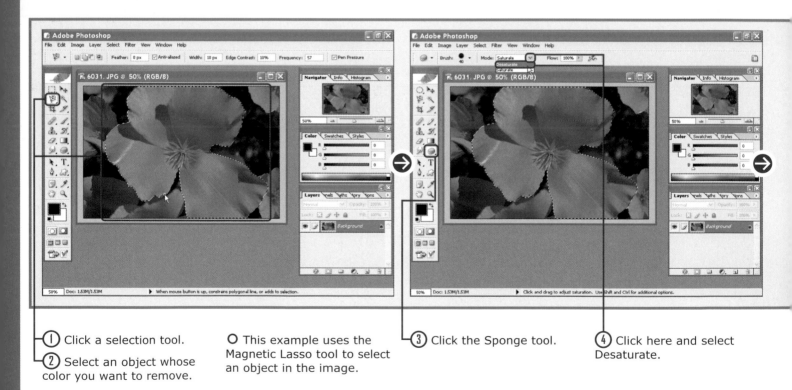

① Click a selection tool.

② Select an object whose color you want to remove.

⊙ This example uses the Magnetic Lasso tool to select an object in the image.

③ Click the Sponge tool.

④ Click here and select Desaturate.

Did You Know? ※

You can use the Sponge tool () to increase or decrease the contrast of grayscale photos. In Desaturate mode, the Sponge tool decreases the contrast of the pixels by moving all tones toward a 50% gray tone. In Saturate mode, the tones in an image are moved away from 50% gray, which increases the contrast.

DIFFICULTY LEVEL

Did You Know? ※

If you have an image with multiple layers, then the Sponge tool only affects the currently selected layer. To modify multiple layers, either merge these layers together or flatten the image. You can also apply the Sponge tool on each layer separately. It is best to work on each layer individually, or to work on a duplicate of the original document, because you cannot reverse color removal with the Sponge tool, outside of using the Undo and History functions.

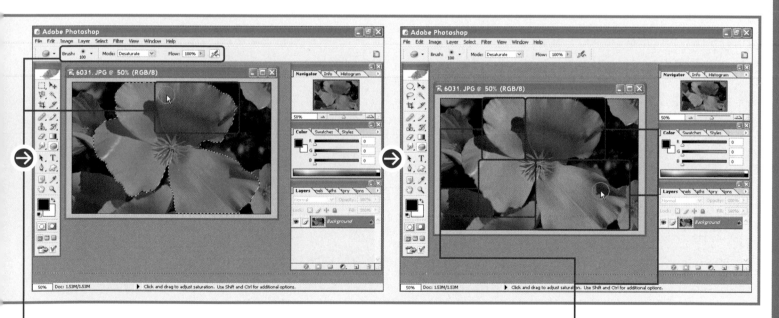

⑤ Adjust the options to what you want.

⑥ Drag the brush cursor across areas you want to desaturate.

○ Though this example sets the Flow amount to 100%, it does not desaturate completely on the first pass. Multiple passes desaturate incrementally to zero percent saturation.

○ This example shows the results of multiple passes of the Desaturate mode Sponge tool at the same settings, counterclockwise from the top right.

○ One pass with the tool.

○ Two passes with the tool.

○ Three passes with the tool.

○ Four passes with the tool.

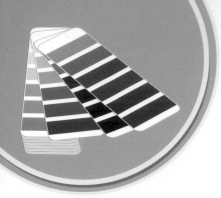

Switch it with the
REPLACE COLOR COMMAND

You can use the Replace Color command to select one or more colors in your image and change them using hue, saturation, and lightness settings. This is useful if you have an image with a number of solid-colored objects and want to change the colors of those objects quickly. The Replace Color command lets you do this without having to select the colored objects one at a time. You just click a sample of the color you want to change. Photoshop selects all the similar colors in your image automatically.

You select the colors that you want to replace using the mask displayed as a grayscale image in the preview box of the command dialog box. Protected areas appear black, unprotected areas of the image appear white, and semi-transparent areas indicate parts that will only be partly affected by the command. Clicking inside your image selects the corresponding area in the preview box, as well as any similarly colored areas in the image. You can then use the sliders in the dialog box to change the selected colors in the image.

① Click Image.

② Click Adjustments.

③ Click Replace Color.

O The Replace Color dialog box appears.

④ Click in the image to select a color.

O The selected color appears as white in the Selection preview.

⑤ Click and drag the Fuzziness slider to specify the amount of tolerance for the color selection.

O Dragging to the right selects a greater color range.

O Dragging to the left selects a smaller color range.

#53

DIFFICULTY LEVEL

Did You Know? ※

To add more colors to your selection, you can select the Dropper Plus tool (✐) in the Replace Color dialog box and then click inside your image. To subtract colors from your selection, you can select the Dropper Minus tool (✐) and click inside your image. If you make an incorrect selection and cannot subtract it from the selection, then hold the Alt key; the Cancel button becomes a Reset button. Click the Reset button, and the dialog box resets to default settings, and returns the photo to its original state.

Customize It! ※

Clicking the Image radio button (○ changes to ◉) in the Replace Color dialog box changes the preview box from the grayscale representation of the selected pixels to a miniature color version of your image. You may find it useful to switch back and forth between the Image and Selection options as you select colors to replace or adjust the Fuzziness slider.

⑥ Click and drag the Replacement sliders to change the colors inside the selected area.

⑦ Click OK.

O Photoshop replaces the selected color.

Touch it up with the
VARIATIONS COMMAND

You can adjust the color balance, brightness, and saturation of an image using the Variations command. This command opens a large dialog box that shows the original image, and variations of hues, luminosity adjustments, and a resulting image next to the original image.

Variations is the most versatile color adjustment feature in Photoshop, mainly because it displays the results while you are adjusting the settings. You can click an adjuster, such as More Red, to add incremental amounts of red to the image hues; Photoshop previews the results next to the original.

The now-current result appears surrounded by variations that are based on the current adjustments. This allows you to fine-tune even minor color adjustments.

Photoshop also allows you to make adjustments on the different tones of the image. You can choose to edit colors and brightness on the Shadow, Midtone, or Highlight ranges of the image, enabling you to correct exposure problems more accurately.

With Variations, you can also increase the saturation of your colors, helping you to correct colors that are washed out or faded.

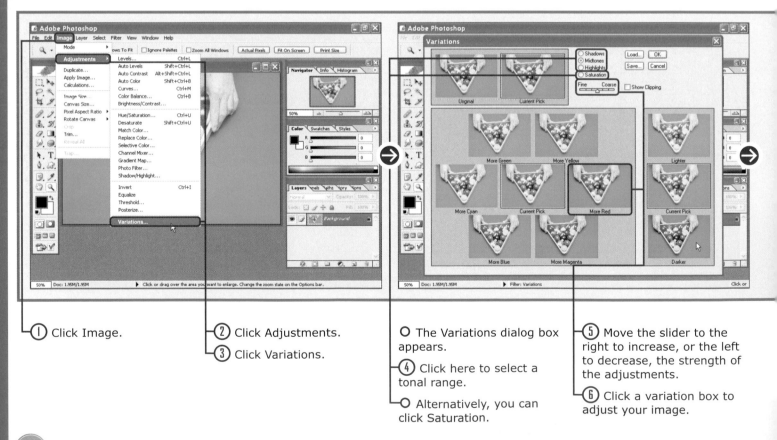

① Click Image.

② Click Adjustments.

③ Click Variations.

○ The Variations dialog box appears.

④ Click here to select a tonal range.

○ Alternatively, you can click Saturation.

⑤ Move the slider to the right to increase, or the left to decrease, the strength of the adjustments.

⑥ Click a variation box to adjust your image.

#54

DIFFICULTY LEVEL

Did You Know? ☀

There are several ways to undo the changes you apply in the Color Variations dialog box. Clicking the thumbnail of an opposite color acts like an undo action for a color you have added. In the same manner, clicking the Darker thumbnail undoes the last application of Lighter. As in all the dialog boxes, if you hold down the Alt key, your Cancel button becomes a Reset button, and you can click it to revert the image to its original state before you opened the dialog box.

Did You Know? ☀

The affects of clicking the thumbnails in the Color Variations dialog box are cumulative. If you click the Darker thumbnail twice, the adjustment is applied twice. The preview of the image shown in all three Current Pick windows is updated immediately and reflects the current appearance of the image. However, because the preview thumbnails are small, you will not be able to accurately determine the effect of Color Variations until you click the OK button.

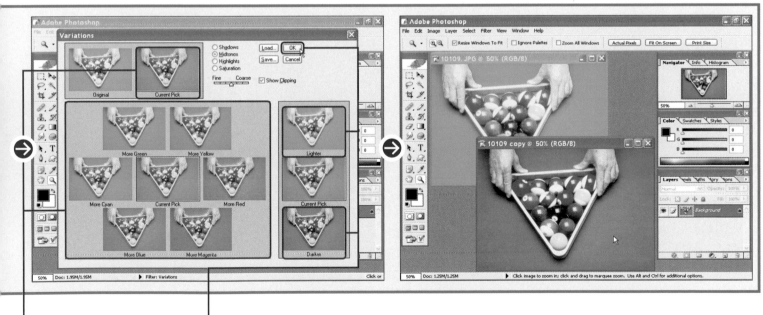

─O Photoshop updates the current color state.

─⑦ Click other variation boxes to make the changes you want.

─O You can increase the brightness of the image by clicking the Lighter variation.

─O You can increase the darkness of the image by clicking the Darker variation.

─⑧ Click OK.

O Photoshop applies your color adjustments to the image.

O This example displays the original next to the adjusted image for comparison.

Restore faded colors with the
SPONGE TOOL

You can use the Sponge tool to restore color to a faded photograph. Often a photograph fades with age, and when you scan it, the resulting image looks washed out and pale. You can use the Sponge tool to resaturate the hues and bring back the vibrancy of the colors. The Sponge tool is a brush-based color adjuster that increases or decreases the saturation level of the colors you brush over. When you set the Sponge tool to Saturate mode, it can raise the saturation level to 100%. You can set the Flow setting to increase or decrease the amount of color

flow that occurs each time you pass the brush over an area, so that you can easily create subtle color changes. You want to be careful not to oversaturate your image, or the color may look fake and intense.

If the area in which you want to increase color is complex in shape, then you can create a selection with any of the Selection tools, and Photoshop only saturates within the boundaries of the selection. This allows you to control the color change without making unwanted adjustments.

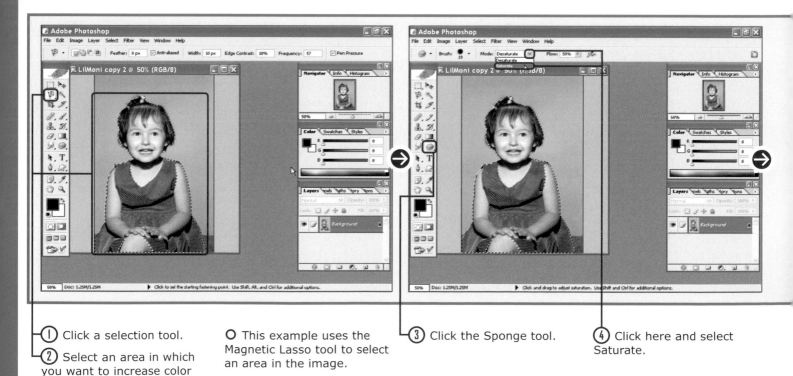

① Click a selection tool.

② Select an area in which you want to increase color saturation.

○ This example uses the Magnetic Lasso tool to select an area in the image.

③ Click the Sponge tool.

④ Click here and select Saturate.

#55

Caution! ☀

You can apply too much
saturation to an image when you
use the Sponge tool (🔲). If the
colors bleed together and detail is lost,
then you have over-saturated the area. If
this happens, use the Undo command, reduce
the Opacity setting, and apply again.

Did You Know? ☀

You can really bring out colors in photos of fall foliage
by selectively applying the Sponge tool to colors in the
trees. When you do this, the colors appear more vivid.
You should avoid applying too much saturation to colors
containing red, because red over-saturates more quickly
than other fall colors.

Customize It! ☀

Because the Sponge tool uses brushes to apply changes, you
can make use of Photoshop's wide variety of brush shapes and
options. Right-click an image to access the Brush palette when
using the Sponge tool.

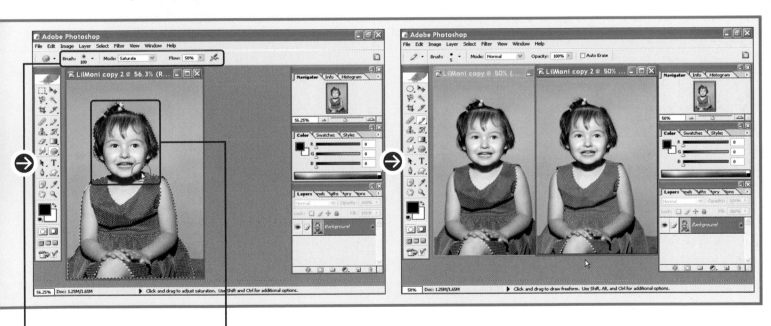

⑤ Adjust the other options
to the settings you want.

⑥ Drag the brush cursor
across the area that you
want to saturate.

○ Photoshop increases the
color in the area you
selected.

○ This example displays the
original image next to the
saturated image for
comparison.

Convert to a
DUOTONE IMAGE

You can use Photoshop to create duotone images from any photo. Traditional duotone images are created using two different colors of ink. Back when color printing was very expensive, a duotone allowed an image to be printed using only two inks instead of the traditional four. The resulting image looked like a tinted image, giving the appearance of multiple colors at a substantially reduced cost. Duotones are still popular today and offer a variety of advantages over traditional color photos. The addition of a second color increases the dynamic range of the same grayscale image printed with only

one ink. Duotones can also create a unified appearance in a group of images. For example, you could make all the photos in a brochure duotones using the same color set to give them a visual sense of common purpose even if their subject matter is very different.

Photoshop is not limited to making duotones. You can also make monotones (one color), tritones (three colors), and quadtones (four colors). As with the duotones, the additional colors increase the amount of visual detail that the printed image can support.

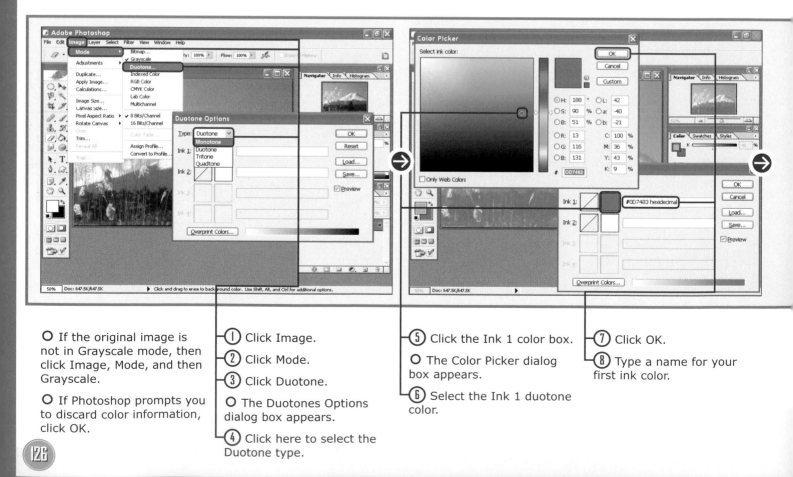

○ If the original image is not in Grayscale mode, then click Image, Mode, and then Grayscale.

○ If Photoshop prompts you to discard color information, click OK.

① Click Image.

② Click Mode.

③ Click Duotone.

○ The Duotones Options dialog box appears.

④ Click here to select the Duotone type.

⑤ Click the Ink 1 color box.

○ The Color Picker dialog box appears.

⑥ Select the Ink 1 duotone color.

⑦ Click OK.

⑧ Type a name for your first ink color.

Did You Know? ※

You can create great duotone images for the Web and for print, and gain benefits from both. Duotone images not only look good, but the file size is dramatically smaller than that for the same effect made with color overlays or adjustment layers in an RGB or CMYK file. The example in this task has a file size of 648KB, while an RGB version of the same effect would be 1.9MB in size.

Caution! ※

Making duotones for printing is not as simple as it appears. If you are planning on commercially printing the duotones, tritones, or quadtone images you are creating, you should first discuss this with the printer who will do the job. Each print shop has specific requirements for the file formats, and there are a myriad of other technical details that are best to know before you start.

56

DIFFICULTY LEVEL

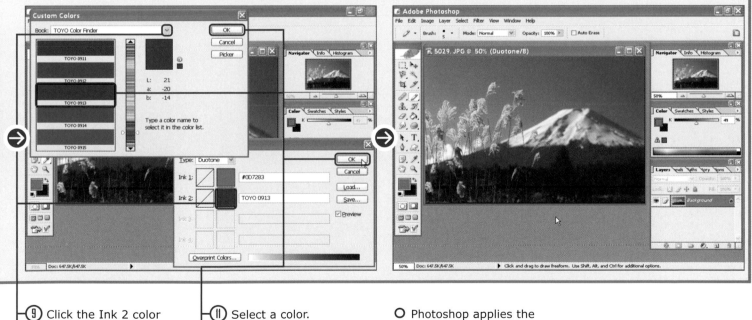

⑨ Click the Ink 2 color box.

○ The Custom Colors dialog box appears.

⑩ Click here to select a swatch book set from the Swatch Library.

⑪ Select a color.

⑫ Click OK.

⑬ Click OK.

○ Photoshop applies the duotone colors.

PUT A LITTLE COLOR
in your black and white

You can use your layer blending modes to take a black-and-white photo and colorize it. The method is relatively simple. Because color cannot be applied to a grayscale image, you must first convert the grayscale image to RGB color by clicking Image, Mode, and then RGB Color. The image still appears to be a grayscale but now you can apply color to it. Next, create a new layer over your grayscale image. Using the Brush tool, or any painting tool you want, you can brush your colors directly onto the layer and

cover the areas you are colorizing with that color. By maintaining relatively low Opacity settings in the Options bar, you can add color while keeping the photo details. You can also use the Overlay blending mode setting to add color without losing image detail. You can experiment with different modes for the results you want.

You may want to use the selection tools to isolate the specific areas you want to colorize, and to prevent painting in unwanted areas.

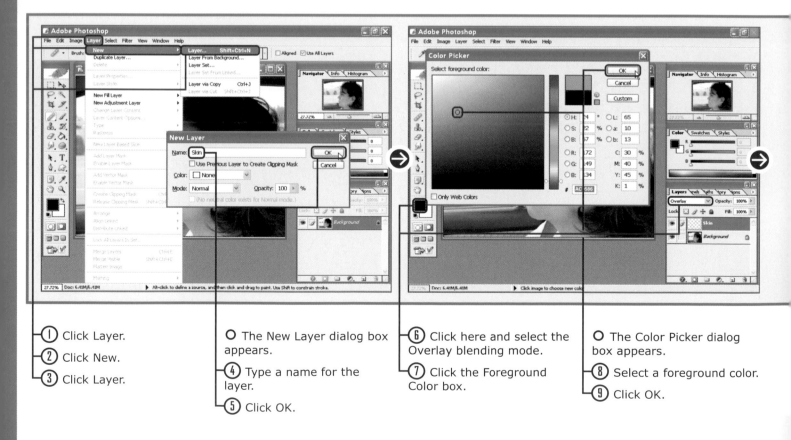

① Click Layer.
② Click New.
③ Click Layer.

○ The New Layer dialog box appears.
④ Type a name for the layer.
⑤ Click OK.

⑥ Click here and select the Overlay blending mode.
⑦ Click the Foreground Color box.

○ The Color Picker dialog box appears.
⑧ Select a foreground color.
⑨ Click OK.

#57

DIFFICULTY LEVEL

Customize It! ☀

You may want to use
other tools to modify the image.
The Burn tool (⬚) is excellent for
shading and color adjustment. With a
low Exposure setting, the Burn tool changes
a color only slightly, similar to using a low
opacity for the Brush tool (⬚). This can help
you add subtle shading and depth to the color in
an image to prevent flat-looking color.

Did You Know? ☀

By setting the Opacity setting of the Brush tool
to a very low setting, less than 10%, for example,
you can add colors that tint the image and make it
appear like a vintage black-and-white photo that has
been hand-tinted with watercolors. It's a popular
technique these days.

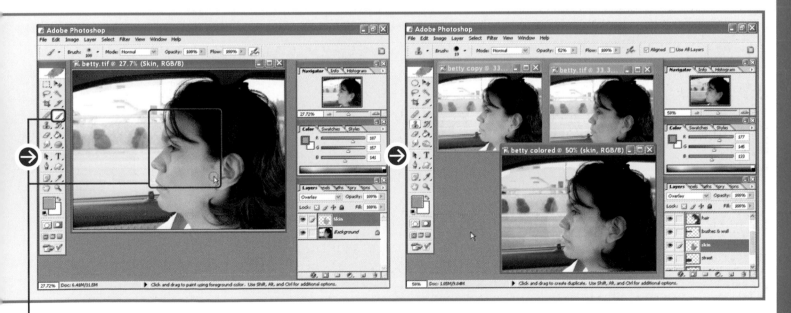

⑩ Click the Brush tool.

⑪ Paint over the areas to
which you want to apply
the foreground color.

○ Repeat steps 1 to 11 until
you achieve the effect you
want.

○ This example displays the
current version with the
original and finished versions
for comparison.

Change colors with the
HUE/SATURATION COMMAND

You can quickly and easily adjust the color of an image with the Hue/Saturation command. Located in the Adjustments menu, under the Image menu, the Hue/Saturation command lets you make changes to the hues, saturation, and lightness settings of your image. Hues refer to the color, which is based on a color wheel that goes 180 degrees in either direction from the currently selected color. Saturation refers to the intensity of the color, ranging from zero percent saturation, or gray, to 100 percent saturation. Lightness is the brightness setting for the color, based on zero percent as pure white and 100 percent as pure black.

You can take your image, or a selection or single layer of your image, and alter its relative position on the selected color scale. You can alter not only the actual image, but the individual color channels as well. This is very useful in altering color casts and color intensity problems on scanned photographs.

You can also remove the color from an object entirely by reducing the saturation of the image to zero. This does not convert it to grayscale, but simply removes measurable color from the current color mode.

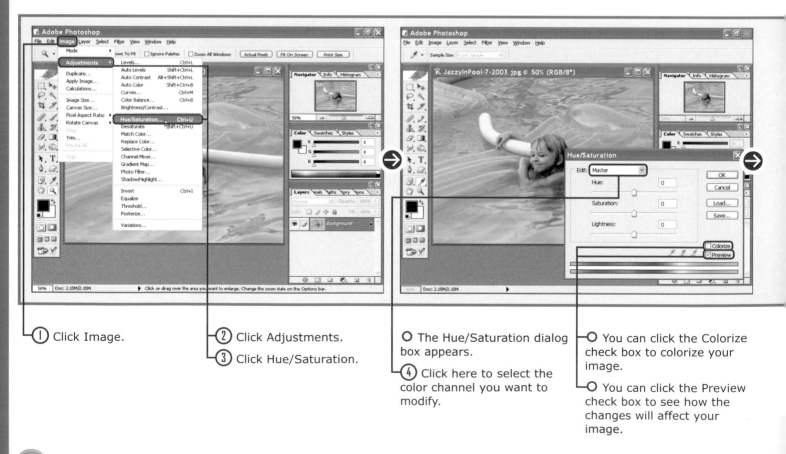

① Click Image.

② Click Adjustments.

③ Click Hue/Saturation.

○ The Hue/Saturation dialog box appears.

④ Click here to select the color channel you want to modify.

○ You can click the Colorize check box to colorize your image.

○ You can click the Preview check box to see how the changes will affect your image.

Did You Know? ※

As you drag the Hue slider, colors in your image change according to their position in the color spectrum. This means that as you drag the slider to the right, red colors in your image turn orange, yellow, green, blue, indigo, and then violet. If you apply a hue change to an entire image, then each color pixel makes the same transition simultaneously, according to its position in the spectrum.

Customize It! ※

The Colorize check box in the Hue/Saturation dialog box allows you to use the feature in the same way as the Fill command. Checking the Colorize check box (☐ changes to ☑) turns all the pixel colors in your image to a single color value, except for the black and white tones. You can then adjust the color value according to what you want.

⑤ Click and drag here to adjust the hue.

⑥ Click and drag here to adjust the saturation.

⑦ Click and drag here to adjust the lightness.

O You can also enter numerical values in the entry fields to make changes.

⑧ Click OK.

O Photoshop applies the Hue/Saturation command.

Fill it up with a
FILL LAYER

You can quickly fill an image with colors, patterns, and gradients by creating a fill layer. Fill layers apply their change using a layer mask, and because the fill is on a separate layer and is not applied to the original image, the fill remains editable. Because they use a layer mask, fill layers give you the flexibility to define where and how much they affect the underlying layers. When you paint black on the mask portion of the layer, these areas are considered hidden, and do not appear onscreen. Painting the

mask with white reveals the fill layer effect. For more information on masking, see tasks #24 and #25.

There are three kinds of fill layers: Solid Color, Gradient, and Pattern. The fill layers are easily editable. When you double-click the layer thumbnail, a dialog box appears, enabling you to change your fill layer settings. There is also a shortcut icon (🔲) at the bottom of the Layers palette that allows you to quickly select from any fill or adjustment layer type.

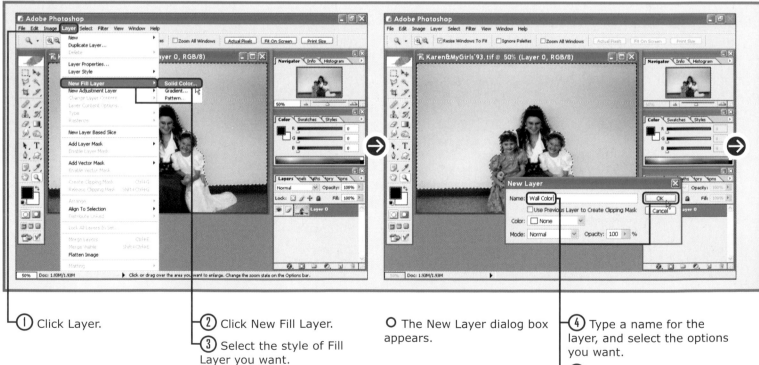

① Click Layer.

② Click New Fill Layer.

③ Select the style of Fill Layer you want.

○ The New Layer dialog box appears.

④ Type a name for the layer, and select the options you want.

⑤ Click OK.

59

Did You Know? ※

Photoshop gives you even more flexibility when using fill layers by allowing you to apply most of the layer options to fill layers as well. You can change the blending modes of fill layers for different effects, adjust the opacity, and even apply layer styles.

Customize It! ※

You can easily switch the type of fill layer or change a fill layer to an adjustment layer. Click Layer, Change Layer Content, and then a new layer type. Your fill layer converts to the new type, and you can modify the fill layer settings in the dialog box.

Did You Know? ※

You can apply your fill layers to a selected area instead of to an entire layer. Create a selection with any selection tool, and then create your fill layer. The fill layer only fills inside the selection boundaries. The example shown in this task demonstrates this technique.

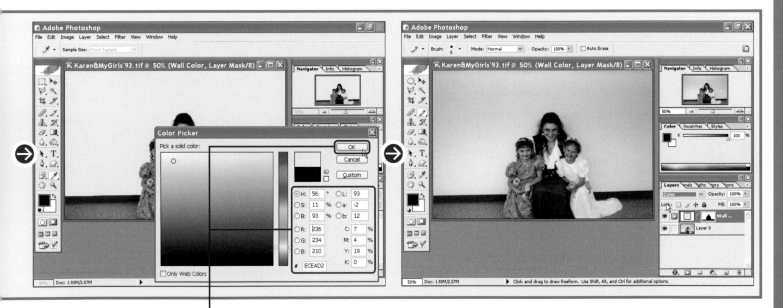

○ Depending on the layer style you selected, the appropriate fill layer dialog box appears.

○ This example uses the Color Fill Layer, which causes the Color Picker to appear instead of a dialog box.

⑥ Select the values you want.

⑦ Click OK.

○ Photoshop applies the fill layer.

○ This example sets the fill layer blending mode to Color, to retain the textured appearance of the wall.

Make a change with ADJUSTMENT LAYERS

You can apply a wide variety of color and tonal changes to your image using adjustment layers. Adjustment layers are special layers that you can use to modify the layers below. You can use several kinds of adjustment layers, including layers that affect levels, contrast/brightness, and hue/saturation. These adjustment layers act as an overlay that allows you to change the appearance of your image or layer, without physically changing the original image or layer. Adjustment layers are fully editable, giving you a lot of flexibility if you want to modify the effect.

You can use adjustment layers to easily make color corrections. For example, you can create a Levels adjustment layer that acts as though the Layers command is applied to your image, correcting color, tone, and contrast. If you want to edit the results, then you can double-click the adjustment layer in the Layers palette. Photoshop allows you to change the settings in the Levels dialog box at any time because the original pixels are unchanged.

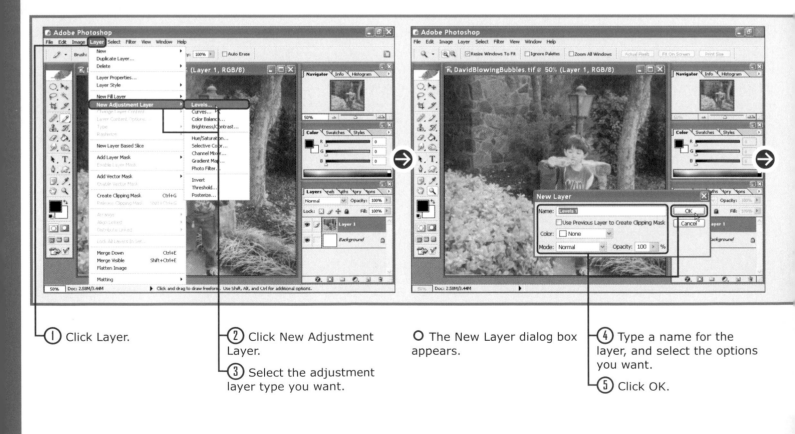

① Click Layer.

② Click New Adjustment Layer.

③ Select the adjustment layer type you want.

○ The New Layer dialog box appears.

④ Type a name for the layer, and select the options you want.

⑤ Click OK.

Did You Know? ☀

You can treat adjustment layers as any other layer type, making changes in opacity for softer effects, applying blending modes, and even hiding the effects by clicking the Eye icon (👁) in the Layers palette.

Customize It! ☀

You can make a color image appear as a grayscale image with your adjustment layers. Create a new Hue/Saturation adjustment layer, and in the Hue/Saturation dialog box, reduce Saturation to zero. When you apply the layer, Photoshop removes color from your image, making it appear black and white. You do not actually lose color data, and you can always return to the original image by hiding or deleting the adjustment layer.

#60

DIFFICULTY LEVEL

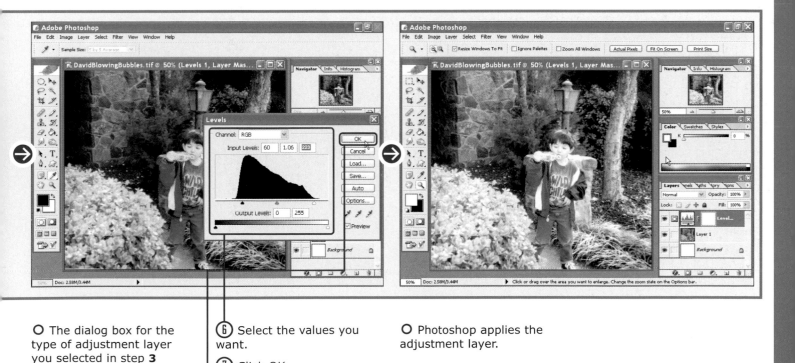

O The dialog box for the type of adjustment layer you selected in step **3** appears.

⑥ Select the values you want.

⑦ Click OK.

O Photoshop applies the adjustment layer.

CHAPTER
7

Creating Effects with Filters

You can create incredible effects using the wide variety of filters in Photoshop. Although the information about filters could fill an entire book, this chapter explores some of the more useful tricks. One thing to keep in mind is that filters often permanently change the layer object or photo to which you apply them. If you are using filters for the first time, then use them on a copy of your image. Many filters have their own set of adjustments and settings that can completely change the final result. You can also apply filters on top of other filters to create all new effects.

Filters range from simple blurs and sharpening, to mimicking artistic painting styles. Distortions, sketch strokes, and textures are available

to transform an ordinary image into an extraordinary image. In addition, you can install third-party plug-in filters to further expand the already generous Photoshop filter collection. Some of these resources are discussed in Chapter 10.

This chapter covers not only some of the more popular and versatile filters, but also new features such as the Filter Gallery, and new filters such as the Lens Blur and Fiber filters. The techniques that you learn here can help you to better understand how you can use single and multiple filters to achieve effects you want. However, experimentation is the best way to discover the usefulness and variety of filters, and the power they add to Photoshop.

TOP 100

USE THE FILTER GALLERY
to access your filters

You can use a new feature in Photoshop called the Filter Gallery, which allows you to preview many of the Photoshop Filters from a single dialog box. The Filter Gallery window lists the six different categories of filters that are available. Most of the filters in the Filter Gallery offer individual settings and controls.

When you use the Filter Gallery, a large preview pane appears, displaying the effect of your settings. Thumbnails of each filter appear, showing the

specific effect that they can create. You can also access all the adjustments and settings in the Filter Gallery.

You can easily switch between filters without the need to navigate the Filter menu. From within the Filter Gallery, you simply click the category of filter you want to preview, and then select and apply filters to your images.

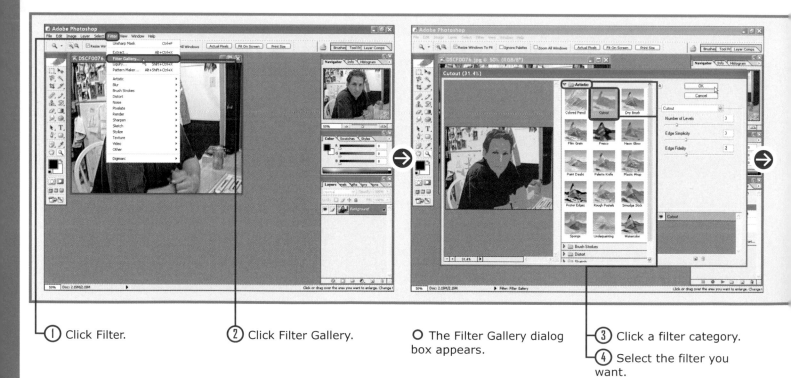

① Click Filter.

② Click Filter Gallery.

○ The Filter Gallery dialog box appears.

③ Click a filter category.

④ Select the filter you want.

Did You Know? ☀

Photoshop lists the categories and the individual filters alphabetically so that you can more easily find the effect you want. When you select a filter, the dialog box changes to display the settings for this filter. In the Settings area for the filter, click ☑ to access any available filter in the Filter Gallery.

DIFFICULTY LEVEL

Did You Know? ☀

You can use the Step Backward keyboard shortcut, Shift+Ctrl+Z, to move backwards in the history of changes that you have made in the Filter Gallery. If you try different settings, and want to return to a prior state of settings, or to correct an unwanted change, use this feature to return to a prior state.

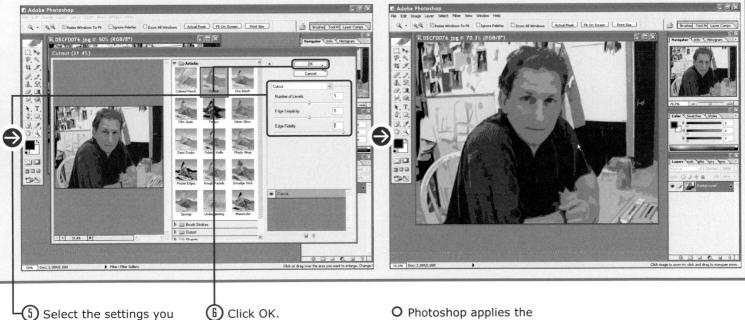

⑤ Select the settings you want.

⑥ Click OK.

○ Photoshop applies the filter.

Create a crystal ball effect with the SPHERIZE FILTER

62

DIFFICULTY LEVEL

You can use the Spherize command, located in the Distort menu, under the Filter menu, to create a distortion effect that resembles a bubble or a crystal ball. This has many uses for both photos and text.

The Spherize command uses your image, object, or selection, and wraps the pixels around a three-dimensional model, creating a distorted, spherical version of the pixels. You can specify the amount of distortion, so you can create a slight bubble-style effect, or a complete sphere, resembling a crystal ball. When you use an

entire image, the Spherize command uses the largest circular reference it can fit into the boundaries of the image as its distortion area. If you use a selection, then the boundaries of the selection determine the size of the distortion.

Options include choosing the distortion to be spherical, vertically columnar, or horizontally columnar. You can choose either of the columnar distortions to apply the image or selection to a cylinder shape.

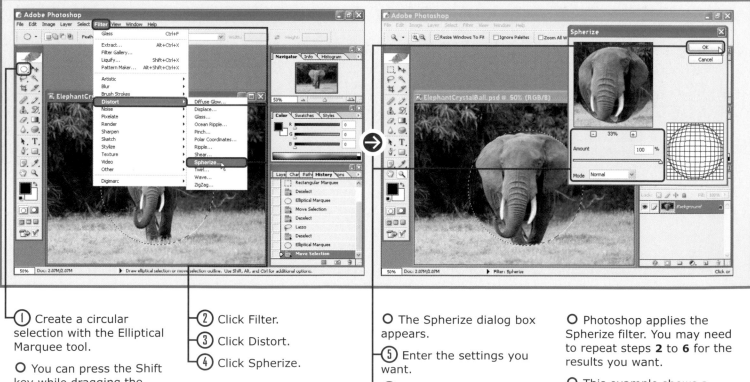

① Create a circular selection with the Elliptical Marquee tool.

O You can press the Shift key while dragging the Marquee tool for perfect circles.

② Click Filter.

③ Click Distort.

④ Click Spherize.

O The Spherize dialog box appears.

⑤ Enter the settings you want.

⑥ Click OK.

O Photoshop applies the Spherize filter. You may need to repeat steps **2** to **6** for the results you want.

O This example shows a selection with one Spherize filter application, and the preview of a second application of the filter.

Brush up with the FIBER FILTER

#63

You can now use a new filter in Photoshop that allows you to create random fiber textures. The Fiber filter creates random fibers, or hair-like designs, for use with backgrounds, textures, and effects. You can find the Fiber filter in the Render menu, under the Filter menu.

When you click the Fiber filter, a dialog box appears, containing two options that affect the variance and the strength of the fibers. The Variance option controls the spread and length

of the fibers, creating a variety of results, from fine hairs to harsh distortion. The Strength option affects the thickness of the fiber separation, from slight blur to strong contrast.

You can only use the Fiber filter on an existing object or image, as opposed to a transparent area or new layer. You can affect the colors by changing your foreground and background colors prior to applying the filter.

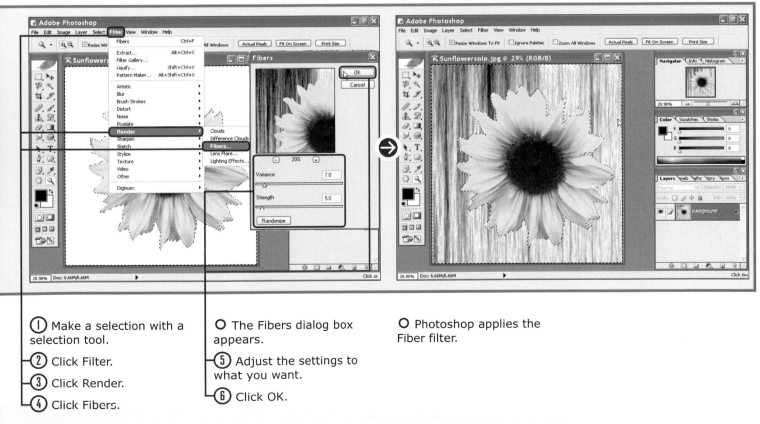

① Make a selection with a selection tool.

② Click Filter.

③ Click Render.

④ Click Fibers.

○ The Fibers dialog box appears.

⑤ Adjust the settings to what you want.

⑥ Click OK.

○ Photoshop applies the Fiber filter.

Apply multiple filters with the
FILTER GALLERY

You can now browse and select from many of the Photoshop filters using the Filter Gallery. The Filter Gallery gives you a much faster and easier method to select and preview the effects of the filters on your image. You can also use the Filter Gallery to apply multiple filters at once to an image.

One of the benefits of this new feature is that it gives you a chance to preview how combinations of filters would look when you apply them to your image. You can open any of the single filters by

clicking them. Inside the Filter Gallery dialog box Photoshop maintains a list of the filters that you have applied to your image. You can click the New Effect Layer icon at the bottom of the filter list to hold the current filter in place, and add a new filter. You can select from any of the available filters in the Filter Gallery, including a second application of the first filter. You can add as many additional filters as you want.

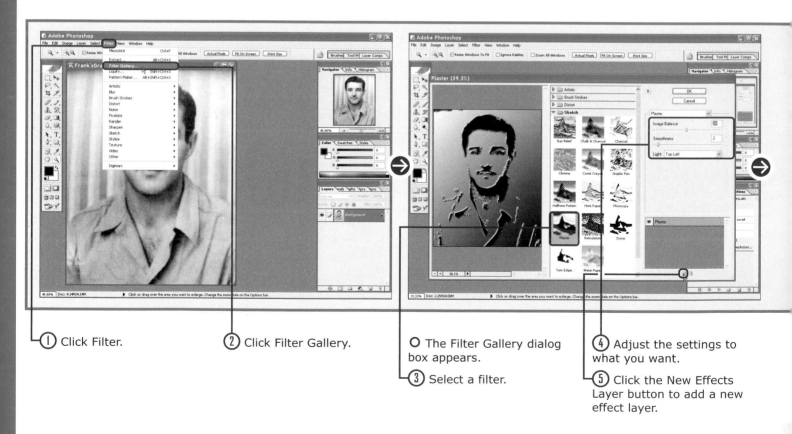

① Click Filter.

② Click Filter Gallery.

○ The Filter Gallery dialog box appears.

③ Select a filter.

④ Adjust the settings to what you want.

⑤ Click the New Effects Layer button to add a new effect layer.

142

DIFFICULTY LEVEL

Did You Know? ※

The order in which you apply filters can dramatically affect the final result. You can apply multiple filters in one order, and then reverse that order for a totally different look. You can click and drag the applied filters up or down in the list of applied filters, similar to a layer in the Layers palette. When you do so, Photoshop reapplies your filters in the new order, as they appear on the list.

Caution! ※

Complex filters often require a lot of system resources, and can slow your computer performance based on the size of your image, the amount of RAM available to Photoshop, processor speed, and the type of filter being applied. The Artistic filters are usually the most complex. If you have limited resources, then you may want to save your work prior to applying the multiple filters, to protect your image.

○ Photoshop holds the first filter, and a new filter becomes available to edit.

⑥ Select a second filter.

⑦ Adjust the settings to what you want.

⑧ Click OK.

○ Photoshop applies the multiple filters.

SOFTEN HARSH EDGES
on extracted objects

When you transfer objects from one photo to another, there are often rough or harsh edges on the object that you are relocating. Photoshop has the filters and tools to help correct this, to allow a more believable assimilation into the photograph. By using the Blur filters and the Blur tool, smoothing out the harsh edges is a simple process.

The Blur tool and filters reduce both color and tonal differences between adjacent pixels. For example, applying the Blur tool to an area of an image changes the tonal differences of the pixels in the

affected area so that they are the same or nearly so. Reducing the difference between the pixels softens or blurs any edges or detail.

Ideally, the object that you transfer should have high-contrasting edges to the surrounding scene. The Blur tools blend the outer edges of the object into its surroundings, making the image more believable. There are other ways to soften harsh edges, but this technique is simple, quick, and one of the most effective.

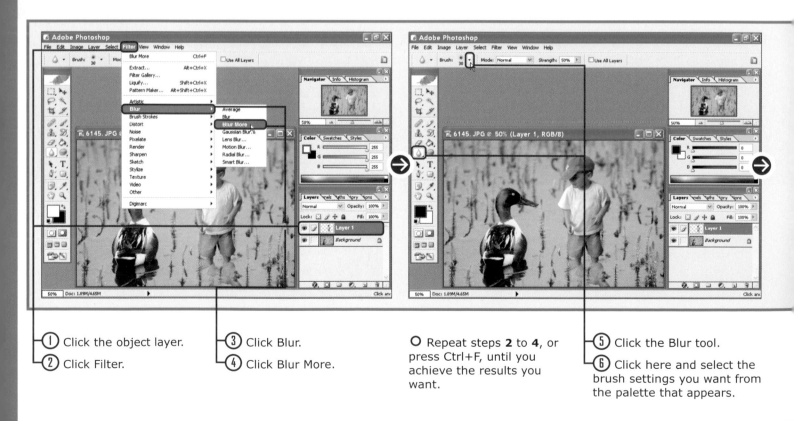

① Click the object layer.

② Click Filter.

③ Click Blur.

④ Click Blur More.

O Repeat steps **2** to **4**, or press Ctrl+F, until you achieve the results you want.

⑤ Click the Blur tool.

⑥ Click here and select the brush settings you want from the palette that appears.

Caution! ☀

The Blur tool (), like other brush tools, permanently affects the pixels it adjusts. Fine detail in an image can be lost rather quickly using the Blur tool, so use it with caution. Do not use the Sharpen filter to attempt to recover detail in an image after using the Blur tool, because it cannot recover the original data. To be safe, you should work on a copy of the image, or save the image under a different name than the original name.

Did You Know? ☀

You can use the Blur tool to do minor photo retouching. If you have a small flaw in an image, such as a dust speck or even a small blemish, you can use the Blur tool to remove contrasting detail from the area. By using a low opacity setting on your Blur tool, you can remove small wrinkles and even reduce shine on faces. Apply it sparingly, so you do not lose so much detail that the area looks fake or altered.

#65

DIFFICULTY LEVEL

O You may want to use the Zoom tool ( ) to magnify the view of the edges you are blurring, for better control. This example uses the Zoom tool to get closer to the object.

⑦ Click and drag the Blur tool along the edges of your object.

O Photoshop blurs the edge pixels to blend more smoothly with the surrounding image.

Turn photos into
SKETCHES

You can create the appearance of an artist's sketch from an ordinary photograph by using Photoshop filters. This technique works on almost any image, and provides you with a base for creating such items as coloring books, or creating patterns for tracing.

This task is not the only sketch transformation you can make. There are many options in the Filter menu for sketching and stylizing your art. Experimentation is the key to discovering the value and range of these artistic filters.

You can use the Sketch filters to create very detailed results, or you can adjust the settings to create more abstract results. High contrast images work more effectively with this type of filter effect, due to the amount of intermediate detail they lose when you apply filters. Low contrast images can become almost unrecognizable after the filer is applied. You can work on high contrast images and then resize them afterwards to retain most of the sketch details. You should also work on a copy of the original image, because many filters have permanent effects.

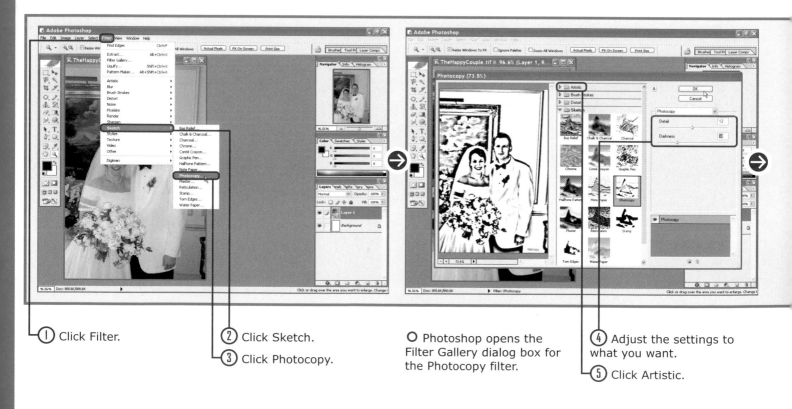

① Click Filter.

② Click Sketch.

③ Click Photocopy.

○ Photoshop opens the Filter Gallery dialog box for the Photocopy filter.

④ Adjust the settings to what you want.

⑤ Click Artistic.

66

DIFFICULTY LEVEL

Customize It! ※

You can retain some color in your sketch by skipping the Photocopy filter, used in steps **1** to **3** below. When you do this, Photoshop creates a colored pastel sketch effect that creates a completely different appearance in your final image.

⑥ Click the New Effects Layer button to add a new filter.

⑦ Click Rough Pastels.

⑧ Adjust the settings to what you want.

⑨ Click OK.

O Photoshop applies the filters and creates a pastel sketch.

O This example displays the original for comparison.

Create textures with the
RENDER LIGHTING FILTER

Photoshop has numerous tools that you can use to create a texture, whether it is mimicking a canvas, creating a chrome finish, or manufacturing a rock formation. The types and styles of textures are limited only by your imagination, and by using the filters in Photoshop, you can create textures for a wide variety of design and illustration purposes.

This task introduces you to the Render Lighting filter. This filter has a wide range of uses, although it is particularly useful when you combine it with gradients for the creation of random textures. Gradients generate a blended pattern of foreground

and background colors. The Render Lighting filter is also very powerful, creating lighting from customizable sources, and even creating three-dimensional texturing effects by using a Texture Channel option. With this option, you can establish the color white as the high point for lighting purposes, thus allowing for some quick and easy texturing.

As shown below, you can also render realistic-looking circular cutouts from a colored wall, similar to Swiss cheese, by using the Render Lighting filter and gradients.

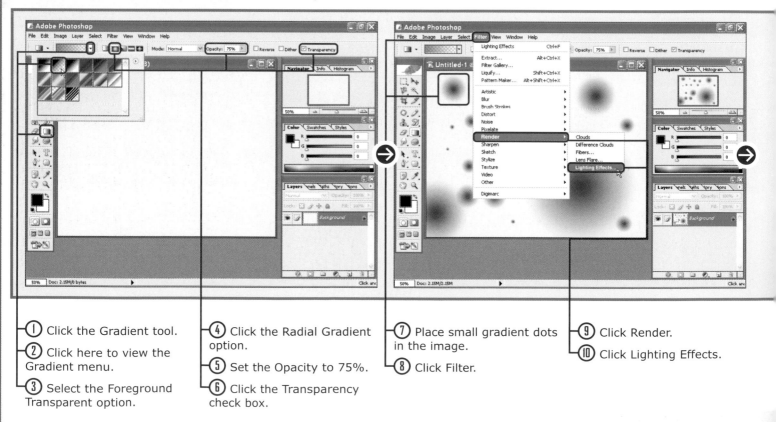

① Click the Gradient tool.

② Click here to view the Gradient menu.

③ Select the Foreground Transparent option.

④ Click the Radial Gradient option.

⑤ Set the Opacity to 75%.

⑥ Click the Transparency check box.

⑦ Place small gradient dots in the image.

⑧ Click Filter.

⑨ Click Render.

⑩ Click Lighting Effects.

Customize it! ※

You can create textured, three-dimensional text. First, create a colored text layer and then select your text. Then, repeat the task steps shown below and add a Bevel layer style. This does not work if you use black as the text color.

Did You Know? ※

You can create unique and fun effects by using other filters. After you apply the Render Clouds filter, apply different filters on the results before applying the Lighting Effects filter. Many filters modify the clouds to create completely different textures.

Customize it! ※

You can use the Render Lighting Effects filter for color effects by adjusting the color boxes located in the Lighting Effects dialog box, and selecting None in the Texture Channel menu. Using the Texture Channel creates a colored texture effect.

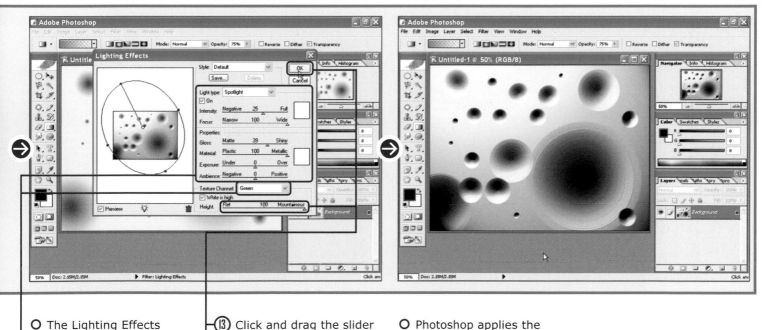

○ The Lighting Effects dialog box appears.

⑪ Select the lighting style and format you want.

⑫ Click here and select a color from the Texture Channel drop-down list.

⑬ Click and drag the slider to adjust the texture.

⑭ Click OK.

○ Photoshop applies the lighting effects to the image.

Distort with the
LIQUIFY FILTER

You can create many kinds of photo effects with the Liquify filter. From bizarre abstractions to creative photo editing, the Liquify filter is a very powerful photo-distortion tool. You can use the Liquify filter's tools to manipulate the pixels of a photograph so that they bloat, pucker, pull, and twirl. The results can be very amusing and creative.

The Liquify filter, located under the Filter menu, works by applying a mesh to the image, essentially dividing it into areas assigned to the mesh. You can

use the Liquify tools on the image, and in doing so, you distort the mesh; the image pixels follow the same distortion pattern as their assigned mesh area.

You can choose from different options, such as using items similar to the Brush tool, different methods for reconstructing the image to its original state, and even showing the image mesh with its distortions. Each option is designed to give you control over the changes you make to your image when you use the Liquify filter.

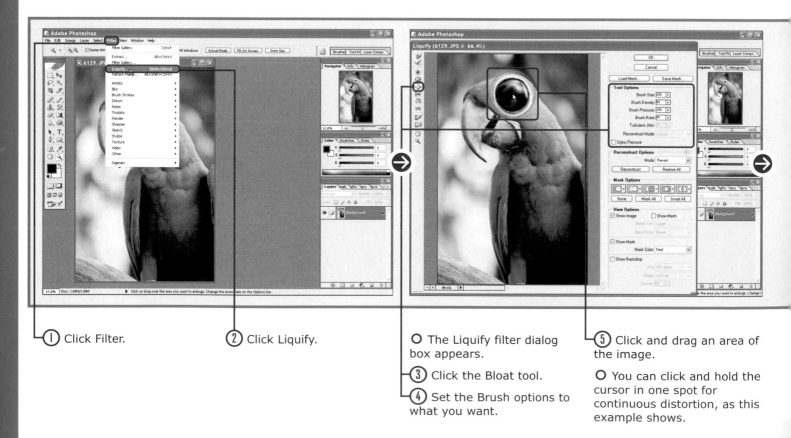

① Click Filter.

② Click Liquify.

○ The Liquify filter dialog box appears.

③ Click the Bloat tool.

④ Set the Brush options to what you want.

⑤ Click and drag an area of the image.

○ You can click and hold the cursor in one spot for continuous distortion, as this example shows.

Did You Know? ※

If the Liquify filter does
not give you the effect you are
looking for, then you can use the
Reconstruct tool ( ) to return the
parts of the image to which you have
applied the tool to the original state. The
Reconstruct tool offers the same options as the
Bloat and Pucker tools (and). However,
instead of distorting the mesh and your image, the
Reconstruct tool returns the mesh to its square grid
shape, and the image to its original appearance. You
can also use the Restore All button to return the entire
image to its original appearance.

DIFFICULTY LEVEL

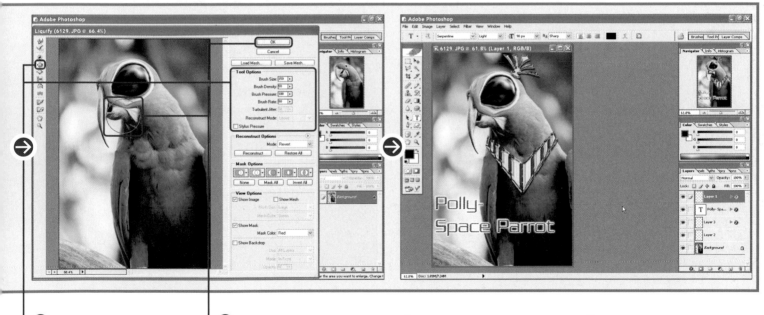

ⓖ Click the Pucker tool.

ⓗ Set the Brush options to
what you want.

ⓘ Click and drag an area of
the image.

ⓙ Click OK.

O Photoshop applies the
Liquify filter.

O This example includes
additional graphic props for
the final result.

Use the LIGHTING EFFECTS
filter for 3D effects

You can create very sophisticated shading and texture effects in Photoshop. The Lighting Effects filter is a very powerful Photoshop tool for creating three-dimensional shading results. It can apply many different multidirectional lighting effects, mimicking many different types of light, from a simple spotlight to a five-light parallel lighting strip. It also has multiple slider options that can intensify and change the final result.

There is also a Texture Channel option, where you can choose any one of the RGB channels of a color photo, or the transparency channel of your layer. You can select the texture channel, and set the amount of texture you want with the height slider.

By using a Blur tool, and then applying the Lighting Effects filter, you can cause the texture channel to create faux shading, and a resulting three-dimensional effect. However, you have a much smoother and more customizable definition of shading when you use multiple layers.

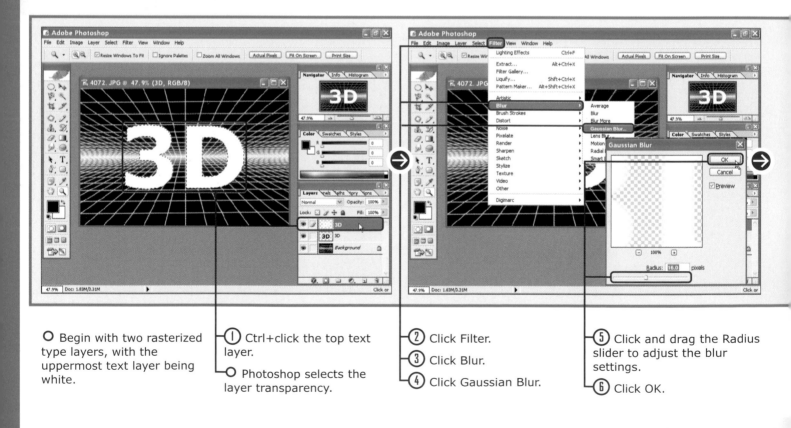

O Begin with two rasterized type layers, with the uppermost text layer being white.

① Ctrl+click the top text layer.

O Photoshop selects the layer transparency.

② Click Filter.

③ Click Blur.

④ Click Gaussian Blur.

⑤ Click and drag the Radius slider to adjust the blur settings.

⑥ Click OK.

Apply It! ※

You can create high-quality
three-dimensional effects easily
by using multiple layers and adding
some color with the Color options. You
can also use this technique with custom
shapes and brushes. You need to simplify
shapes before you can apply some of the filters to
them. Brushes are already simplified as soon as they
are drawn, and you can apply filter effects right away.

DIFFICULTY LEVEL

Customize It! ※

By selecting a different color of text for the
bottom text layer, you can completely change the
background color of the text. Because the top layer
is blurred, the color shows through on the edges.
This is not similar to what a colored lighting effect
would do, but instead adds color to the text base layer.

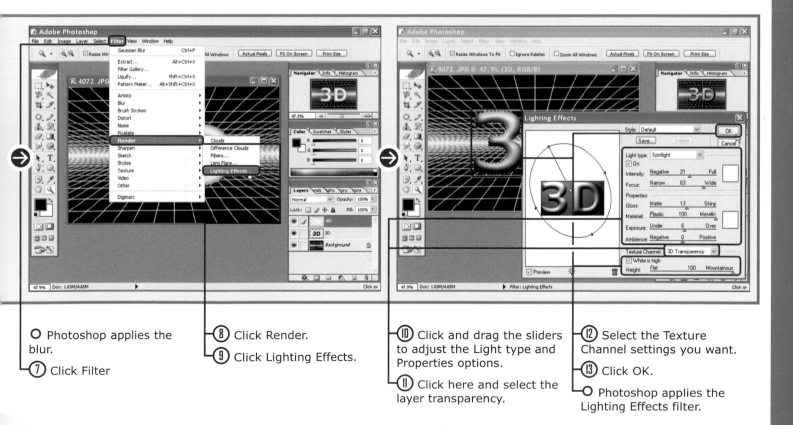

○ Photoshop applies the
blur.

⑦ Click Filter

⑧ Click Render.

⑨ Click Lighting Effects.

⑩ Click and drag the sliders
to adjust the Light type and
Properties options.

⑪ Click here and select the
layer transparency.

⑫ Select the Texture
Channel settings you want.

⑬ Click OK.

○ Photoshop applies the
Lighting Effects filter.

Create camera effects with the
LENS BLUR FILTER

You can create the effect of depth of field using Photoshop's new Lens Blur filter. The Lens Blur filter changes an image so that the designated areas appear to be in focus, while other areas appear to be out of focus, mimicking the same effect created by a camera lens. You can create images where the subject is the only item in focus, drawing attention to it.

You can define your focus area in two ways. You can create a selection with any selection tool, and apply the Lens Blur filter to create a multi-focused image

based on your selected area. This method is very quick and easy.

The other method involves using a selection that is saved as an alpha channel. The Lens Blur filter uses the saved selection as a depth map to create its focus point. To control the areas that are to be out of focus, select the alpha channel in the Channels palette. Using any of the brush tools, apply black to areas that you want to remain unaffected. Any area in white will have a blurring affect applied to it.

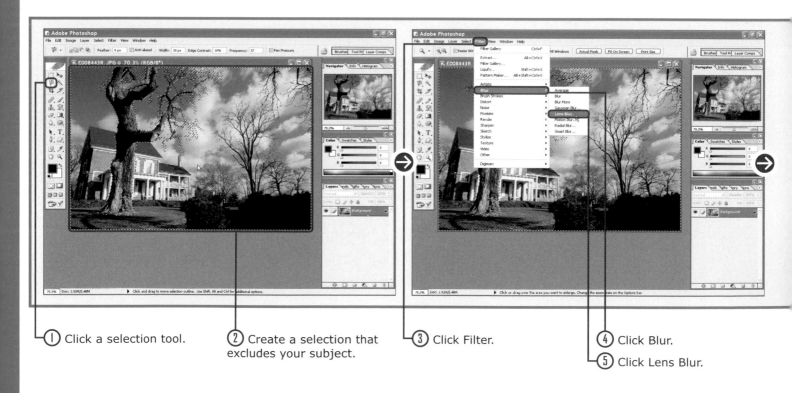

① Click a selection tool.

② Create a selection that excludes your subject.

③ Click Filter.

④ Click Blur.

⑤ Click Lens Blur.

70

DIFFICULTY LEVEL

Apply It!

Try applying a gradient to a channel before applying the Lens Blur filter. Click your Channels palette, and in the Palette menu, click New Channel. Using your Gradient tool (), create a black-and-white gradient across the new channel. Now, when you use the Lens Blur filter, you can specify this gradient as a Depth Map in the Source drop-down menu, and the Lens Blur filter creates a gradual blur effect.

Did You Know?

The Lens Blur filter has several additional adjustment options. One lets you adjust the iris, or shape of the camera aperture, allowing for different blur amounts. Click the Shape ∨ to select one of the different shapes that you can use with the Lens Blur filter. Other options allow you to affect highlights and noise within the blurring process.

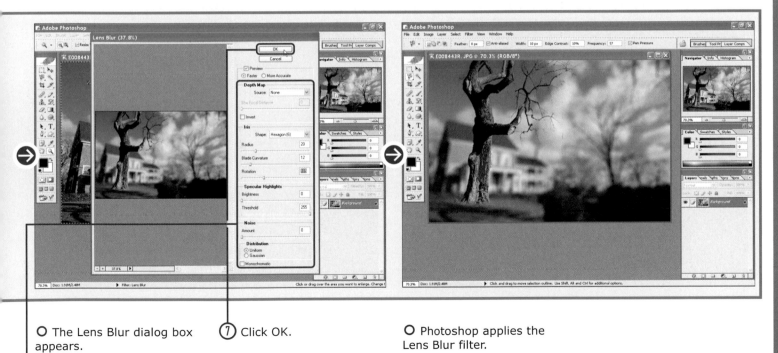

O The Lens Blur dialog box appears.

⑥ Select the options you want.

⑦ Click OK.

O Photoshop applies the Lens Blur filter.

CHAPTER
8

Preparing Images for Print and the Web

When you are finished with a file, you may want to either print the file or use it on the Web. Photoshop includes many features that make printing photographs or any image a snap. It also provides tools for creating attractive images that you can upload straight to the Web.

Photoshop offers automated tools that create *contact sheets* and *picture packages*. Contact sheets are composed of thumbnails of your images that you can use to preview and record your images. You print these images at a slightly lower resolution because they are only for your reference. A picture package contains one or several different images in a variety of sizes that you can print on one page. You should

always take advantage of the Print Preview feature in Photoshop, to spot errors or other problems before the photo goes to print.

You can use the Save for Web dialog box to create images in GIF, JPEG, and PNG formats, the three standard formats for displaying images on the Web. Photoshop can also build an online photo gallery. You can have Photoshop automatically generate the thumbnails and layouts for you, and all you need to do is upload the Web pages and images.

The File Browser is a great tool for working with your print images or your Web graphics. You can easily browse, rank, and add information to your images.

TOP 100

CREATE A CONTACT SHEET
of your images

You can use Photoshop to automatically create a digital version of a photographer's contact sheet. Contact sheets are made up of small versions, or thumbnails, of your images. You can use a contact sheet to preview and keep a record of your image files. This can be useful if you have a large number of digital photos to keep track of, and when you do not want to print them out at full size.

The Contact Sheet II dialog box allows you to specify the number of rows and columns of images you want to display on the contact sheet. It also allows you to add the filename as a caption for each image, which can be useful for matching up each thumbnail with an image file on your computer. You may want to print the contact sheet with a slightly lower resolution, because it is primarily for reference. For more information on previewing how the contact sheet prints on a page, see tasks #72 and #73.

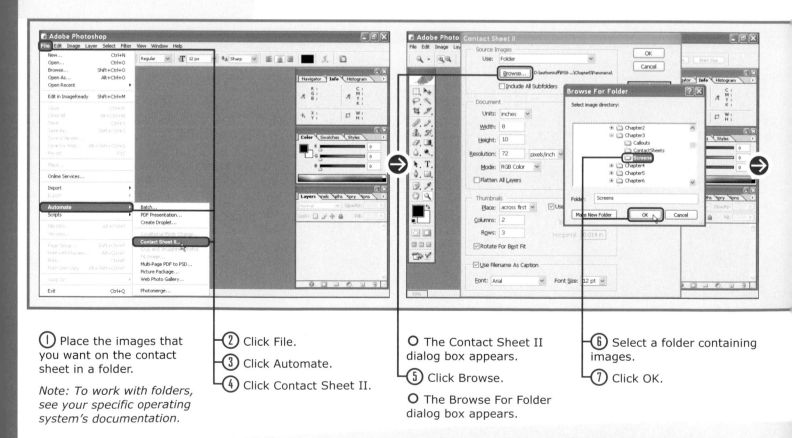

① Place the images that you want on the contact sheet in a folder.

Note: To work with folders, see your specific operating system's documentation.

② Click File.

③ Click Automate.

④ Click Contact Sheet II.

O The Contact Sheet II dialog box appears.

⑤ Click Browse.

O The Browse For Folder dialog box appears.

⑥ Select a folder containing images.

⑦ Click OK.

Did You Know? ※

You can make the thumbnail images of your contact sheet larger or smaller by adjusting the number of rows and columns. Photoshop determines the final size of the thumbnails on the contact sheet based on the number of rows and columns, as well as the paper size.

Did You Know? ※

You can edit your contact sheets after you create them. In the Contact Sheet II dialog box, click the Flatten All Layers check box (☑ changes to ☐). When Photoshop creates the layout, each image is on its own layer, and each filename, if used, is still an editable text layer. You can now edit the images or rename the caption.

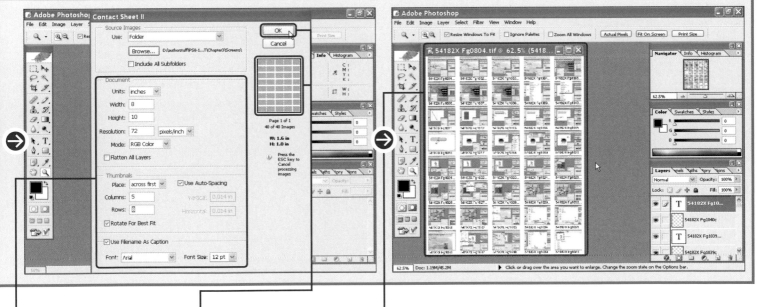

⑧ Select the contact sheet properties you want.

○ You can set the contact sheet size and resolution, the order and number of columns and rows, and the caption font and font size.

○ Photoshop displays a preview of the layout.

⑨ Click OK.

○ Photoshop creates and displays your contact sheets.

○ If there are more images than Photoshop can fit on a single page, then Photoshop adds more contact sheets.

Design a
PICTURE PACKAGE

You can use the Picture Package command to automatically create a one-page layout containing a selected image displayed at various sizes. You may find this useful when you want to print out copies of your favorite photo taken with a digital camera or imported by a scanner. Picture sizes range from wallet size to 10 by 13 inches, and paper sizes range from 8 by 10 inches to 11 by 17 inches, giving you many different photograph layouts from which to choose.

The Picture Package dialog box allows you to preview the arrangement of the layout as well as

specify the page size, resolution, and color mode. You can specify what color mode you want to print, such as RGB, CMYK, or Grayscale.

The quality of the resulting printout depends on the quality of the original image, as well as the picture package settings. To help ensure your prints looks as sharp as possible, start with a large image and increase the resolution of the picture package setting. You can directly change the resolution of the imported images by entering a value in the Resolution field of the Picture Package dialog box.

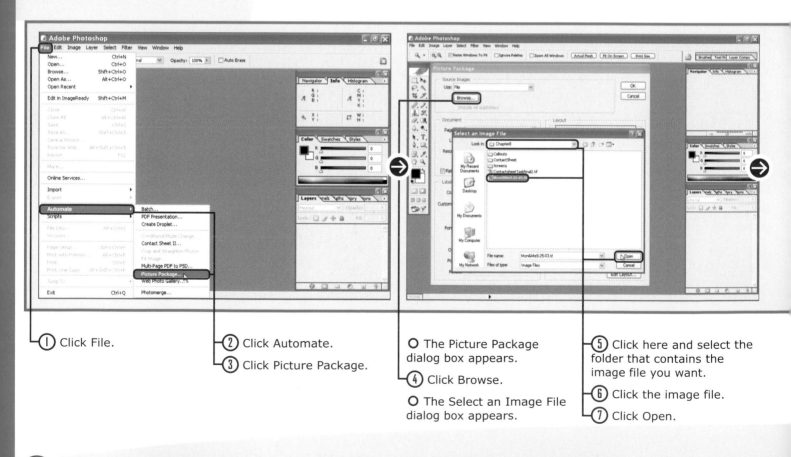

① Click File.

② Click Automate.

③ Click Picture Package.

○ The Picture Package dialog box appears.

④ Click Browse.

○ The Select an Image File dialog box appears.

⑤ Click here and select the folder that contains the image file you want.

⑥ Click the image file.

⑦ Click Open.

Did You Know? ✳

You can have many different images in each picture package. Click the placeholder for the photo in the Picture Package dialog box, and Photoshop allows you to specify a single image for that placement. You can assign as many different images as there are spaces for the layout. This is very useful for creating sample packages, or printing a series of photos from a particular photo shoot.

Did You Know? ✳

You can create multiple picture packages by specifying a folder in the Use ▾ in the Source area of the Picture Package dialog box. Photoshop takes each image in the folder and creates a separate picture package image for it.

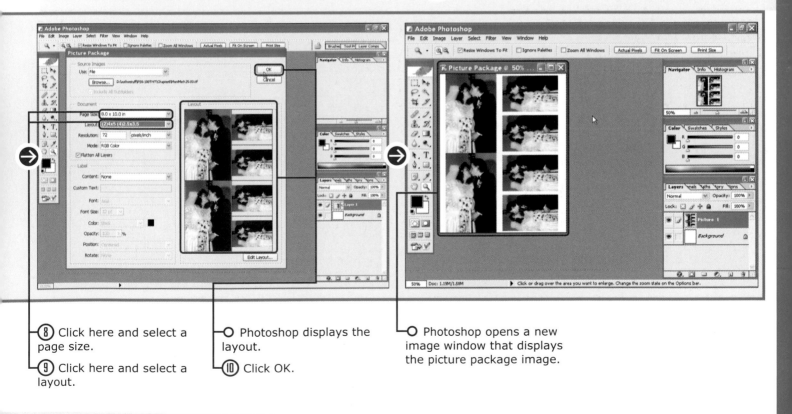

⑧ Click here and select a page size.

⑨ Click here and select a layout.

─○ Photoshop displays the layout.

⑩ Click OK.

─○ Photoshop opens a new image window that displays the picture package image.

Customize your
PICTURE PACKAGE LAYOUT

You can place your images into one of Photoshop's prepared Picture Packages, but you may be limited by the availability of specific sizes or the number of available copies of a size. Photoshop now allows you to edit a picture package and save it for future use.

The Picture Package layout is located under the Automate menu, which is found under the File menu. When you click the Edit Layout button, located at the bottom right of the dialog box, a separate dialog box appears, in which you can make changes to your Picture Package layout.

In the Picture Package Edit Layout dialog box, you can add and remove photo positions, and resize them by entering values or dragging the bounding boxes. Other options allow you to define the page-size and save the layout. After saving the layout, you can access it through the Picture Package dialog box drop-down menus. When you select the same paper size on which you created your custom layout, it appears on that menu. You can find the file in Adobe\Photoshop CS\Presets\Layouts. Simply copy these files to share with other Photoshop users.

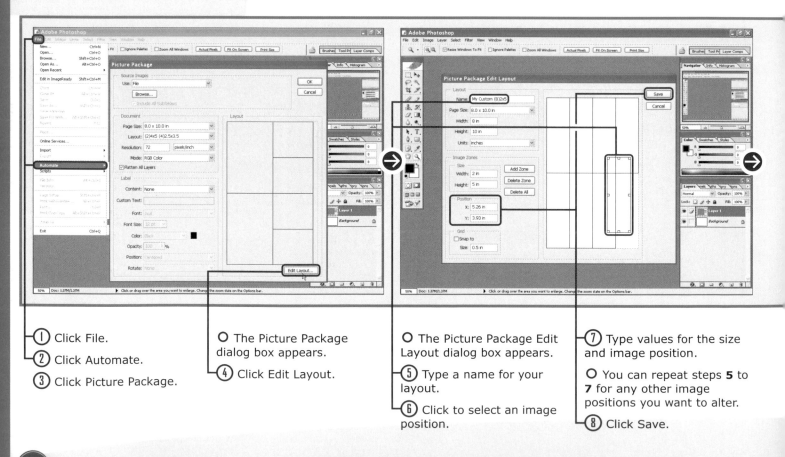

① Click File.

② Click Automate.

③ Click Picture Package.

○ The Picture Package dialog box appears.

④ Click Edit Layout.

○ The Picture Package Edit Layout dialog box appears.

⑤ Type a name for your layout.

⑥ Click to select an image position.

⑦ Type values for the size and image position.

○ You can repeat steps **5** to **7** for any other image positions you want to alter.

⑧ Click Save.

Customize It! ※

The Picture Package dialog box allows you to add a custom label to each image in the picture package. This can be useful if you want to prominently display a caption or copyright information associated with the image. Click in the Custom Text field to type your caption or label.

#73

DIFFICULTY LEVEL

Did You Know? ※

You can also resize the images by clicking and dragging any of the points of the bounding box that surrounds an image position when you select it. As you drag and resize, the actual size appears in the Width and Height text.

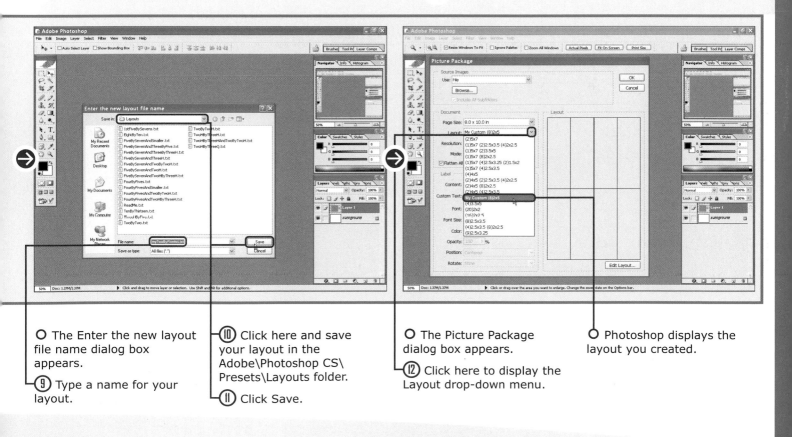

○ The Enter the new layout file name dialog box appears.

⑨ Type a name for your layout.

⑩ Click here and save your layout in the Adobe\Photoshop CS\ Presets\Layouts folder.

⑪ Click Save.

○ The Picture Package dialog box appears.

⑫ Click here to display the Layout drop-down menu.

○ Photoshop displays the layout you created.

RESAMPLE
your image

You can resize your image by changing the number of pixels per inch, or resolution; this technique is called resampling the image. Resampling changes the size of your image when you change the resolution of the image.

When you work with Web images, you are working within the limits of a computer monitor screen resolution and color palette. Large images and resolutions create very large file sizes, which slows download times for the Internet user. Resampling an image helps reduce the file size without having to sacrifice much detail.

In the Image Size dialog box, you can change image size in the Pixel Dimensions area and Document Size area. Pixel Dimensions stretches or shrinks the pixels within the image to fit the new size. Document Size allows you to change the physical size of the image in inches and resolution.

When you check the Resample Image check box, Photoshop adds pixels to or removes pixels from the image to reflect the change in resolution. If you change the resolution from 72 ppi to 300 ppi, then Photoshop places new pixels into the extra space, making the image larger. If you change the resolution from 300 ppi to 72 ppi, then Photoshop removes pixels to shrink the image.

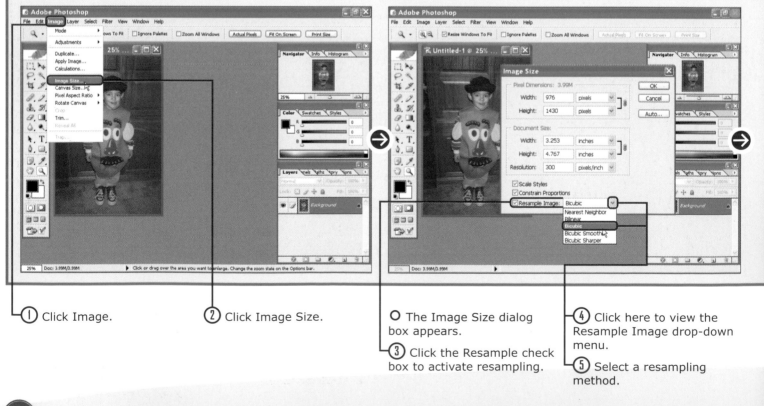

① Click Image.

② Click Image Size.

○ The Image Size dialog box appears.

③ Click the Resample check box to activate resampling.

④ Click here to view the Resample Image drop-down menu.

⑤ Select a resampling method.

Did You Know? ☀

There are three methods of resampling. Nearest Neighbor sampling selects the adjacent pixel closest to the original pixel, and duplicates it to fill in the spaces for the new size. Although this method creates jagged edges, it is the fastest. Bilinear sampling averages the pixels on all four sides of the new space, and places that color to fill the space. This increases the size of the image, but results in smooth, softer edges than Nearest Neighbor. Finally, Bicubic sampling takes an average of all the eight surrounding pixels to the new space and increases the contrast slightly to avoid being too soft or blurred, as can happen with Bilinear sampling. This method takes the longest time to process, but generally creates the best results. With the speed of today's computers there is no apparent difference in the time it takes each method to resample, so you can use Bicubic without any problems.

DIFFICULTY LEVEL

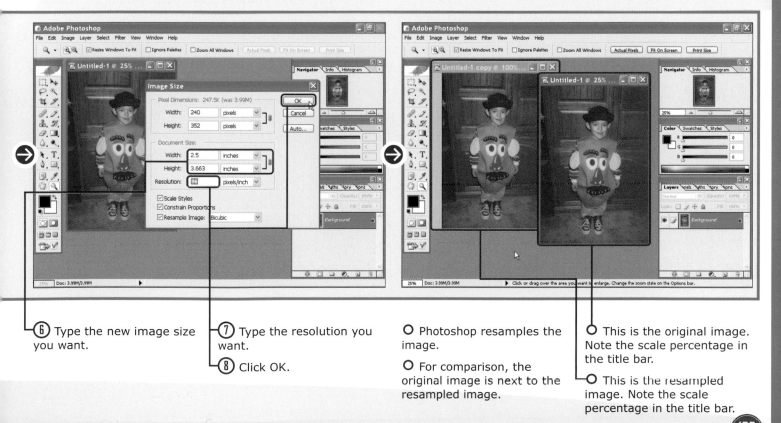

⑥ Type the new image size you want.

⑦ Type the resolution you want.

⑧ Click OK.

○ Photoshop resamples the image.

○ For comparison, the original image is next to the resampled image.

○ This is the original image. Note the scale percentage in the title bar.

○ This is the resampled image. Note the scale percentage in the title bar.

SCALE YOUR IMAGES
for print and the Web

When you change the resolution of an image without adding or subtracting pixels, it is called scaling. You can scale an image to change its size relative to your computer monitor or to the printing paper. The advantage of scaling over resampling is that the original pixels remain unchanged and therefore the image quality is unaffected. You may need to do this often, because images do not always fit a standard size. You can do this for both print and the Web: both have their own specific requirements and resolutions.

When you want to print your image, it needs a high resolution for the fine detail to show clearly on the printed page. You should resample the image so that it prints at the proper size. The detail of most images is important, so you should use higher resolutions — as compared to the resolution for the Internet — for higher-quality printing of your images. Regardless, the image resolution should never exceed 300 dpi for printing. Using a higher resolution only results in larger file sizes with no increase in quality.

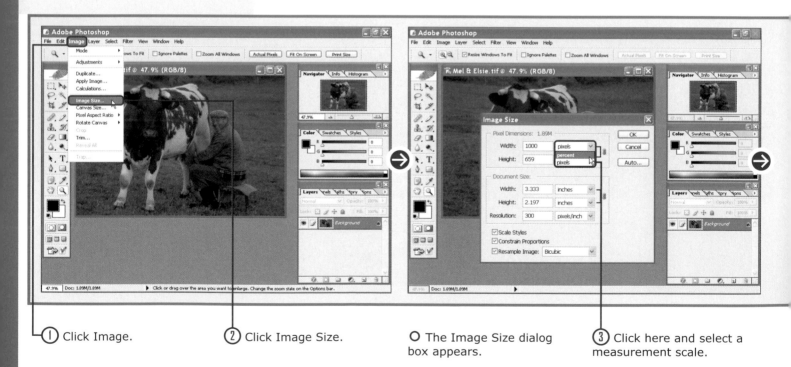

① Click Image.

② Click Image Size.

○ The Image Size dialog box appears.

③ Click here and select a measurement scale.

#75

Shortcut! ☀

You can change the size of your image without accessing the Image menu. When you right-click the title bar of the image, a menu appears, displaying options that include Change Image Size. When you click this option, the Resize Image dialog box appears.

Customize It! ☀

You can change the resolution of your image in the Image Size dialog box. Changing the resolution does not affect the number of pixels in the image, so it does not affect the size of the image on the computer screen or on a Web page. However, it does affect how the image prints out. Increasing the resolution shrinks the image on the page, while decreasing the resolution enlarges the printed image.

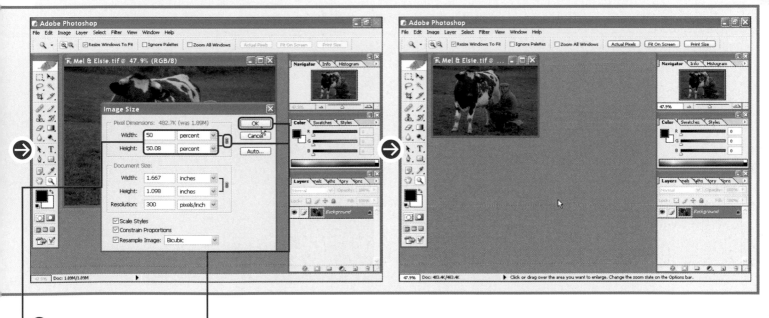

④ Type a value for the height or width.

O You can click here to have changes to one aspect proportionately change the other automatically.

⑤ Click OK.

O Photoshop resizes the image for print.

Create an
ONLINE PHOTO GALLERY

You can design an online photo gallery with Photoshop. You can use your digital images to create a Web site that contains everything necessary to view it as a Web site on the Internet. Photoshop not only optimizes your image files for the site, but it also allows you to select the design for the Web pages that display the images from a gallery of different templates.

Photoshop also generates *thumbnails*, or miniature versions of your images, for display as links in the gallery. When a visitor clicks a link, a full-size image appears in the browser window. Photoshop also adds graphical arrows to use as navigational links.

When you design your gallery, Photoshop offers you several options, including what information — titles, file names, descriptions — is displayed, different layout styles, and the treatment of specific elements within the page.

After you have set the options, Photoshop generates the thumbnails, optimizes the images, and creates everything necessary for the gallery to appear as a Web page. Photoshop saves the finished product in a folder that you can upload to the area designated for your Web page. Photoshop even opens your computer's Internet browser so you can view the new Photo Gallery.

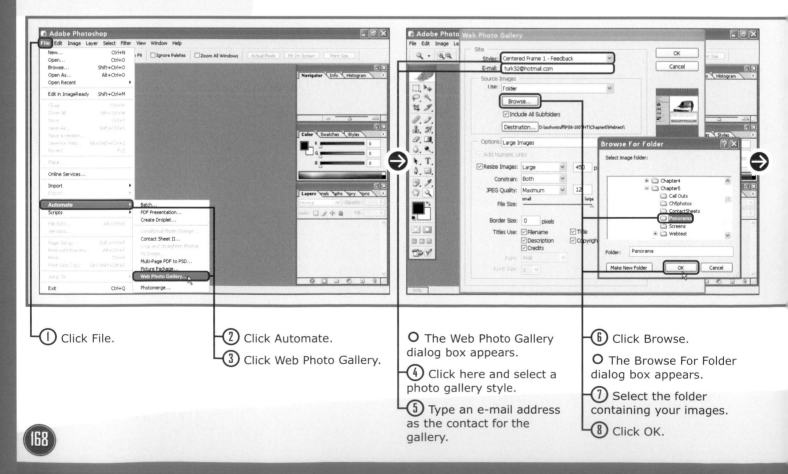

① Click File.

② Click Automate.

③ Click Web Photo Gallery.

○ The Web Photo Gallery dialog box appears.

④ Click here and select a photo gallery style.

⑤ Type an e-mail address as the contact for the gallery.

⑥ Click Browse.

○ The Browse For Folder dialog box appears.

⑦ Select the folder containing your images.

⑧ Click OK.

Customize It! ※

You can select from a variety
of page styles when you click the
Styles ▾ in the Site area of the Web
Photo Gallery dialog box. You can find
preset styles in the Program Files\Adobe\
Photoshop CS\Presets\Web Photo Gallery
folder. In that folder, you can make a copy of the
template, and modify it using a Web publishing or
HTML editor. You can then make changes within the
pages and save them as templates. See the Photoshop
Help files for more information on editing your Web pages.

76

DIFFICULTY LEVEL

Did You Know? ※

You can select multiple source files directly from the
File Browser before you perform steps **1** to **3** below.
When you click the Use ▾ in the Source Images area
of the Web Photo Gallery dialog box, the Selected files
from File Browser option becomes available. Click this
option, and Photoshop only uses the images you selected.

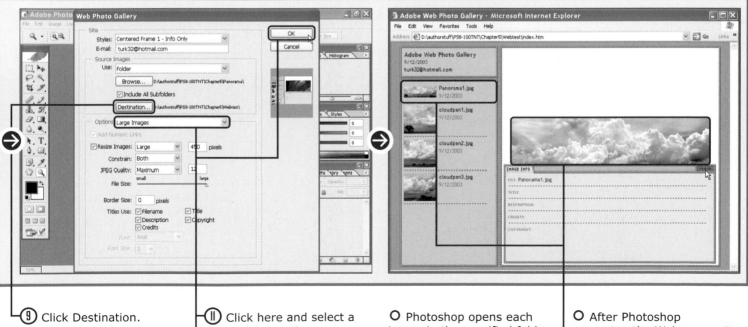

⑨ Click Destination.

⑩ Repeat steps **7** and **8** to
specify the folder in which
you want to save your
gallery.

⑪ Click here and select a
customizing option.

⑫ Click OK.

○ Photoshop opens each
image in the specified folder,
creates versions for the
photo gallery, and generates
the necessary HTML.

○ After Photoshop
generates the Web pages, it
displays the gallery in your
default browser.

○ You can click a thumbnail
to see a larger version of the
image.

OPTIMIZE IMAGES
for print or the Web

When you save your images, it is important to optimize them for the particular medium in which you intend to use them. Saving your files for the Web and for print have very different optimization requirements.

You can optimize your images for the Web with the Save for Web option in the File menu. If you have a large image file, then the image can take a long time to download to a browser. Because speed is essential for the Internet, small file sizes are critical. Photoshop optimizes your image by previewing the image at different image qualities and file sizes. JPEG and GIF images are the most common formats

for the Web, because of their smaller file sizes. While GIF is still the format of choice for Web icons and buttons, you should save all your photos as JPEG files.

Optimizing for offset printing requires higher resolution — usually 300 dpi. It also requires a specific size, and sometimes color swatches and CMYK formatting. As a result, the file sizes tend to be much larger because of the detail needed for the final print. TIFF, EPS, and PDF are the most common print file formats. Always consult with your printer or service bureau to find out what format and other technical specifics they prefer.

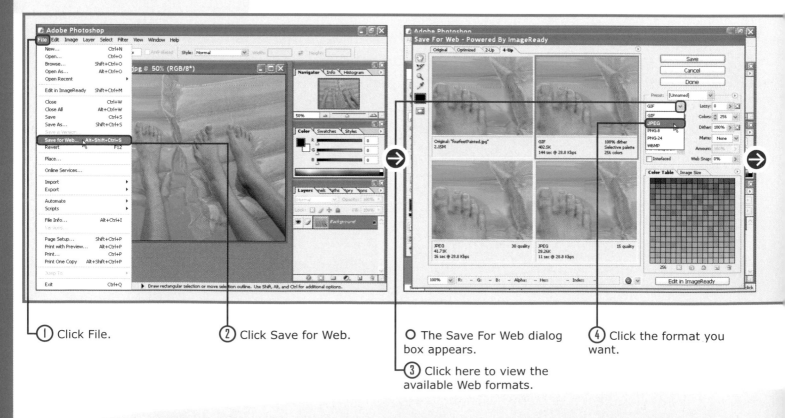

① Click File.

② Click Save for Web.

O The Save For Web dialog box appears.

③ Click here to view the available Web formats.

④ Click the format you want.

#77

Did You Know? ☀

The Save for Web command does not allow you to save a file in the TIFF, EPS, PDF, BMP, or other print formats. To save a file for print output, use the Save As command. File optimization for these formats has few options, and you can specify these in the Save As dialog boxes.

Customize It! ☀

When faced with the choice of which format to use for the image to be viewed on the Web, you should always choose JPEG unless the image is composed primarily of large areas of solid color, like a logo or a Web button or icon. GIF is the best choice for such images. You should also consider using GIF if the image contains areas that you want to be transparent so that the background appears behind it.

⑤ Click here to view the available quality settings.

⑥ Click the quality setting you want.

⑦ Check the file quality and size in the preview window.

O You can click here for alternate views of your images.

O Repeat steps **5** and **6** until you get the results you want.

⑧ Click Save.

⑨ Click here and navigate to your destination folder.

⑩ Type a filename.

O Photoshop automatically assigns an extension based on the format you chose in step **4**.

⑪ Click Save.

O Photoshop saves the file.

PUT FILE INFO
into your images

You can store valuable information inside your photos using metadata. For example, you can add captions and copyright information, along with color profiles and camera information. You may find this feature useful if you plan to sell or license your images, and want the files to retain information about authorship and creation.

Adding caption information is convenient if you are planning to use some of the other features in Photoshop. For example, you can automatically add caption information to your printouts through the Print Preview dialog box.

Another place you can edit and change caption and copyright information is in the File Browser. You can click in the editable fields of the Metadata tab, indicated with a Pencil icon, and type data directly into the file, without having to open it in Photoshop. This feature of the File Browser also makes it convenient to update metadata for items, such as when you need to change URLs saved in the image, or to determine details on the digital camera setup to repeat a picture style.

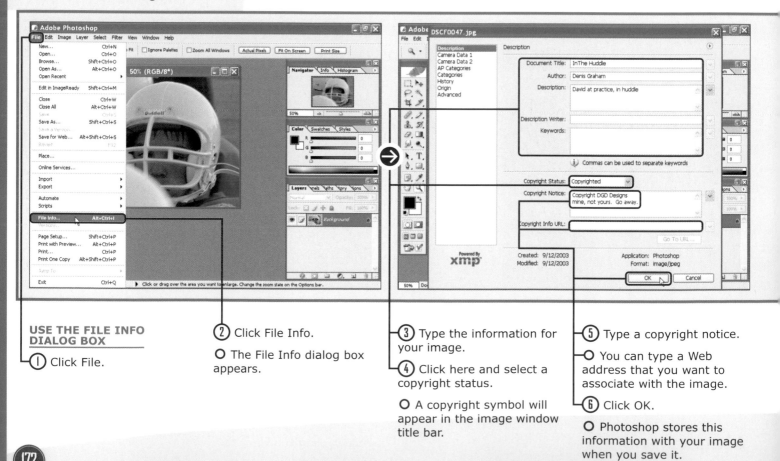

USE THE FILE INFO DIALOG BOX

① Click File.

② Click File Info.

O The File Info dialog box appears.

③ Type the information for your image.

④ Click here and select a copyright status.

O A copyright symbol will appear in the image window title bar.

⑤ Type a copyright notice.

O You can type a Web address that you want to associate with the image.

⑥ Click OK.

O Photoshop stores this information with your image when you save it.

#78

DIFFICULTY LEVEL

Did You Know? ※

In the File Browser, after you enter information in the editable fields of the Metadata tab and apply it, you cannot edit that information again in the File Browser. However, you can access and edit the information through the File Info command, which is under the File menu. If you delete the file information in the File Info dialog box, the fields become editable again in the File Browser.

Did You Know? ※

You can view information included in photos taken with most digital cameras by selecting the Camera Data 1 tab in the File Info dialog box. This information includes the make and model of the camera as well as the date and time the photo was shot. You can find additional technical details about the photo in the EXIF section in the Advanced tab of the same dialog box.

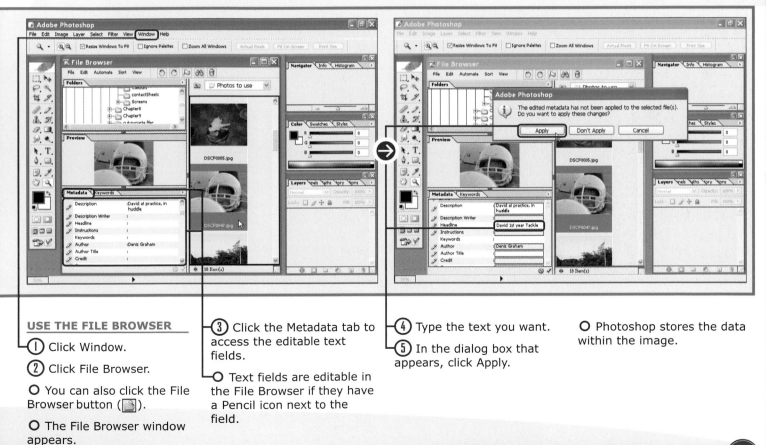

USE THE FILE BROWSER

① Click Window.

② Click File Browser.

O You can also click the File Browser button ([image]).

O The File Browser window appears.

③ Click the Metadata tab to access the editable text fields.

O Text fields are editable in the File Browser if they have a Pencil icon next to the field.

④ Type the text you want.

⑤ In the dialog box that appears, click Apply.

O Photoshop stores the data within the image.

Work with the
FILE BROWSER

You can easily view all your images on your system with the Photoshop File Browser feature. The File Browser is a preview window that you can use to view almost any type of information about your images.

The File Browser has a multi-frame dialog box that allows you to access a wealth of information about your files. In the Explorer section, you can browse through your computer's folders to locate your images. Click any folder, and thumbnails preview all the image files within that folder. The thumbnails

contain basic information about each file, such as name, creation date, last modified date, and copyright information. Click a thumbnail to select it, and the Preview window on the left side of the File Browser window displays a preview thumbnail of the selected image. Below this preview thumbnail is displayed the data concerning every aspect of the image, including some editable fields for data entry. For more information on entering data in these fields, see task #78.

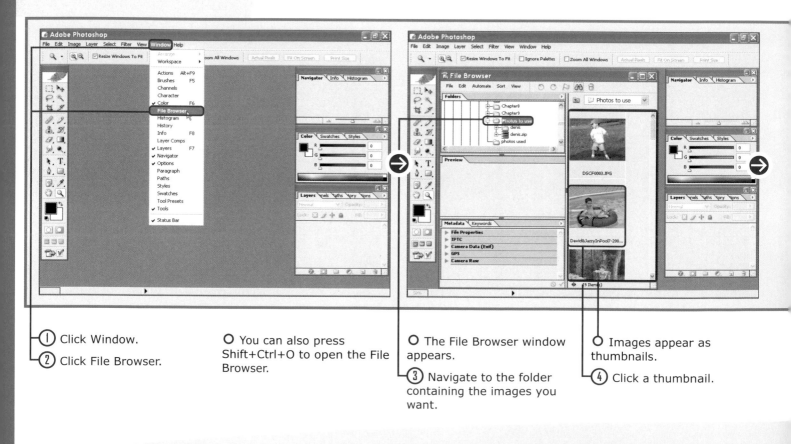

① Click Window.

② Click File Browser.

○ You can also press Shift+Ctrl+O to open the File Browser.

○ The File Browser window appears.

③ Navigate to the folder containing the images you want.

○ Images appear as thumbnails.

④ Click a thumbnail.

#79

DIFFICULTY LEVEL

Did You Know? ※

You can open files in Photoshop for easy editing. Click File and then Open. Navigate to your file folder, and if viewing details is set to thumbnails, double-click the thumbnail. Photoshop opens the image. You can also open multiple files quickly. Use Ctrl+click to select multiple files and then right-click them. In the menu that appears, click Open. All the images you selected open in Photoshop.

Did You Know? ※

When you right-click a thumbnail in the File Browser, you are presented with many different options. In addition to Open, you can also choose to select or deselect all the images, rename your files, create new folders, and even rotate images. A final series of options allows you to rank your images. These options can save a lot of time switching back and forth to your system browsers or opening the Image In Photoshop to make these changes. For more information on ranking your images, see task #80.

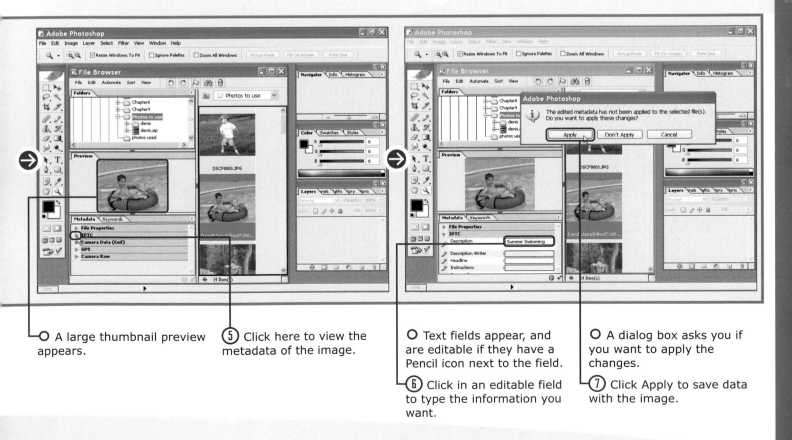

○ A large thumbnail preview appears.

⑤ Click here to view the metadata of the image.

○ Text fields appear, and are editable if they have a Pencil icon next to the field.

⑥ Click in an editable field to type the information you want.

○ A dialog box asks you if you want to apply the changes.

⑦ Click Apply to save data with the image.

Rank files with the
FILE BROWSER

You can organize and easily locate your image files by ranking them with the File Browser. Over time you may accumulate a large number of images, and even organizing files by separate folders can leave you with a large number of images in the same folder. You can spend a lot of time browsing through the images to find your favorite or most useful images. Ranking the images gives you another tool to organize your images for faster retrieval and classification of the images into groups.

When you view your thumbnails in the File Browser, you can assign a rank, or classification code, that tags the image for future reference. You can sort your images in the File Browser according to rank, allowing you to group similar pictures together, or to give your images a grade. This speeds up search time because sorting by rank places all your groups together, with the result that you do not have to browse through files unnecessarily. You can only view ranking in the thumbnails when you select Large Thumbnail in the View menu.

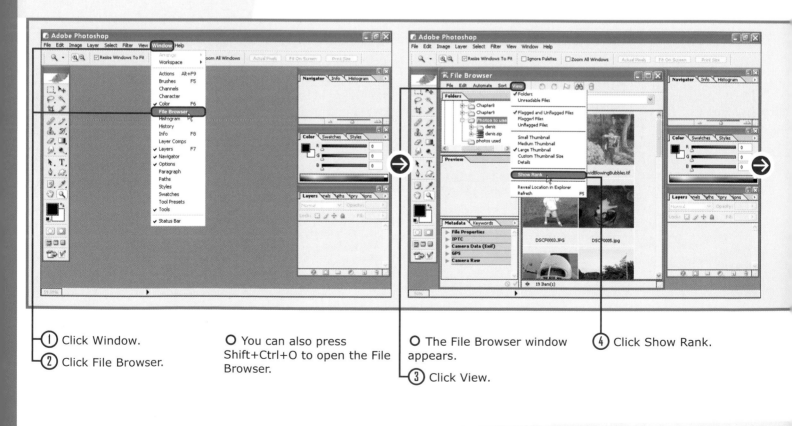

① Click Window.

② Click File Browser.

○ You can also press Shift+Ctrl+O to open the File Browser.

○ The File Browser window appears.

③ Click View.

④ Click Show Rank.

Did You Know? ※

There are many useful options available
in the Menu bar across the top of the File
Browser. You can click Automate in the menu
to create folders, to create Web Photo Galleries or
PDF slideshows, and even to run a Batch file or Batch
Rename on all the photos in the current folder. There are
also buttons that allow you to quickly perform often-used
functions like image rotation; flag, which identifies specific
images; and search and delete.

#80

DIFFICULTY LEVEL

Customize It! ※

Press Ctrl+click to select multiple files, and then right-click any
selected file. Select Rank in the menu and apply the same rank to
every selected file.

Did You Know? ※

You can assign any alphanumeric rank you want, with a limit of 15 characters.
Typically, A through E is used for ranking, but you can select other letters,
numbers, words, or phrases, based on personal preference and the
character limit.

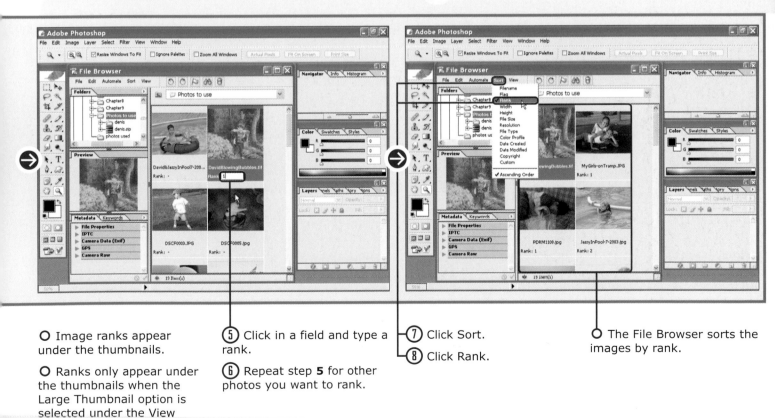

O Image ranks appear
under the thumbnails.

O Ranks only appear under
the thumbnails when the
Large Thumbnail option is
selected under the View
menu, as indicated by the
check mark.

⑤ Click in a field and type a
rank.

⑥ Repeat step **5** for other
photos you want to rank.

⑦ Click Sort.

⑧ Click Rank.

O The File Browser sorts the
images by rank.

CHAPTER 9

Speeding Up Your Work

You can obtain stunning results with Photoshop, but these results come with a price. This is because Photoshop uses many resources. Photoshop is processor- and RAM-intensive, and Photoshop files often take up a lot of hard drive space. If your system does not have enough memory or hard drive space, then it can run slowly. Photoshop users are constantly looking for tools and ways to make the application work faster and better. If you are a regular Photoshop user, then the tips and tricks in this chapter can help you speed up your workflow, improve the performance of your system, and optimize your results.

Over time, your system and application software can become sluggish and cumbersome as a result of normal use. For example, unused data on a clipboard and fragmented hard drives can cause a computer to run much more slowly because of the limited resources and jumbled storage space that Photoshop has available to use.

If you are not careful, you can also end up with cluttered screens and disorganized files, which can slow you down. This makes you slower and less productive because of the additional time you need to navigate around the program and image files.

You can use the tasks in this chapter to ensure that your work moves faster and your computer functions more smoothly. Even simple improvements like organizing your files can help speed up the creative process. The whole point is to customize your computer and Photoshop setup, to maximize your workflow.

TOP 100

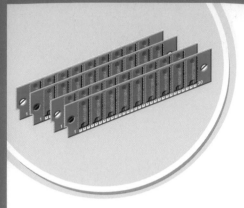

MAXIMIZE
your workspace

Even if you are using a large, flat-screen monitor, you may still find yourself limited as to the amount of information or graphics you can have onscreen. Working in Photoshop often leaves users wanting more space in which to put their tool palettes and images. Because of this, Photoshop gives you a great deal of flexibility in how you place toolbars and palettes, making the most of the limited screen space.

You can maximize your Photoshop workspace in several ways. For example, Photoshop creates palettes that can display multiple tabs so that you can easily switch between the tabs while you are working. You can merge several of your favorite

palettes together under one title bar for quicker access. You can join any number of palettes like this, but it is best to avoid merging too many palettes, because the tab names become difficult to read clearly. You can also adjust the size of onscreen palettes. Photoshop has set minimums for width, but you can adjust the palette to any height.

Use the layout that makes you comfortable regularly. You can quickly become frustrated if you frequently switch your palette arrangements. Familiarity with a setup is the greatest factor in increasing your productivity.

MERGE PALETTES

① Position the mouse cursor over the tab of the palette you want to merge into another palette.

② Click and drag the tab next to a tab on the target palette, and release the mouse button.

○ Photoshop adds the new tab to the other tabs on the palette. You can merge as many tabs on a palette as you like, but keep palette legibility in mind.

#81

Customize It!

You can use several other simple tricks to help maximize your workspace. For example, turning off unused palettes can dramatically open up your work area. Press the Tab key, and Photoshop removes all palettes and toolbars from the screen; press the Tab key again to restore them. Pressing the Shift and Tab keys simultaneously removes all palettes but leaves the basic toolbar visible.

Apply It!

You can save your favorite workspaces for later use. Click Window, Workspace, and then click Save Workspace. The dialog box prompts you to name the workspace. Photoshop saves the current layout in the Workspace submenu. To return to this workspace, click the name of the workspace in the drop-down menu; the palettes automatically rearrange to the preset layout.

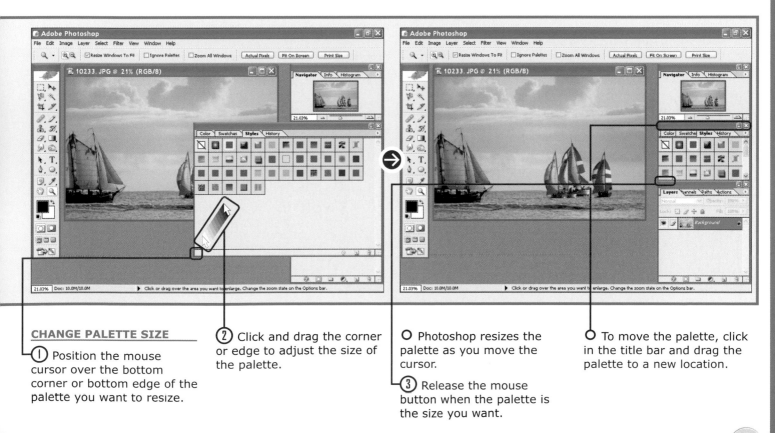

CHANGE PALETTE SIZE

① Position the mouse cursor over the bottom corner or bottom edge of the palette you want to resize.

② Click and drag the corner or edge to adjust the size of the palette.

○ Photoshop resizes the palette as you move the cursor.

③ Release the mouse button when the palette is the size you want.

○ To move the palette, click in the title bar and drag the palette to a new location.

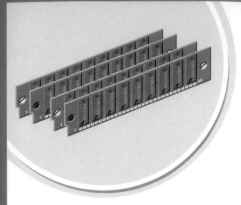

ASSIGN MORE MEMORY
for better performance

You can improve the speed and performance of Photoshop by assigning a greater percentage of RAM for use by the application. Although you can also improve performance by increasing the number of cache levels, increasing the percentage of RAM memory is perhaps the single most important performance enhancer for Photoshop.

You can specify a percentage of your available system RAM for use within Photoshop. By default, your system assigns 50 percent of the available RAM to Photoshop. You should not increase the percentage of available RAM above 80 percent. If

you change this setting, it takes effect the next time you start Photoshop.

If you find that Photoshop is running slowly, but you have assigned it plenty of memory, it could be that Photoshop assigned the RAM to other areas, like History States and the Clipboard. Photoshop allows you to free up that RAM for other uses. You can purge your History States, Clipboard, and cache memory to immediately reassign your computer memory. Be careful when doing this, because purging is irreversible, and any information that you purge is lost.

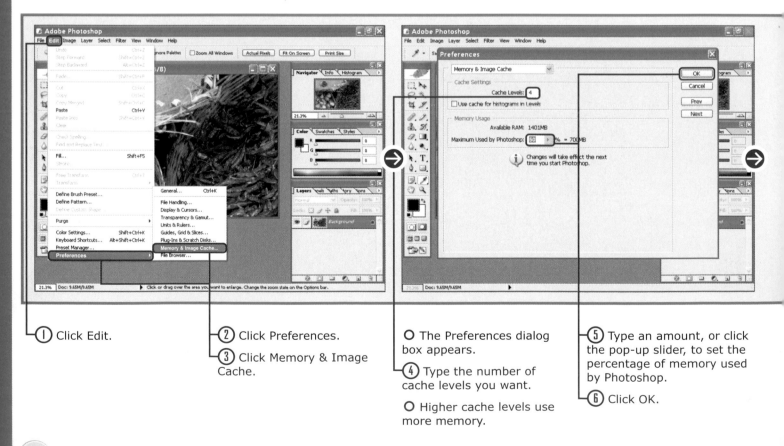

① Click Edit.

② Click Preferences.

③ Click Memory & Image Cache.

○ The Preferences dialog box appears.

④ Type the number of cache levels you want.

○ Higher cache levels use more memory.

⑤ Type an amount, or click the pop-up slider, to set the percentage of memory used by Photoshop.

⑥ Click OK.

DIFFICULTY LEVEL

Did You Know?

Realistically, you should
have no less than 128MB of
RAM available on your computer
for Photoshop to run. If you are running
with too little RAM, have additional RAM
installed. 256MB or more is recommended.
Some computers allow you to install up to 2GB
to 4GB of RAM.

Did You Know?

Every program you run, including your
operating system, uses RAM. If your computer
has limited RAM, running other programs with
Photoshop may reduce your memory to low
amounts and cause your software to run very slowly
or, more rarely, lock up. If you have limited RAM, be
sure to run only Photoshop whenever possible to
speed up performance.

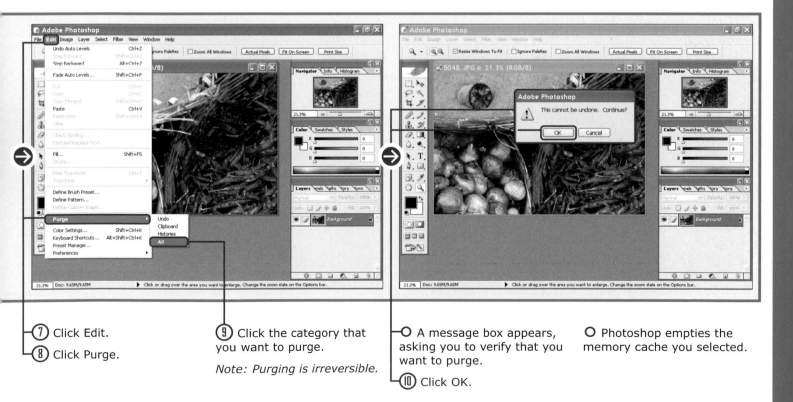

⑦ Click Edit.

⑧ Click Purge.

⑨ Click the category that
you want to purge.

Note: Purging is irreversible.

○ A message box appears,
asking you to verify that you
want to purge.

⑩ Click OK.

○ Photoshop empties the
memory cache you selected.

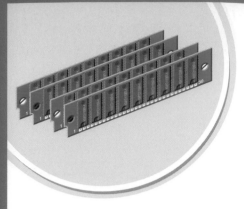

Improve performance with
SCRATCH DISKS

Scratch disks are hard drives or assigned storage that Photoshop uses as temporary memory when you are using all available RAM. Photoshop treats the scratch disks as a memory cache, allowing Photoshop to utilize much more space for working with large files or complex filters, and speeding up performance. A scratch disk is almost as important for smooth performance as RAM memory.

You can easily set up a scratch disk in Photoshop. In Windows, the default scratch disk is set to the C drive when you install Photoshop. You can edit this setting and assign a different hard drive if you want. It is recommended that the scratch disk be on a different drive or drive partition than the program, so that when Photoshop is processing a filter on an image on one drive, it can use the second drive for other functions and so not interfere or have to wait for the other drive to stop processing.

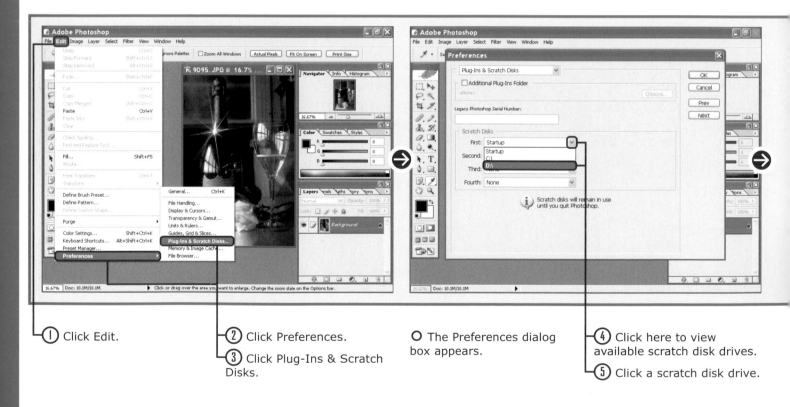

① Click Edit.

② Click Preferences.

③ Click Plug-Ins & Scratch Disks.

○ The Preferences dialog box appears.

④ Click here to view available scratch disk drives.

⑤ Click a scratch disk drive.

DIFFICULTY LEVEL

Did You Know?

Photoshop can use up to four different scratch disk drives. Should the first scratch disk become full or unusable, Photoshop uses the other assigned scratch disks.

Customize It!

You can have only one hard drive available on your computer system, and still use a separate scratch disk. To do this, you can partition your hard drive, a system process that involves splitting off a section of the hard drive and transforming it into a recognizable second drive that you can assign as a scratch disk.

Caution!

Unless a third-party partitioning software application is used, your hard drive must be reformatted to add a partition erasing all files and programs on your computer. Read your operating system instructions on partitioning before attempting to partition your drive, or contact a professional computer technician.

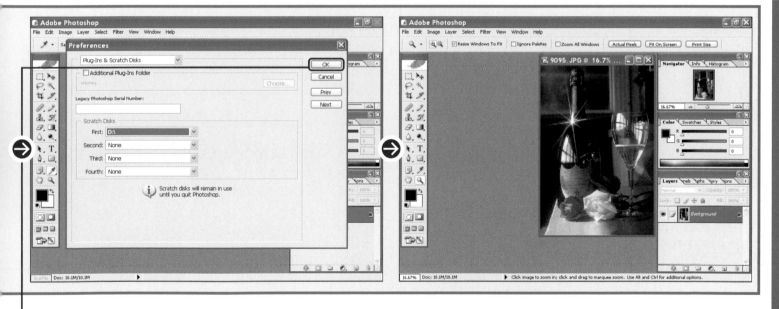

⑥ Click OK.

O Photoshop automatically reassigns the scratch disk.

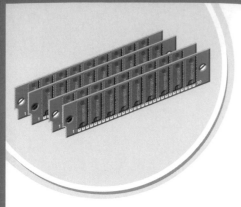

DOUBLE YOUR WORKSPACE
with multiple monitors

It seems you can never have enough workspace in Photoshop. However, if you shrink the viewable size of the image to fit onscreen, you lose detail; if you enlarge the image to see more detail, it spills outside the viewable area, and you cannot see the whole image. To resolve this problem, you can use multiple monitors to increase your available screen space.

Using multiple monitors essentially expands your computer desktop to a second monitor. When you move your cursor off the right edge of the left

monitor screen, the cursor appears on the left edge of the other monitor's screen. This means that you can move Photoshop tools around, allowing you to work more efficiently, and with a less cluttered screen.

The screens below demonstrate two common multiple-monitor arrangements: putting all of the palettes on the second monitor, or using the second monitor to work on another image. To use multiple monitors, consult your manual or Help files to get more information.

RELEGATE PALETTES TO A SECOND MONITOR

⭕ The monitor on the left displays a larger image when you select the Fit on Screen zoom option in the Options bar.

⭕ You can place favorite palettes on the right monitor without overlapping or crowding.

⭕ You can enlarge palettes to full size to show more options or choices.

Customize It!

When using dual monitors you may want to display your most commonly used palettes at the center of the dual-screen workspace, and place any open images on either side. You can also save your workspace layout by clicking Window and then clicking Workspaces. In the drop-down menu, select a favorite layout you have saved in the past.

Apply It!

If you work with more than one program at a time, dual monitors are almost essential. Use Photoshop full-screen on one monitor with the tool palettes on the second monitor. Place your second program on the second monitor, and any palettes or toolbars for that program on the first monitor. This makes it easier to distinguish between the two programs when you toggle between them, and also gives you maximum workspace for both.

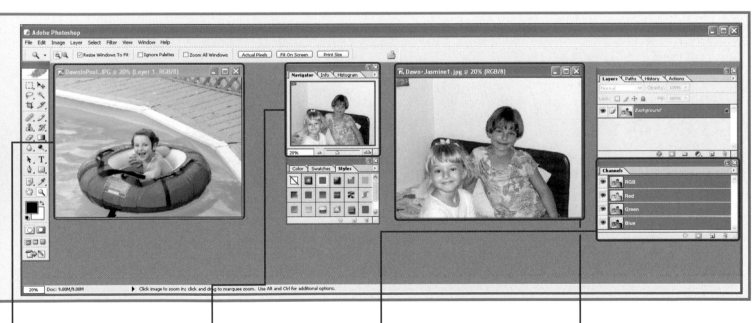

WORK WITH IMAGES ON A SECOND MONITOR

O The monitor on the left displays a larger image when you select the Fit on Screen zoom option in the Options bar.

O You can enlarge palettes to show more options or choices.

O A second monitor allows you to display additional palettes without covering up parts of the images.

O A second monitor allows you to work with multiple documents simultaneously without overlap.

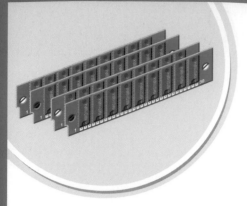

Manage your tool presets with the
PRESET MANAGER

When you select certain tools in Photoshop, they may offer you many options that affect how you can work with them. Many tools, such as gradients, brushes, and shapes, have dozens of options, and you can also import more options to these tools, or delete them. Photoshop makes it easy to track, edit, and manage these preset groups of tool options.

With the Preset Manager, you can easily organize your tool presets. The Preset Manager is located in the Edit menu. When you access the Preset Manager, a dialog box appears, with options for brushes, color

swatches, gradients, and patterns. You can use these option menus to change the settings for each tool as well as import more tools. For example, you can change the current brush set to a different group of brushes.

The Preset Manager can help you quickly and easily revert to different presets, an important feature to users with multiple projects that require different settings for tools such as brush sets, gradient sets, and colors.

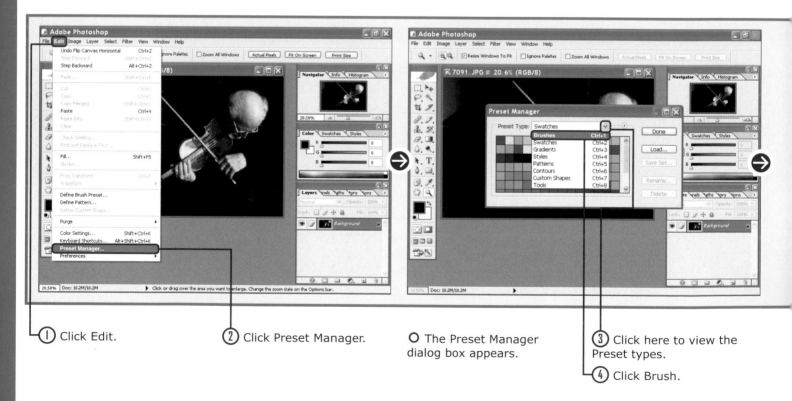

① Click Edit.

② Click Preset Manager.

O The Preset Manager dialog box appears.

③ Click here to view the Preset types.

④ Click Brush.

Customize It!

You can make many changes, such as deleting, renaming, saving, and loading, to your Preset sets when using the Preset Manager. Design a set of your favorite brushes by deleting existing brushes and defining new ones. You can save this new set as a custom brush file. Now you can load your favorite brush set whenever you want. Keep in mind that you should not save over the default sets because this deletes the original set.

Did You Know?

You can import brush sets from outside of Photoshop. Simply download an ABR format brushes file from a network or the Internet, and save it to the Adobe\Photoshop CS\Presets\Brushes folder. Load the set in the Preset Manager from the drop-down menus to use it.

#85

DIFFICULTY LEVEL

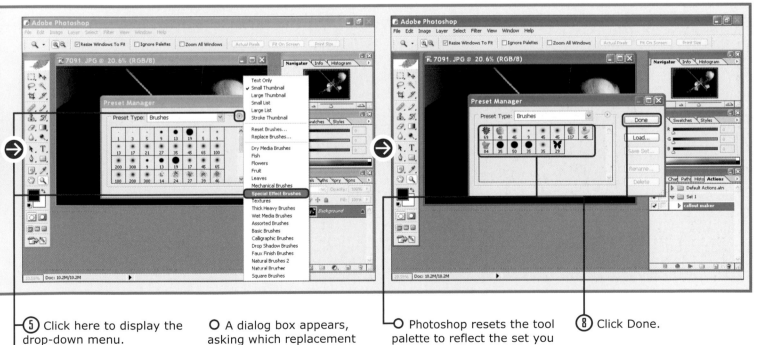

⑤ Click here to display the drop-down menu.

⑥ Select a new brush set.

○ A dialog box appears, asking which replacement option you want.

⑦ Select the option you want.

○ Photoshop resets the tool palette to reflect the set you selected.

⑧ Click Done.

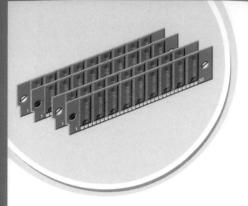

Create custom
KEYBOARD
SHORTCUTS

You can save time by learning and using the Photoshop keyboard shortcuts. Each time you use a keyboard shortcut, you save valuable seconds by not having to use drop-down navigational menus, or to select tools and options all over the screen with the mouse. Virtually every tool in the main toolbar has a keyboard shortcut, as do many of the drop-down menu items. Photoshop indicates each keyboard shortcut with a letter in parentheses after the tool or menu name. Become familiar with them, and they will become an indispensable part of your workflow.

Sometimes, however, there are tools and menu items that do not have a shortcut. In these cases you can create your own keyboard shortcuts, based on available, unassigned keys. Simply select the tool option to which you want to assign the shortcut. To assign the shortcut, click Edit, and then click Keyboard Shortcuts.

You can assign keyboard shortcuts to menu items, tools, and palette commands, including the ones you can access in the File Browser. This versatility, combined with the time that it saves you, makes keyboard shortcuts an outstanding new addition to Photoshop.

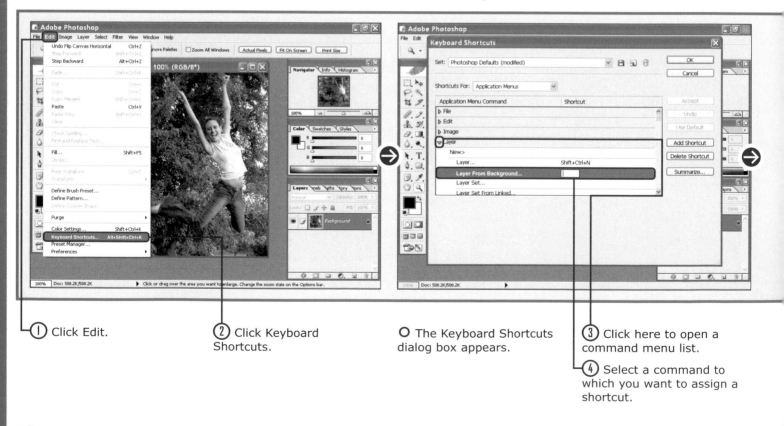

① Click Edit.

② Click Keyboard Shortcuts.

O The Keyboard Shortcuts dialog box appears.

③ Click here to open a command menu list.

④ Select a command to which you want to assign a shortcut.

86

DIFFICULTY LEVEL

Did You Know?

You can create your own personal set of keyboard shortcuts. In the Keyboard Shortcuts dialog box, click the Set ▾. Click the Save icon (🖫) to open the Save dialog box, and save the personalized Keyboard shortcut file in the location you want.

Customize It!

You can print out your lists of keyboard shortcuts. In the Keyboard Shortcuts dialog box, click the Summarize button to export a printable HTML page of all the shortcuts on the active shortcut set. Be sure to use a descriptive filename, especially if you create multiple custom sets.

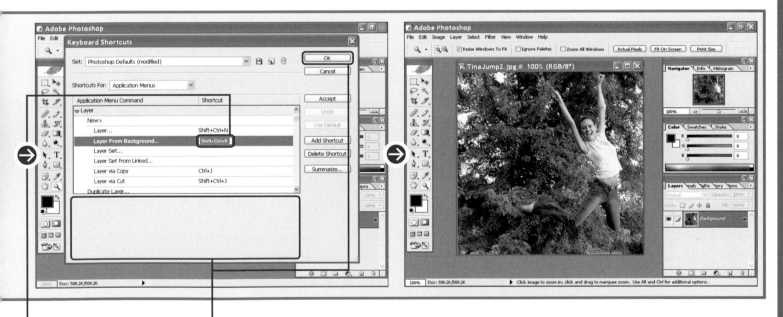

⑤ Enter a key combination for the command shortcut by simultaneously pressing the desired keys.

○ Photoshop uses this space to notify you if the shortcut is already in use or restricted from use.

⑥ Click OK.

○ Photoshop assigns the shortcut.

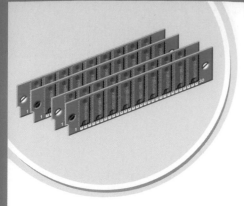

Record timesaving
ACTIONS

If you use the same group of steps repeatedly when working with different images or shapes, then you can save time by using Photoshop Actions to record those steps and apply them to different images with a single mouse click. Actions are a record of each individual step you make during the recording process. Photoshop stores the information of each filter, style, and movement inside the action for playback later on. After you record the action, you can play this action in another image, and Photoshop applies the exact same steps that you recorded earlier.

You can turn individual steps on and off in actions, as well as edit or adjust the steps. You can duplicate an action, and create variations of the same action by adjusting the settings. Almost everything you do in Photoshop can be recorded, including saving, opening, and even switching between images. This makes Actions one of Photoshop's most powerful features. In the Action palette drop-down menu, you can save and load actions. This gives you the ability to import and share action files with other users.

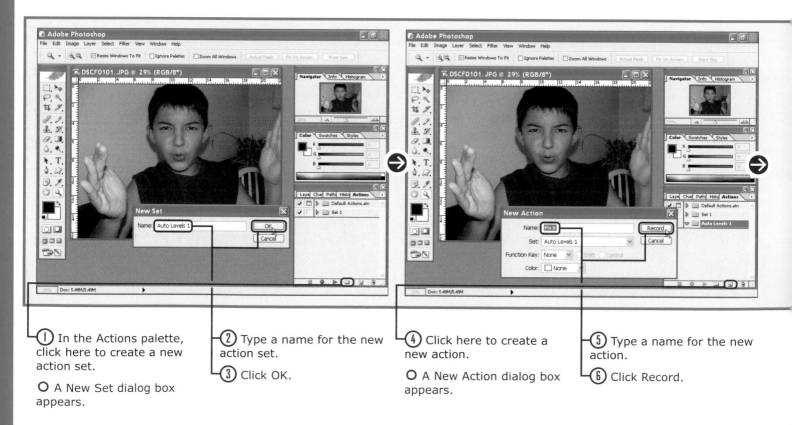

① In the Actions palette, click here to create a new action set.

O A New Set dialog box appears.

② Type a name for the new action set.

③ Click OK.

④ Click here to create a new action.

O A New Action dialog box appears.

⑤ Type a name for the new action.

⑥ Click Record.

Check It Out! ☀

There are dozens of Web sites that offer free actions for you to import into Photoshop. For example, http://share.studio.adobe.com has over 4,400 actions available for download. Sites like www.actionfx.com, www.webteknique.com, and www.myjanee.com also have many resources for actions.

DIFFICULTY LEVEL

Did You Know? ☀

You can hold down the Shift and Alt keys when you click Save Actions in the Actions palette menu to save the file as a text file. You can then open the action as a text document and see each step, along with the step settings, used in the action. You can even print it out for reference.

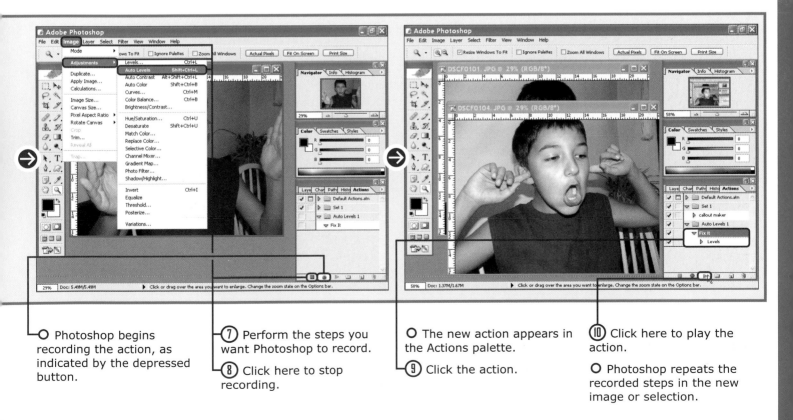

O Photoshop begins recording the action, as indicated by the depressed button.

⑦ Perform the steps you want Photoshop to record.

⑧ Click here to stop recording.

O The new action appears in the Actions palette.

⑨ Click the action.

⑩ Click here to play the action.

O Photoshop repeats the recorded steps in the new image or selection.

BATCH PROCESS
your images to save time

You may have projects that require you to perform repetitive steps to dozens, maybe even hundreds, of images. To edit the images individually can be extremely time consuming. When you have a number of images that require the same editing to be applied to each one, you can use batch processing with Photoshop actions to automate the application of the editing to all the images, and save a great deal of time.

Batch processing applies a specific action to all the files within a file folder that you specify. When

Photoshop applies the action, it does so to each recognized image format file within the specified folder. You can even tell Photoshop to apply the actions to subfolders as well. For more information on actions, see task #87.

You can specify where you want Photoshop to save the processed images. Photoshop also offers a wide selection of renaming options. For example, this is an excellent way to correct the naming method used by digital cameras by making the filenames more descriptive and useful.

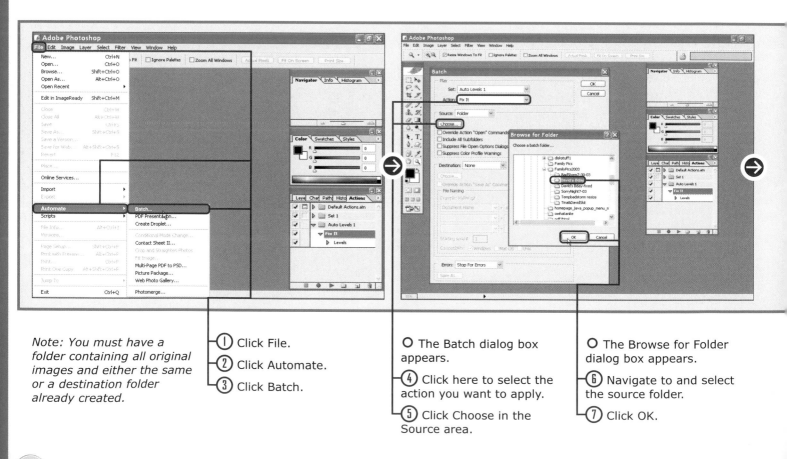

Note: You must have a folder containing all original images and either the same or a destination folder already created.

① Click File.

② Click Automate.

③ Click Batch.

○ The Batch dialog box appears.

④ Click here to select the action you want to apply.

⑤ Click Choose in the Source area.

○ The Browse for Folder dialog box appears.

⑥ Navigate to and select the source folder.

⑦ Click OK.

Caution! ☀

The batch processing feature
applies the specified action to
every file within the source folder. To
avoid wasted time and duplicated files,
you should remove files from the folder that
you do not want Photoshop to process.

Customize It! ☀

Some Actions require user input. You can apply
batch processing using these actions, but Photoshop
automatically uses your original input from the creation
of the action. This can result in incorrect image results.
Structure your actions to avoid this, where possible.

Apply It! ☀

When renaming files, be as descriptive as possible. Poorly chosen
filenames make it difficult to differentiate between files.

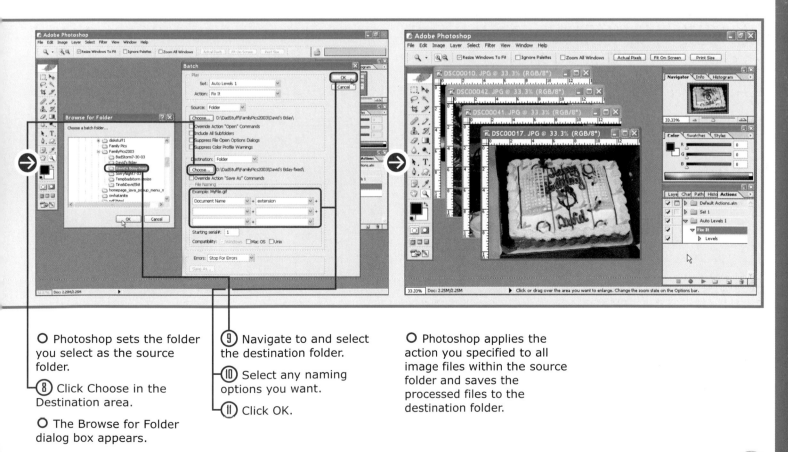

○ Photoshop sets the folder
you select as the source
folder.

⑧ Click Choose in the
Destination area.

○ The Browse for Folder
dialog box appears.

⑨ Navigate to and select
the destination folder.

⑩ Select any naming
options you want.

⑪ Click OK.

○ Photoshop applies the
action you specified to all
image files within the source
folder and saves the
processed files to the
destination folder.

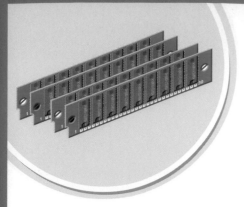

SCAN MULTIPLE PHOTOS
with the Crop and Straighten command

You can import images directly into Photoshop using your scanner. Most scanners can scan multiple photos, which Photoshop imports as a single image. The task of placing the individual photos into their own documents can be time consuming and tedious. Photoshop has a new automation tool called Crop and Straighten Photos that can perform this task for you.

With the scanned image file open, you can click File, then Automate, and then Crop and Straighten

Photos. Photoshop automatically searches the image for the right-angled corners of individual photos, selects a photo, rotates, copies, and pastes it into a new document, and then returns to the original scan for the next photo.

For bulk-scanning projects, the new Crop and Straighten Photos command is an invaluable feature. For example, you can use it to scan images for projects such as home photo albums or a yearbook class page.

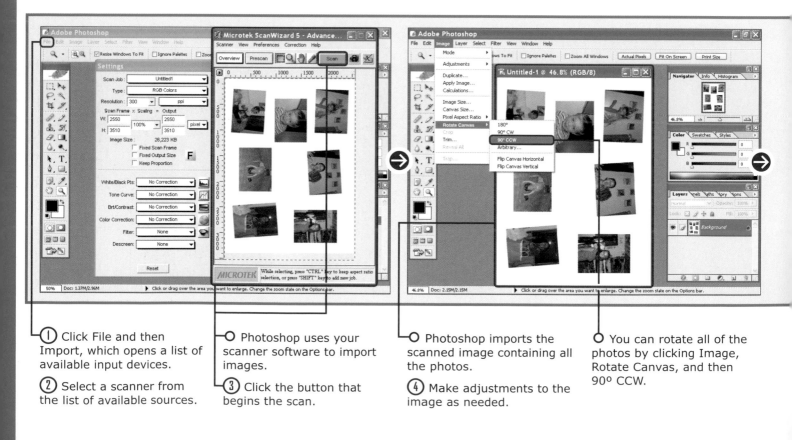

① Click File and then Import, which opens a list of available input devices.

② Select a scanner from the list of available sources.

○ Photoshop uses your scanner software to import images.

③ Click the button that begins the scan.

○ Photoshop imports the scanned image containing all the photos.

④ Make adjustments to the image as needed.

○ You can rotate all of the photos by clicking Image, Rotate Canvas, and then 90° CCW.

Customize It! ☀

89

DIFFICULTY LEVEL

You can make the Photoshop Crop and Straighten feature work more efficiently by properly arranging your images on the scanner. Placing images too close together can cause Photoshop to save the images to the same file, because it may not recognize that the images are separate. Space your photos apart, especially if they do not have clearly defined edges. You should also place the photos on the scanner as straight as possible. The Photoshop algorithm for performing this command does not always rotate an image to align with a perfectly horizontal or vertical angle. If the image is still slightly off, you can rotate it in the new document by clicking Image, Rotate Canvas, and then Arbitrary.

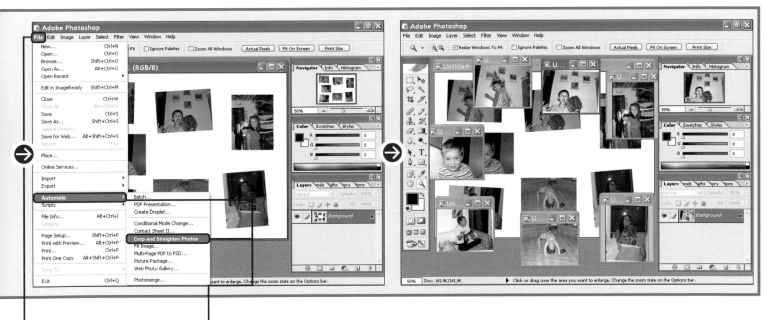

⑤ Click File.

⑥ Click Automate.

⑦ Click Crop and Straighten Photos.

○ Photoshop crops, straightens, and extracts your individual images into separate documents.

○ During this process, Photoshop also trims excess white space from the extracted image.

THIRD-PARTY PLUG-INS

Photoshop offers dozens of filters and effects that create dramatic results in your images. However, you can also use other software packages with Photoshop, such as *third-party plug-ins.* Third-party plug-ins can expand on existing effects or create new ones. There are quite a few plug-ins available, and if you use a lot of them, they can quickly become disorganized.

You should separate the plug-ins from the program to ensure good organization. By default, Photoshop stores plug-ins in the Adobe\Photoshop CS\Plug-Ins folder. To keep better track of your plug-ins, you may want to store them outside of Photoshop. You can designate a second plug-ins folder that Photoshop loads during startup, so that you can expand your plug-ins outside of Photoshop and remain organized at the same time. This is very helpful when you need to back up your plug-ins and troubleshoot with conflicting plug-ins. If you ever need to reload Photoshop, you then only need to redefine the second plug-ins folder, and not worry about installing all your plug-ins again.

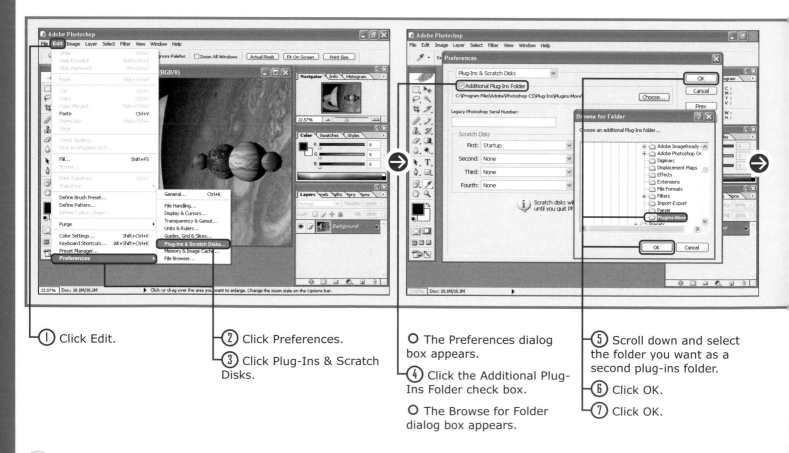

① Click Edit.

② Click Preferences.

③ Click Plug-Ins & Scratch Disks.

○ The Preferences dialog box appears.

④ Click the Additional Plug-Ins Folder check box.

○ The Browse for Folder dialog box appears.

⑤ Scroll down and select the folder you want as a second plug-ins folder.

⑥ Click OK.

⑦ Click OK.

#90

Did You Know? ※

Keeping your plug-ins external
from Photoshop ensures the safety
of the plug-ins. Otherwise, if you need
to reinstall Photoshop, then all default
folders are reset, and you must reinstall the
plug-ins.

Did You Know? ※

After installing plug-ins, you must restart Photoshop to
access them. When Photoshop loads a plug-in, it appears
in the Filters menu; if the menu becomes too full, Photoshop
places additional plug-ins in the Filters, Other submenu.

Did You Know? ※

The Choose button in the Plug-Ins dialog box only becomes active
after you have assigned a folder as the additional Plug-Ins folder. This
allows you to edit or change your selection. The first time you assign a
new folder, the Browse for Folder dialog box opens automatically when
you select the check box (☐ changes to ☑) for the Additional Plug-Ins
Folder in the Preferences dialog box.

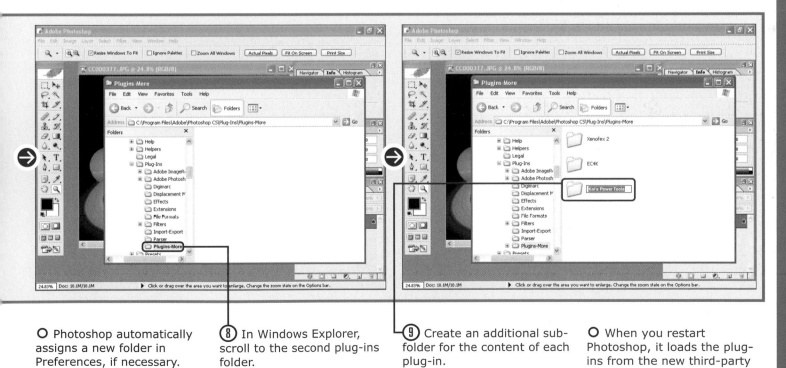

O Photoshop automatically
assigns a new folder in
Preferences, if necessary.

⑧ In Windows Explorer,
scroll to the second plug-ins
folder.

⑨ Create an additional sub-
folder for the content of each
plug-in.

O When you restart
Photoshop, it loads the plug-
ins from the new third-party
plug-ins folder.

CHAPTER 10

Designing with ImageReady Tools

You can create fantastic Web pages and animations with ImageReady CS. ImageReady CS is the sister program to Photoshop CS, and it is included on the Photoshop installation disk. Its primary function is Web-based graphics and design. Where Photoshop can take your images and create stunning graphics, ImageReady can take those graphics and create dynamic, interactive Web pages, complete with mouse rollover effects, hyperlinks, and animated graphics.

ImageReady contains many of the same tools, features and filters as Photoshop, as well as specialty tools, features, and palettes not available in Photoshop. This chapter introduces you to the main features in ImageReady, including slicing images for Web page layout design, creating mouse rollover effects for buttons, assigning interactive image maps to graphics, and exporting fully functional Web pages. You can even export your animations as a Macromedia Flash .swf format file, a new feature for ImageReady.

ImageReady is a standalone program, but the integration between Photoshop and ImageReady blurs that dividing line. You can work on an open image in Photoshop, and switch over to ImageReady from Photoshop by choosing File and then Jump To. Your image transfers over to ImageReady, ready to work on. You can jump back and forth if you want to make further changes in either program.

TOP 100

TAKE A SLICE
of your images

Slices are one of the most versatile and useful features in ImageReady. You can use the Slice tool to make your large images more manageable and to create dynamic effects for the Web. Slices are rectangular-shaped sections of your image. You can create slices when you want to assign different functions to parts of your image. Mouse rollovers, hyperlinks, and animations can all be defined by using slices. You can now even use slices to create tables within your image.

The type of content they contain categorizes slices. You can select from several types of slices, including Image, No-Image, Table, and Auto Slices. Image slices can contain images you want to use for rollovers, animations, or simply to represent the image content. No-Image slices are essentially empty, and ImageReady exports them as table cells in your Web page that you can use for text or other content. Table slices allow you to make sub-slices, or slices within slices, to create nested tables.

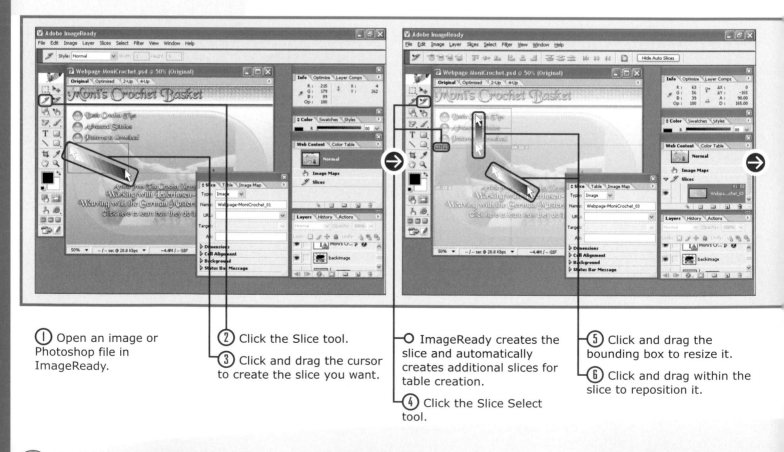

① Open an image or Photoshop file in ImageReady.

② Click the Slice tool.

③ Click and drag the cursor to create the slice you want.

○ ImageReady creates the slice and automatically creates additional slices for table creation.

④ Click the Slice Select tool.

⑤ Click and drag the bounding box to resize it.

⑥ Click and drag within the slice to reposition it.

Caution! ※

Changing slices can affect your rollovers and hyperlinks. If you move a new slice over another slice that contains a rollover state or link, then the new slice area will not trigger the rollover or link, because ImageReady does not assign those effects to the new slice. If you have a lot of object movement or slice adjustments to make, then be sure to clear all slices, and reassign all effects. This may create extra work now, but it can help to avoid embarrassing errors later.

Did You Know? ※

The Alt text field in the Slice palette contains the text that appears if the image is not available. You can also click the Status Bar Message ▷ in the Slice palette, and enter text that you want to appear in the status bar of the Web browser when the mouse cursor moves over the active slice. You can assign a status bar message without having an active link.

☆91

DIFFICULTY LEVEL

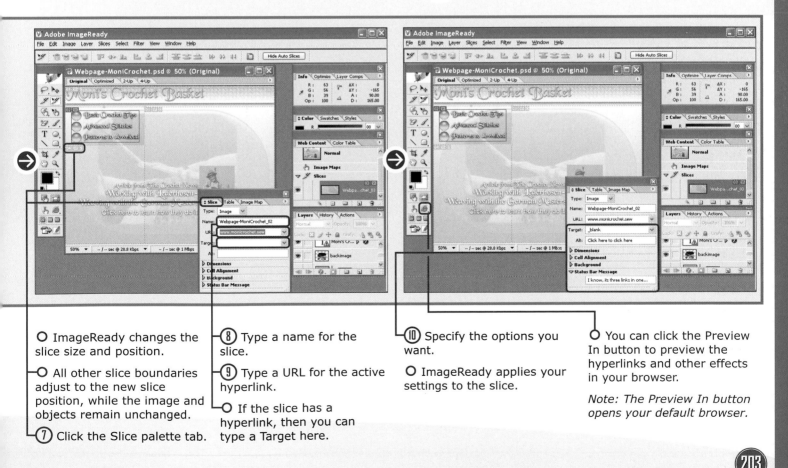

O ImageReady changes the slice size and position.

-O All other slice boundaries adjust to the new slice position, while the image and objects remain unchanged.

⑦ Click the Slice palette tab.

⑧ Type a name for the slice.

⑨ Type a URL for the active hyperlink.

-O If the slice has a hyperlink, then you can type a Target here.

⑩ Specify the options you want.

O ImageReady applies your settings to the slice.

O You can click the Preview In button to preview the hyperlinks and other effects in your browser.

Note: The Preview In button opens your default browser.

Create a
SLICE SET

You can group together a Slice layout and store it in a slice set. Slice sets remember the size, placement, and features of the slices you create in an image. ImageReady even remembers rollover and hyperlink data in the slice data. When you combine this new feature with the new Layer Comp feature, which remembers layer order and layouts, you can save multiple versions of a Web page in the same image. For more information about layer comps, see task #10.

You can easily create new slice sets by clicking the Slice menu, and selecting New Slice Set. A new folder appears in the Web Content palette. You can name this new slice set folder by double-clicking the current name. Click and drag any slice thumbnail in the Web Content folder and drop it into the slice set folder. ImageReady places the slice into the slice set. If you cannot see the slice after you drop it, then click the triangle next to the slice set folder; all slices contained in that folder appear. Click the triangle again, and the folder closes, hiding the contained slices.

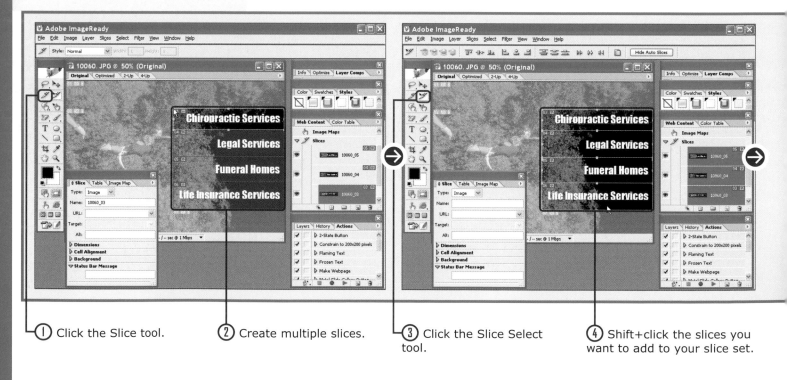

① Click the Slice tool.

② Create multiple slices.

③ Click the Slice Select tool.

④ Shift+click the slices you want to add to your slice set.

DIFFICULTY LEVEL

Caution! ❊

When you save your slice
configurations, you save your
rollover states, hyperlinks, and other
slice effects. Be sure when you export
to HTML that you do not show slices from
another set. You can lose the rollovers,
hyperlinks, and image map information if the
slices from another set overlap your effects. Test
each image and slice set in your browser prior to
exporting the HTML for your page.

Customize It! ❊

Be descriptive in your slice set names. It is easy
to become confused as to their purpose if your
set names are vague. If you are using slice sets
in conjunction with layer comps, then you can give
each slice set a similar name to, or refer to, the layer
comp in the slice set name to clarify its purpose.

⑤ Click the New Slice Set
button to create a new slice
set.

○ ImageReady saves the
slices you selected into a
new slice set.

○ You can double-click the
slice set name to rename it.

USE SHAPE STYLES
in ImageReady

When you create your shapes, you can automatically assign layer styles to them. Shape styles appear in the Options bar when you click any of the custom shape tools. To use them, you can click any of the shape tools, and click the Style drop-down menu. When you select a style from the list, and draw your shape, ImageReady automatically applies the layer style to that shape. This can save you time by helping you create repetitive shapes with similar layer styles.

After you apply the style, it is editable just like any other layer style. Simply double-click the Layer Style icon (🔲) in the Layers palette, and the Styles palette appears. You can now make manual adjustments to any currently applied layer.

You can use any available style in the Styles palette. If you have custom style sets available, then you can load them into the Styles palette to make them available as well.

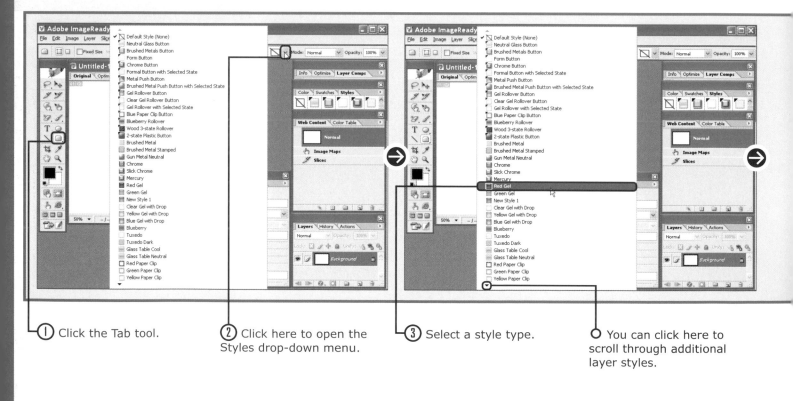

① Click the Tab tool.

② Click here to open the Styles drop-down menu.

③ Select a style type.

○ You can click here to scroll through additional layer styles.

#93

Did You Know? ※

The Styles list contains samples that have a small black triangle in the top-left corner of the style thumbnail, the Gel Rollover Button (▦), for example. This is a Rollover style, and when you apply this style to your shape, ImageReady automatically creates a rollover state layer for that shape, complete with a different style applied to it for the rollover effect. There are 21 preset rollover styles in the ImageReady Web Rollover style set from which you can choose. For more information about rollovers and rollover styles, see task #94.

Customize It! ※

Because shapes are vector-based, you can alter the shape and size of the shape layer, and it always retains its crisp edges and smooth look. When you make alterations to the shape, any layer styles automatically apply to the new shape. If the shape is part of a layer-based slice, then it alters the slice dimensions as well, including layer-based rollover states.

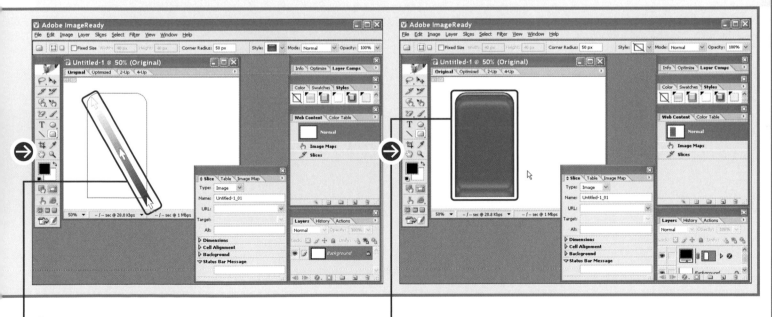

④ Click and drag to create a shape.

○ ImageReady creates a shape with the selected styles automatically applied.

Create a
ROLLOVER

Dynamic rollover buttons are a very popular and effective Web page navigation feature, and you can easily create them using the different tools in ImageReady.

You can create a rollover style based on any slice or image map areas. You can assign the rollover to any object in an image except for backgrounds. Simply create the rollover state, select it in the Web Content palette, and change the image for the new state. You can apply layer styles, layer locations, changes in format, or even hide or show layers and objects.

ImageReady offers several types of rollover states, including Over, Down, and Click. Over refers to when the cursor is moved over the rollover area without clicking the mouse button; Down refers to holding the mouse button down in the rollover area; and Click refers to after the mouse button is clicked and released, and the cursor remains over the rollover area. There are other states available that are equally specific and customizable. For more information on these other states, see the ImageReady Help files.

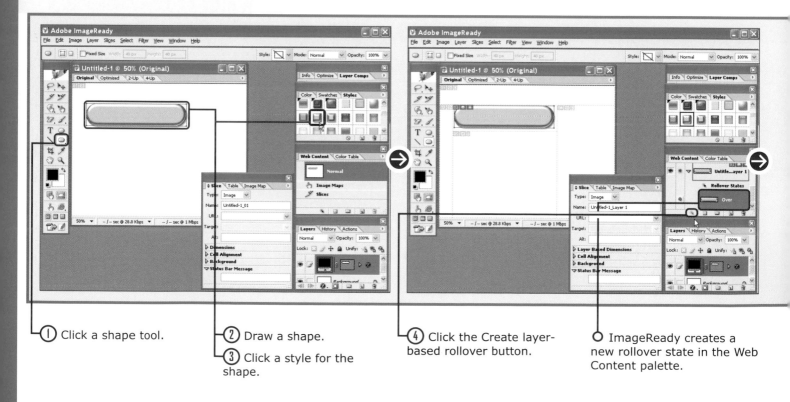

① Click a shape tool.

② Draw a shape.

③ Click a style for the shape.

④ Click the Create layer-based rollover button.

○ ImageReady creates a new rollover state in the Web Content palette.

Caution! ☼

Any time you make a change to a layout, be sure that you do not have a rollover state layer selected. When you select a rollover state layer, any changes you make to the image take effect when the rollover occurs. You can do this intentionally to create a remote rollover event, another popular navigational method. To be sure that your rollover states are working as you intend, preview them in your browser. To do this, you can click the Preview In button (⊡), located towards the bottom of the toolbox, or use the Preview In submenu of the File menu. Test all rollovers and styles prior to publishing online.

Did You Know? ☼

When you export your Web page, ImageReady automatically generates the HMTL and JavaScript coding necessary for all of your Image maps and rollover effects. This saves a lot of time and work for those who do not know HTML and JavaScript coding.

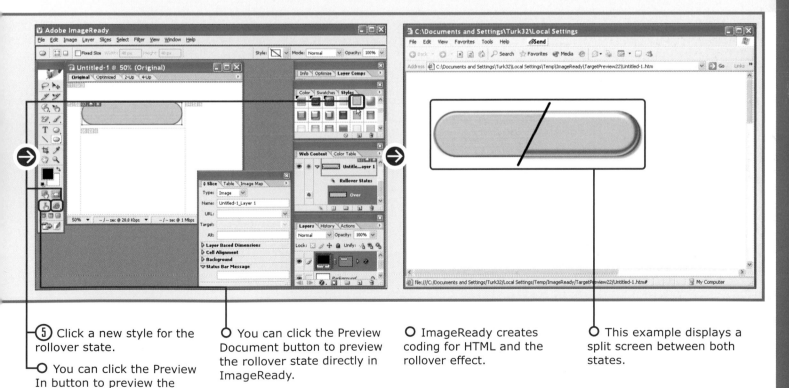

⑤ Click a new style for the rollover state.

○ You can click the Preview In button to preview the rollover state in the browser.

○ You can click the Preview Document button to preview the rollover state directly in ImageReady.

○ ImageReady creates coding for HTML and the rollover effect.

○ This example displays a split screen between both states.

Design a
ROLLOVER
WITH STYLE

You can create your own rollover styles to use on other objects. When you apply a rollover style to a shape or text, ImageReady automatically creates a Normal state and a Rollover state using two preset layer styles. To create a rollover style, design a layer-based rollover using any shape with a style applied to the Normal state, and a different layer style applied to the Rollover state. You can then save the rollover style inside the current style group in the Styles palette for use on other objects or future projects.

This feature is an excellent tool for rollover styles that are frequently used or repeated in a Web page. You can add new buttons or effects by creating the shape and applying the rollover style, and letting ImageReady create the rollover states automatically for you. This saves time compared to re-creating the styles from scratch, and ensures that all the objects have a uniform look.

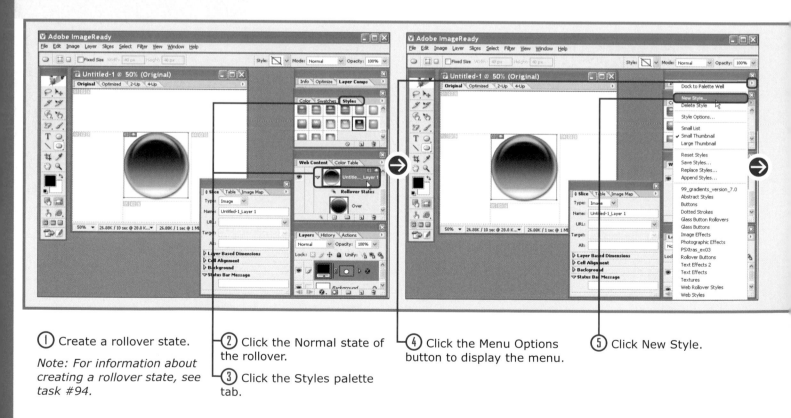

① Create a rollover state.

Note: For information about creating a rollover state, see task #94.

② Click the Normal state of the rollover.

③ Click the Styles palette tab.

④ Click the Menu Options button to display the menu.

⑤ Click New Style.

Did You Know? ※

You can save rollover styles for sharing and archiving. After you create your rollover style, click the Styles palette Menu Options button (⊙) and select Save Styles. ImageReady saves your new style set in the default styles folder located in Program Files\Adobe\Photoshop CS\Presets\Styles. Select Load Styles from the Style palette menu to load your new style. Your new rollover style will appear in the Style palette menu list after you restart Photoshop. If you save to a different file location than shown here, you will need to manually load the styles.

Did You Know? ※

You can change rollover styles as easily as regular styles. You can individually edit the states by clicking the state in the Web Content palette, and then double-clicking the Layer Styles icon (🖉) in the object layer in the Layers palette. The Layer Style dialog box appears, allowing you to make changes to that particular state. You can also click a different rollover style to redefine all of the rollover states for that object at the same time.

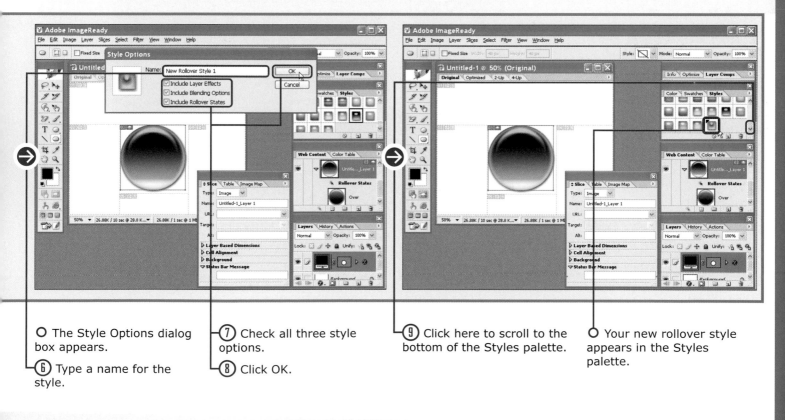

○ The Style Options dialog box appears.

⑥ Type a name for the style.

⑦ Check all three style options.

⑧ Click OK.

⑨ Click here to scroll to the bottom of the Styles palette.

○ Your new rollover style appears in the Styles palette.

ANIMATE A GIF
in ImageReady

You can design an animated GIF for your Web pages in ImageReady. Animated GIFs are a sequence of individual frames that rotate in a specific order on the computer screen. Each frame is slightly different than its neighbors in the sequence, so when these frames are shown in quick succession, they give the illusion of animated movement.

With ImageReady, you can create the individual frames, place them in any order that you want, and save them in the GIF format to show as animated images on a Web page. ImageReady has a very

easy-to-use Animation palette where you can choose different options for your animation. You can create animation stages between two different frames, a technique known as tweening.

Animations frames are self-contained in a single layer, so you do not see different layers for each frame. You can preview an animation by clicking the Play icon at the bottom of the Animation palette. The Animation palette also contains icons for adding frames, tweening, and setting the looping options for the animation.

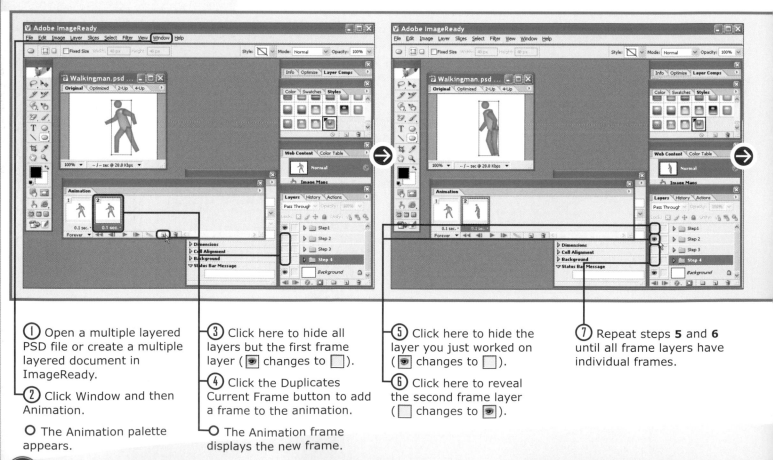

① Open a multiple layered PSD file or create a multiple layered document in ImageReady.

② Click Window and then Animation.

O The Animation palette appears.

③ Click here to hide all layers but the first frame layer (👁 changes to ☐).

④ Click the Duplicates Current Frame button to add a frame to the animation.

O The Animation frame displays the new frame.

⑤ Click here to hide the layer you just worked on (👁 changes to ☐).

⑥ Click here to reveal the second frame layer (☐ changes to 👁).

⑦ Repeat steps **5** and **6** until all frame layers have individual frames.

Did You Know? ※

You can create an animation from a Photoshop file. Create your Photoshop image, with each layer of the image being a frame for the animation, and open the image in ImageReady. Click the Animation palette Menu Options button (▶), and select Make Frames From Layers. ImageReady turns each individual layer in the Layers palette into an animation frame, in the order they appear in the Layers palette.

#96

DIFFICULTY LEVEL

Customize It! ※

You can create multiple frames instantly with the Tweening function. Click the Animation palette Menu Options button, and select Tweening from the menu that appears. Tweening automatically generates frames between one frame and another. You can adjust the Tweening function by specifying options such as the number of frames, and the inclusion of opacity changes, position changes, and effects. This technique is excellent for simple object movements, color changes, and simple effects such as a glow surrounding an object. The more tweening frames you use, the smoother the transformation.

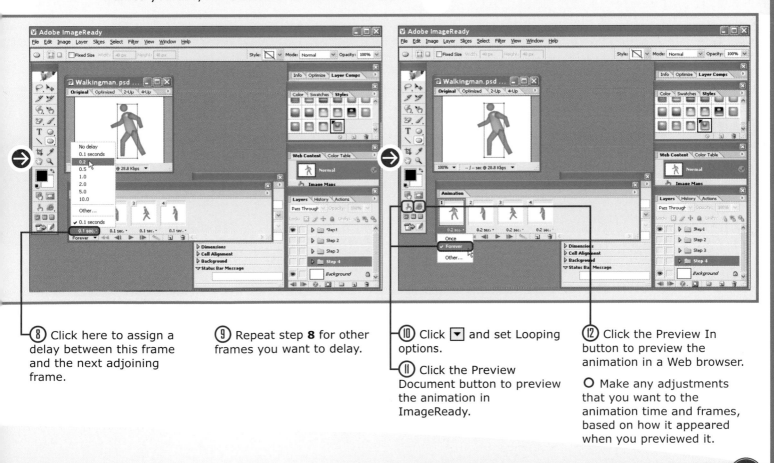

⑧ Click here to assign a delay between this frame and the next adjoining frame.

⑨ Repeat step **8** for other frames you want to delay.

⑩ Click ▼ and set Looping options.

⑪ Click the Preview Document button to preview the animation in ImageReady.

⑫ Click the Preview In button to preview the animation in a Web browser.

O Make any adjustments that you want to the animation time and frames, based on how it appeared when you previewed it.

ASSIGN AN IMAGE MAP
to your image

You can use ImageReady to create image maps in your images. Image maps are selected areas in an image that you can use for hyperlinks or rollover effects on your Web page. Image maps differ from slices in that they do not divide the image into separate rectangular pieces, but designate a specific-shaped area in the larger image as a "hot spot" for the mouse to recognize as special.

ImageReady has several ways to make image maps. For example, you can use the Image Map tool and choose from Rectangular, Elliptical, and Polygonal-shaped tools. When you drag or draw your selected

area, ImageReady automatically writes the HTML that depicts the shape for your Web page.

Another method for creating an image map is to create a selection with any selection tool, click the Select menu, and then select Create Image Map from Selection. You can then select options for the final shape. Rectangle creates the smallest rectangular area possible to surround the entire selection. Circular performs the same function, but defines the surrounding shape as elliptical. See the tips section of this task for more on the polygonal option.

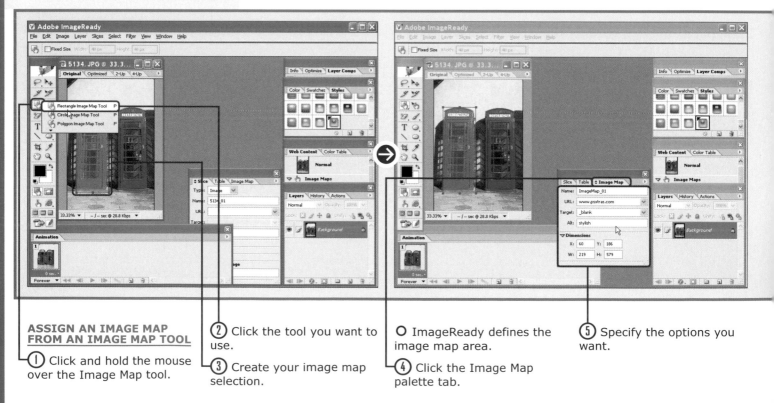

ASSIGN AN IMAGE MAP FROM AN IMAGE MAP TOOL

① Click and hold the mouse over the Image Map tool.

② Click the tool you want to use.

③ Create your image map selection.

O ImageReady defines the image map area.

④ Click the Image Map palette tab.

⑤ Specify the options you want.

#97

DIFFICULTY LEVEL

Did You Know? ※

The Quality value of the Polygon option in the Create Image Map dialog box sets the number of points on the custom-shaped image map. A higher Quality field value means more points along the selection, and a higher accuracy to the original shape of your selection. Lower Quality values can turn a curvy selection into a straight-edged polygonal selection, thus losing much of the original shape's detail.

Customize It! ※

You can create a rollover effect using an image map as the triggering area for the rollover. Select your image map layer in the Web Content palette. Click the Web Content Menu Options button (▸) and select New Rollover State. With your new state selected, make changes to your image. ImageReady creates your rollover. You can also use this technique to create a remote rollover, where areas outside the image map change when the rollover event happens.

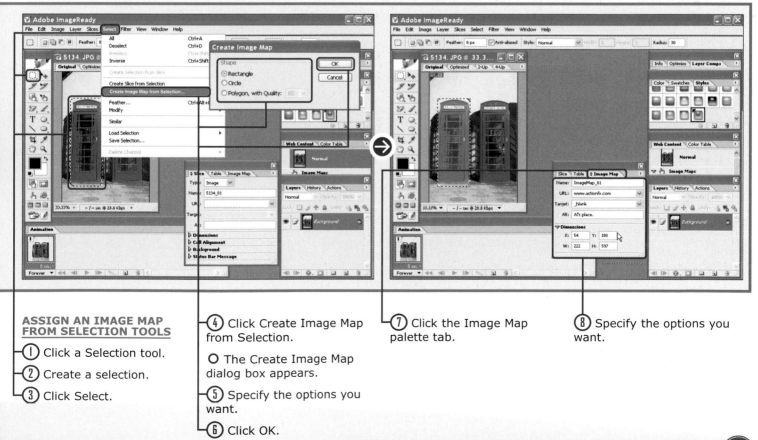

ASSIGN AN IMAGE MAP FROM SELECTION TOOLS

① Click a Selection tool.

② Create a selection.

③ Click Select.

④ Click Create Image Map from Selection.

○ The Create Image Map dialog box appears.

⑤ Specify the options you want.

⑥ Click OK.

⑦ Click the Image Map palette tab.

⑧ Specify the options you want.

MOVE MULTIPLE OBJECTS
in layers

Up to now, linking the layers in your image was the only method of grouping multiple objects together, but it required you to link layers, move the object, and then unlink. A new option in ImageReady allows you to quickly select multiple objects in your image, reducing the steps and allowing you to quickly group and move different objects without having to link the layers at all.

There are two ways to select the multiple objects. Inside the Layers palette, Shift+click each layer you want to include in the group. ImageReady highlights

each selected layer in blue, just as it does when the layer is active. You can now click the Move tool and drag all objects within the selected layers as one item, retaining their relative position with the other selected objects.

You can also select multiple objects from directly within the image. Choose the Layer Select tool from the Options bar of the Move tool. Then Shift+click each object you want to select. ImageReady selects the layer for each object that you select in the Layers palette, grouping them together.

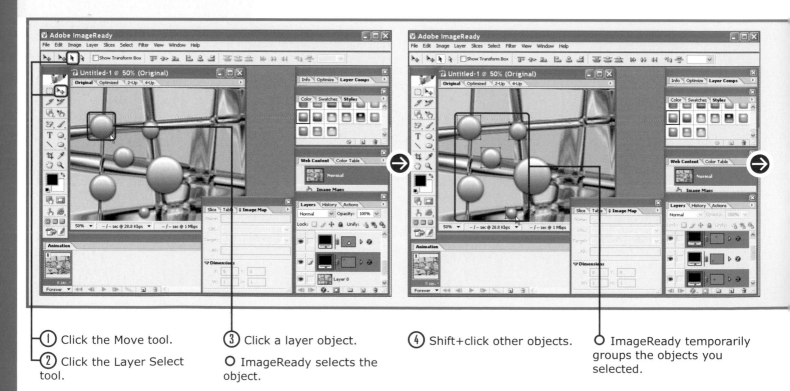

① Click the Move tool.

② Click the Layer Select tool.

③ Click a layer object.

○ ImageReady selects the object.

④ Shift+click other objects.

○ ImageReady temporarily groups the objects you selected.

98

Did You Know? ☀

You can use the temporary grouping of the layers to do more than just change their location. By Shift+clicking your layers, you can also apply styles with the Styles palette, rollover effects, and even use the alignment functions in the Move tool Options bar. This makes it quick and convenient to change the appearance or position of multiple objects.

Did You Know? ☀

You can use the multiple selection feature for many things, but it is temporary. Clicking any individual layer after using the multiple selections feature deselects all other layers. Link the files together by clicking the empty box to the left of the layer thumbnail; the chain icon (⬛) appears, indicating linking. Linking does not allow for the application of effects as described above, but the layers move in tandem if you change their position.

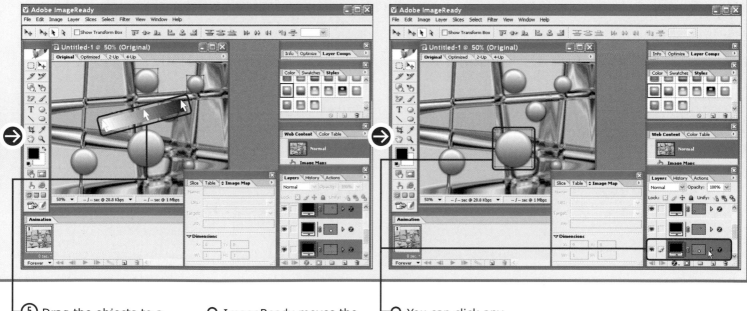

⑤ Drag the objects to a new location.

○ ImageReady moves the grouped objects together.

○ You can click any individual layer or object to undo the temporary link.

CREATE A WEB PAGE
in ImageReady

ImageReady is used for Web graphics design. You can create your images in Photoshop, and use ImageReady to create rollovers and effects, and generate a Web page. The finished Web page is complete, including HTML and JavaScript coding for page layouts and any dynamic effects.

ImageReady makes it easy to create your Web page. You can create your image and effects and then use the Save Optimized As command in the File menu to save your Web page. ImageReady cuts the image into the appropriate pieces based on slices and

effects, generates the HTML page, and saves the resulting files to your designated location for uploading and publishing online.

You can specify how your pages export by selecting Output Settings under the File menu, and selecting an option from the list. A dialog box appears, giving you many different options such as file extension options, slice and image map output choices, and image Metadata. These options allow you to generate your page to the specific needs of your client or your personal preferences.

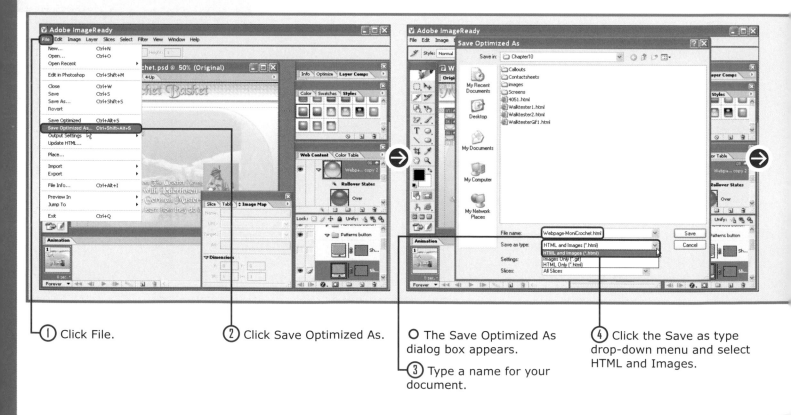

① Click File.

② Click Save Optimized As.

○ The Save Optimized As dialog box appears.

③ Type a name for your document.

④ Click the Save as type drop-down menu and select HTML and Images.

#99

Did You Know? ※

If you have already saved your Web page and images once using the Save Optimized As command, then you do not need to use this command again for any new changes. Instead, you can use the Save Optimized command; ImageReady saves your Web page under the last-used settings for this file. If you are saving to a different filename, then use the Save Optimized As command again, to avoid data loss on the other files.

Customize It! ※

When you use the Save Optimized As command with a document containing slices, you can choose to save the file based on different slice sets within your image. Slice sets contain different slice layouts, which you customize to a specific page and can save within the PSD document. By selecting a specific slice set, you can ensure that only the required slices are used to generate your current version of the Web page.

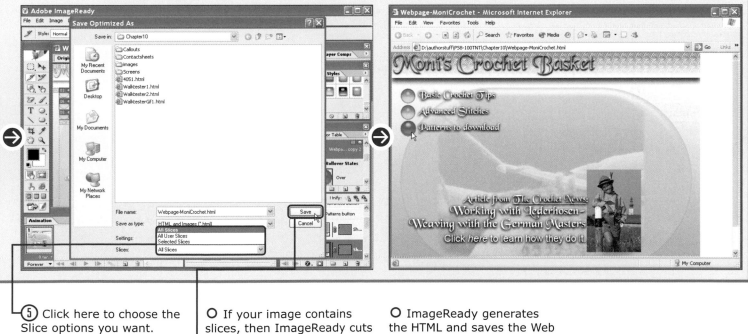

⑤ Click here to choose the Slice options you want.

○ If your image contains slices, then ImageReady cuts up and saves all images individually, based on slice shapes and sizes.

⑥ Click Save.

○ ImageReady generates the HTML and saves the Web page and images.

Export
ANIMATIONS
as SWF files

You can now export your ImageReady animations and images as Macromedia Flash SWF format files. This file format is highly popular on the Internet for its smaller file sizes and dynamic and animated content. ImageReady now gives you the power to save your images in this format for immediate use on the Web, or for import into Macromedia Flash for other work.

Flash is a great tool for saving animations as vector images, which keeps file sizes smaller than bitmap formats. It is a great tool for GIF-like images that

contain large areas of solid color and definition. Raster graphics like JPEG are bulkier for Flash, creating larger file sizes, and should be used sparingly when file size is a concern.

When you export your image, an Export dialog box appears with options. These options include appearance preservation, generating the HTML for the export, and even embedding fonts into the file. You can also choose different quality levels for bitmap images included in the file, which can help reduce final file sizes.

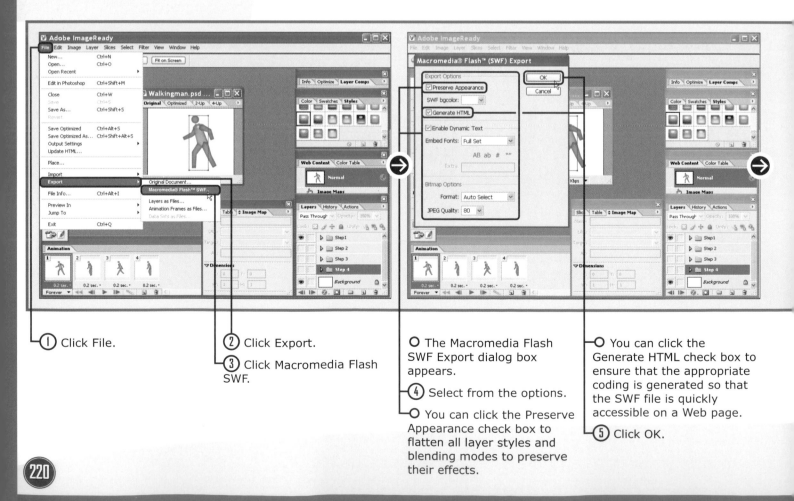

① Click File.

② Click Export.

③ Click Macromedia Flash SWF.

○ The Macromedia Flash SWF Export dialog box appears.

④ Select from the options.

○ You can click the Preserve Appearance check box to flatten all layer styles and blending modes to preserve their effects.

○ You can click the Generate HTML check box to ensure that the appropriate coding is generated so that the SWF file is quickly accessible on a Web page.

⑤ Click OK.

Did You Know? ☀

You can export your Photoshop layers as separate files for Flash by choosing another export option. By choosing File, Export, and then Layers as Files, each layer of your ImageReady document exports as a separate file. By choosing SWF in the Format Options drop-down menu, each of these individual files can be independently imported into Flash, allowing you to easily separate specific elements of your original image as needed. You can even select Separate Format for Each Layer as an Apply option in the Export Layers as Files dialog box, and save certain layers as SWF and the remaining layers as other formats. You can click the Set button, found in the Format Options area when the SWF format is selected, to change the Flash export settings. Clicking the Set button opens a Flash-specific dialog box in which you can adjust these settings.

DIFFICULTY LEVEL

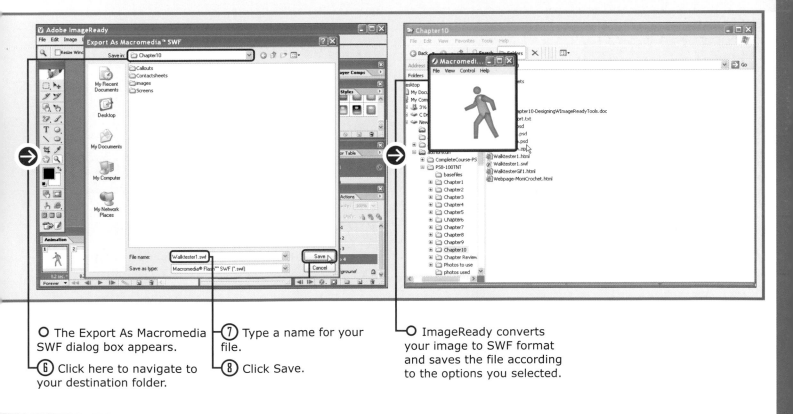

○ The Export As Macromedia SWF dialog box appears.

⑥ Click here to navigate to your destination folder.

⑦ Type a name for your file.

⑧ Click Save.

○ ImageReady converts your image to SWF format and saves the file according to the options you selected.

INDEX

INDEX

INDEX

INDEX